Strategic Stu.
and
U.S. Army War College Press

CONFLICT MANAGEMENT AND PEACEBUILDING: PILLARS OF A NEW AMERICAN GRAND STRATEGY

Volker C. Franke
Robert H. Dorff
Editors

October 2013

*****

The Strategic Studies Institute and the co-editors of this volume join in thanking the faculty, students, and staff of Kennesaw State University (KSU) for their extraordinary efforts in organizing and implementing the symposium, and in the preparation of this book. We also extend a very special thanks to KSU President Dr. Daniel S. Papp and Dr. Richard A. Vengroff, Dean Emeritus of the College of Humanities and Social Sciences for their energetic support of and commitment to the event and the publication of this book. In addition, we would like to thank Dr.

Jeffrey D. McCausland, Distinguished Visiting Professor of Research and Minerva Chair at SSI; Mr. Doug Brooks, President Emeritus of the International Stability Operations Association; and Dr. Akanmu Adebayo, Professor of History and Director of KSU's Center for Conflict Management, for their skillful moderation of the panels. We appreciate the assistance of Mr. Edward L. Mienie, INCM Ph.D. Candidate who, as graduate assistant for the symposium, helped coordinate the conference logistics and co-authored the conference brief; and INCM staff, including Program Administrator Rose Procter, Program Coordinator Chelsea van Bergen, and Student Assistant Audrey Adams, whose tireless efforts and great dedication ensured the successful organization and effective implementation of the symposium. Finally, our thanks go to the INCM Ph.D. students, all of whom volunteered to serve as program liaisons and campus guides to the panelists.

ISBN 1-58487-583-6

CONTENTS

FOREWORD

On February 24, 2012, Kennesaw State University (KSU) and the Strategic Studies Institute (SSI) of the U.S. Army War College (USAWC), conducted a symposium entitled "Peacebuilding and Conflict Management: Pillars of a New American Grand Strategy." The symposium built on the results of the 2011 KSU-SSI symposium that examined the utility of the U.S. Government's whole-of-government (WoG) approach for responding to the challenging security demands of operations in Iraq and Afghanistan. Based on this earlier evaluation of the benefits and shortcomings of the WoG approach in the field and the integration of operational and tactical demands generated by new security challenges, the 2012 symposium examined more closely the strategic objectives of interagency cooperation specifically in the areas of peacebuilding and conflict management.

In addition to the dual focus on peacebuilding and conflict management, the symposium was designed to examine one of the ongoing research interests in the SSI academic engagement series: the role of WoG efforts in addressing contemporary national and international security challenges and opportunities. In addition, the topics covered by the panelists created important synergies with SSI's 2012 Annual Strategy Conference, which examined challenges and opportunities for the future of U.S. grand strategy in an age of austerity. Four symposium panels addressed the following topics: "The Role of Peacebuilding and Conflict Management in a Future American Grand Strategy," "More than a Military Tool: Strengthening Civil-Military Cooperation in Peacebuilding," "Peace and Development: Key Elements of a New

Grand Strategy," and "Conflict Management, Peace-building, and a New American Grand Strategy: Views from Abroad."

The symposium discussions ranged from the conceptual to the practical, with a focus on the challenges and desirability of interagency cooperation in international interventions. Invited panelists shared their experiences and expertise on the need for and future of an American grand strategy in an era characterized by increasingly complex security challenges and shrinking budgets. Panelists agreed that taking the status quo for granted was a major obstacle to developing a successful grand strategy and that government, the military, international and nongovernmental organizations, and the private sector are all called on to contribute their best talents and efforts to joint global peace and security efforts. The panelists engaged the audience in a discussion that included viewpoints from academia, the military, government agencies, nongovernmental organizations, and industry. Despite the broad range of viewpoints, a number of overarching themes and tentative agreements emerged. The reader will find them in the chapters of this edited volume.

KSU and SSI are pleased to present this book, and we hope that readers will engage us further in the kinds of issues and debates that surfaced during the symposium and that are captured and extended in the pages that follow. In the interest of both national and international security, we must continue to debate issues pertinent to strategy and strategic decisionmaking and develop effective tools for the implementation and coordination of strategies of peacebuilding and conflict management.

DOUGLAS C. LOVELACE, JR.
Director
Strategic Studies Institute and
    U.S. Army War College Press

CHAPTER 1

CONFLICT MANAGEMENT AND PEACEBUILDING: PILLARS OF A NEW AMERICAN GRAND STRATEGY

Volker C. Franke
Robert H. Dorff

The United States must renew its leadership in the world by building and cultivating the sources of our strength and influence. Our national security depends upon America's ability to leverage our unique national attributes, just as global security depends upon strong and responsible American leadership.

President Barack Obama,
2010 U.S. National Security Strategy

INTRODUCTION

In June 2009, President Obama traveled to Egypt to make good on a campaign promise to mend U.S. relations with the Muslim world and to repair America's tarnished image in the world. Immediately after taking over the White House, President Obama had launched a series of foreign policy initiatives—e.g., ordering the closure of the U.S. detention facility in Guantanamo Bay, Cuba; sending additional troops to Afghanistan while ordering the withdrawal of all combat troops from Iraq; promoting democratic reform, economic development, and peace and security across the Middle East and North Africa; and negotiating and ratifying a new Strategic Arms Reduction

Treaty (START) with Russia[1] — that presented a sharp turn-around from the George W. Bush administration's "go-it-alone" approach to fighting a global war on terror (GWOT) that had turned away allies and friends and angered public opinion worldwide.

Indeed, Obama's embrace of diplomacy and cooperation made him popular abroad and revived America's image, eventually leading to him being awarded the 2009 Nobel Peace Prize. The prize committee celebrated President Obama "for his extraordinary efforts to strengthen international diplomacy and cooperation between peoples" and for giving people around the world hope for a better future "founded in the concept that those who are to lead the world must do so on the basis of values and attitudes that are shared by the majority of the world's population."[2]

Despite obvious differences between the Obama and Bush administrations' foreign and national security policies, both Presidents seem to share one common conviction: that other countries long for U.S. leadership and that U.S. policies ought to manifest America's leadership position in the world.[3] Notwithstanding mounting global criticism of American unilateralism and straining transatlantic relations, the Bush administration was convinced that friends and allies would eventually come around and rally to the side of the United States, even if they bristled at its actions, because they shared America's goals and values and had faith in its motives. But flexing American muscles in Iraq and Afghanistan not only turned Washington's partners away, it also led to nuclear saber rattling by Iran and North Korea and left the U.S. Government with a mounting deficit.

As the 2008 election neared, it had become clear that the United States could no longer afford the Bush practice of "bullying other countries to ratify changes we hatch in isolation."[4] Instead, President Obama advocated "a strategy no longer driven by ideology and politics but rather one that is based on a realistic assessment of the sobering facts on the ground and our interests in the region."[5] Obama believed that a United States that listened more to others, stressed common interests and favored multinational action would command followers. In practice, however, Obama discovered that in a globalized world, where power has been more widely dispersed, many countries are indifferent to American leadership. In the same vein, describing the political and economic ascendance of countries such as China, India, Brazil, Russia, or South Africa, Fareed Zakaria has argued that the world is shifting from the hostile Anti-Americanism that characterized much of the Bush presidency to a post-Americanism where power is far more diffuse and dispersed across a wider array of countries.[6] But not only that, nonstate actors are becoming increasingly important players in the geopolitical terrain as well.

"Even if Washington led wisely and sympathetically," James Lindsay has argued, "others might not follow. Consultations could not guarantee consensus."[7] Given these new global realities, how are U.S. interests to be promoted in a world in which others no longer blindly follow the single most powerful and influential country? What are the prospects for American leadership, and what are appropriate strategic responses to emerging security threats? What principles should inform the development of those responses? What, in other words, should be the elements of a new grand strategy guiding the formulation of American foreign and national security policy?

Since the end of World War II, U.S. policies have been informed by changing and at times competing ideas about America's role in the world, shifting among visions promoting "neo-isolationism," "selective engagement," "cooperative security," and "primacy."[8] None of these visions, however, are sufficient to address the rapidly changing nature of today's global security context and provide a coherent and comprehensive organizing framework to protect and promote U.S. national security at home or abroad. Unless the President—irrespective of party or political persuasion—finds a way to align foreign policy prescriptions with evolving global trends, Lindsay warns, "the gap between American aspirations and accomplishments will grow, and the prospects for successful US global leadership will dim further."[9]

In an effort to discuss visions and ideas for a future U.S. grand strategy based on diplomacy and cooperation, on February 24, 2012, a number of leading civilian and military experts came together at a symposium held at Kennesaw State University, Kennesaw, GA, to evaluate the usefulness and practicality of conflict management and peacebuilding as key pillars to the development of a new American grand strategy.[10] The 2012 symposium built on the results of a successful 2011 symposium that examined the utility of the U.S. Government's whole-of-government approach for responding to the challenging security demands of operations in Iraq and Afghanistan.[11]

This volume presents the central arguments and key findings of the 2012 symposium, tracing the central plans and policies that ought to comprise Washington's efforts to harness political, military, diplomatic, and economic tools together to advance U.S. national interests in an increasingly complex and globalizing world. Authors contributing to this volume tackle strategic choices for effectively addressing emerging security threats, integrating conflict management approaches into strategic decisionmaking, sharing the burden of peacebuilding and stability operations between military and civilian actors, strengthening civil-military cooperation in complex operations, and enabling the timely scaling-down of military deployments.

The first part of this volume lays out some of the specific threats, challenges, and opportunities of the emerging strategic global security environment and offers some more general recommendations for strategic responses to those challenges. In Chapter 2, former Chief-of-Staff to Secretary of State Colin Powell, Frederick W. Smullen III, presents a comprehensive overview of the challenges that characterize the global national security landscape — ranging from terrorism and piracy to hunger and humanitarian issues, to pandemics, climate change, energy and resource security, and the global economic crisis. Facing this plethora of challenges, Smullen advocates that the United States, as the remaining single global superpower, can and should lead by example, taking strategic advantage of a moment in history that offers the opportunity to heal America's global image, strengthen its influence with like-minded nations, and (re)earn respect as a solid citizen nation of the world.

Focusing specifically on challenges to transatlantic relations, in Chapter 3 former German Defense and Economics Minister Karl-Theodor zu Guttenberg warns of the danger of "disconnection through connection," i.e., that new and intertwined global challenges and shifts of power risk marginalizing traditional partnerships and multinational institutions. Identifying the paradox that the circumstances requiring better global governance — e.g., conflicting interests and incentives, divergent values, or differing norms — are also the ones that make its realization incredibly complex and often unpleasant, Guttenberg calls for a bold and long-term strategic vision that reinvigorates the transatlantic relationship by promoting a global democratic political culture based on respect for cultural differences. Any new American grand strategy, Guttenberg argues, ought to move beyond short-term thinking and ad hoc procedures to change the transatlantic narrative so national populations can understand the complexities and dilemmas within which institutions from the North Atlantic Treaty Organization (NATO) and the United Nations (UN) to the European Union (EU) operate and reach out past the "old West" to bring emerging powers such as Brazil, Russia, China, or India into the global dialogue, so they will shoulder greater global responsibility while recognizing the limits of their own power.

Although acknowledging the many and varying threats to U.S. national security in the years and decades to come, Robert Kennedy argues in Chapter 4 that perhaps the greatest challenge for the United States will arise from a continued relative shift in power from the world's predominant political, economic, diplomatic, and military superpower to *primus inter pares* in world affairs. Thus, to meet the challenges ahead including its readjustment in status, Kennedy argues, Washington must wisely apply the instruments of national power — political, economic, psychological, and military. Chapter 4 addresses specifically the origins and nature of national power: its sources and the means by which those are transformed into preferred outcomes in the international arena and the instruments states use to do so, and examines the likely demands arising from soft and hard power to be molded into what is fashionably called "smart power."

Presenting an overview of the origins, present state, and prospects of the international security order, Michael Lekson and Nathan Wilson conjecture in Chapter 5 that traditional peacebuilding in the sense of stabilization, institution building, and democratization, while remaining an active and important component of international relations, will decrease in importance to a future American grand strategy and an even smaller part in actual practice. Instead, Lekson and Wilson argue the need for conflict management, understood as a mix of defense and diplomacy, will increase in the future. As a result, both diplomats and the military will have to place a premium on flexibility and practice selective engagement, especially in an environment where threats and challenges are multifold and resource allocations remain tight. The adage "doing more with less," Lekson and Wilson criticize, not only serves as a guide to policy but also as a convenient pretext to avoid prioritization. In short, the authors conclude, "There will be no shortage of conflicts to manage, and we will all need to keep getting better at it if we want this story to have a happy ending."

Given the enormous cost in casualties and resources in America's post-September 11, 2001 (9/11) wars, Charles J. Dunlap, Jr. argues in Chapter 6, the United States needs to consider alternative approaches — to include especially peacebuilding and conflict management — to accomplish its strategic goals. Dunlap conjectures that it is incumbent upon the Armed Forces to develop methodologies to accomplish these missions in a way that is supportable by the American public. To achieve this, Dunlap proposes an "off shore" approach based on a light military footprint that leverages America's asymmetric advantages in high technology as a means of addressing emerging security challenges without necessarily putting large forces on the ground. Off-shore peacebuilding and conflict management will not work in every instance, but can serve as a starting point when the next challenge arises. At the end of the day, however, Dunlap concludes, any off shore strategy must recognize that the central task of peacebuilding and conflict management must be developing local capabilities.

International peacebuilding, William Flavin argues in Chapter 7, is at its heart a host nation challenge and responsibility, and national factors will shape its pace and sequencing. As a result, Flavin contends, the U.S. military will always remain an outsider to the peacebuilding process and the country it is trying to assist. Irrespective of what the military will try to do to shape the outcome, the host nation has its own objectives and ideas and, as the influence of the military force wanes, local imperatives will take over. Flavin cautions that the military can never have sufficient knowledge about the host country and the other international actors because of its own institutional processes and the temporary nature of its involvement. Nevertheless, its unique ability to plan, organize, respond, and mobilize resources ensures that the U.S. military will continue to undertake a wide variety of tasks beyond its basic combat skills, making short-term security the *sine-qua-non* and peacebuilding a secondary function of military operations in the future.

Given the grand strategic imperatives of the 21st century, Christopher Holshek contends in Chapter 8, the civil-military nexus of conflict management and peacebuilding is more relevant to international engagements and American grand strategy today than ever before. However, America's current civil-military approach to foreign policy and national security remains largely based on an outdated national security paradigm, itself predicated on Cold War thinking, that has been revitalized since 9/11. Instead, Holshek calls for a more enlightened approach to civil-military coordination that is not based on a tradeoff between idealism and realism, but one where those who bring democracy serve as true ambassadors of the concept and exemplify its tenets in their daily interactions with local populations. Such applied civil-military coordination must mirror the civil-military relationship in democratic societies and the actions of uniformed personnel must be consonant with the values of the democratic societies they represent. When Americans think globally and act locally, make their actions consonant with their core values, and embrace a new ethos of engagement, they can transform both their environment and themselves. However, failure to recognize this, he warns, risks further deterioration of American global leadership and the security and prosperity resulting from it.

Examining the strategic challenges at the intersection between peacebuilding, development, and security, Melanie Alamir argues in Chapter 9 that strategic thinking that tends to treat actors and societies in developing countries as mere objects in pursuing their own countries' national interests, contradicts the key development tenet of local ownership. Strategic thinking that is marked by a general confidence in instrumental rationality that for the most part disregards the relevance of perceptions, emotions, identities, and beliefs, and is characterized by an "engineering" mindset based on hierarchy, predictability, order, and sequence cannot be applied to planning for peace-building and development. Instead, it tends to take political decisions for granted, focusing on how to implement them rather than to question their wisdom. Peacebuilding and development, however, require permanent monitoring, evaluation, and the flexibility to question not only tactics, but also goals, if needed. Alamir concludes that strategic thinking needs more flexibility, making the likelihood of delay, setbacks, detours, or failure integral elements of any effective future grand strategy. The main challenge, she conjectures, is to reconcile dominant top-down approaches along with their "engineering logic" with the ambiguity, unpredictability, and uncontrollability of contemporary security threats and challenges.

Heeding Alamir's call for a more flexible and sensitive strategic approach to peacebuilding, Michael Ashkenazi argues in Chapter 10 for greater nuancing in the strategic discourse particularly by recognizing how interactions between low-level actors — individuals and small groups — can have major impacts on the outcomes of strategies. Ashkenazi examines his claim by developing a concept of security providers encompassing different types of more or less structured formations that engage in security. Using identifiable rewards — cash, emotional gratification from association, legal support, and ideology — Ashkenazi contends that variations in the relative strength of these rewards over time cause formations to move in the mapped space toward one or another of the four ideal types. Ashkenazi concludes that identifying these rewards and manipulating them over time must be incorporated into strategic thinking. Where an international actor such as the United States has a strategic interest in ensuring stability, peace, development, democracy, and other social goods, it is crucial to identify and resolve micro-level problems that, in the aggregate, can cause a strategy to fail.

Examining America's strategic efforts specifically in the prevention of mass atrocities and genocide, Dwight Raymond reviews in Chapter 11 the policy formulation contained in the government's recent Mass Atrocity Prevention and Response Options (MAPRO) planning process.[12] Raymond criticizes that competing national interests oftentimes dissuade action, that risk-averse bureaucracies tend to support status quo approaches, and that the complex nature of security problems may not be conducive to clear-cut decisions in the interest of stopping perpetrators and protecting innocent victims. Reviewing the recently released MAPRO Handbook, Raymond provides an outline for effective interagency cooperation to help policymakers wrestle with MAPRO decisions and associated risks—although much of the Handbook is also applicable to other complex situations involving conflict—by providing a rational yet feasible process for contingency planning as well as crisis response.

The final part of this volume examines how America's strategic choices are perceived from abroad. Evaluating Washington's reorientation away from the Atlantic to the Pacific, especially with China and India as rising competitors, Liselotte Odgaard contends in Chapter 12 that any future world order will be dominated by America's pursuit of an integrationist world order and China's pursuit of a coexistence world order. The different U.S. and Chinese versions of international order give rise to an international system without clear rules because of the lack of one coherent set of principles of international conduct. In this in-between system, she argues, India and Europe will be takers rather than makers of that future order, facing the challenge of carving out a position in-between these two competing world orders, and security threats will be addressed primarily through ad hoc frameworks of conflict management.

Turning to Africa, Kwesi Aning and Festus Aubyn examine in Chapter 13 the history of U.S. engagements in Africa, especially in the peace and security arena and juxtapose America's grand strategic calculations with Africa's own perceptions of and responses to its security challenges. In addition, Aning and Aubyn explore how in the face of common challenges both the African Union (AU) and the United States can identify and respond to their security challenges in a manner that makes this relationship a win-win one instead of the present one driven by suspicion, competition, and outright hostility. Unfortunately, Aning and Aubyn conclude that U.S. policy toward Africa has remained largely intact under the Obama administration, still pursuing that same militarized and unilateral security approach toward Africa policy employed by the Bill Clinton and George W. Bush administrations. It is important, Aning and Aubyn conjecture, for the United States not to see Africa at the periphery of its foreign policy engagements but rather to devote resources to strengthening the operational and tactical components of AU peace support operations, focus on bolstering the civilian capabilities for the AU's conflict management activities, increase its economic support to bridge the AU's bureaucratic and institutional capability gaps in conflict management, and reconcile its interest with African human security needs such as poverty, unemployment, access to clean water, and the HIV/AIDs pandemic.

Dove-tailing on the geopolitical challenges outlined by Odgaard and the African context presented by Aning and Aubyn, Abel Esterhuyse examines in Chapter 14 specifically the role of South Africa as a key partner in the pursuit of U.S. strategic interests in Africa. Reviewing the historically rather limited involvement in African security by either country, Esterhuyse contends that perceptions in South Africa about the United States and, specifically how the United States prefers to conceptualize and respond to perceived threats, have been shaped predominantly by the kinetic-driven U.S. involvement in Iraq, Afghanistan and, more recently, Libya. The creation of U.S. Africa Command (AFRICOM) further reinforces this perception. South Africans view their own military involvement in Africa as human security-related and that of the United States as military security-orientated. For the current Action Council of Nigeria (ANC) government, U.S. military involvement in Africa is seen as a force of destruction shaped largely by conventional warfighting applications, while South African military involvement is driven by the human security and peacetime applications of military force. As a result, as long as these perceptions remain, strategic cooperation between both countries will be difficult to achieve.

ENDNOTES - CHAPTER 1

1. A comprehensive list of foreign policy initiatives is available from *www.whitehouse.gov/issues/foreign-policy*. See also James M. Lindsay, "George W. Bush, Barack Obama and the Future of US Global Leadership," *International Affairs*, Vol. 87, No. 4, 2011, pp. 765-779.

2. The text of the Nobel Prize citation is available from *www.reuters.com/article/2009/10/09/us-nobel-peace-citation-text-sb-idUSTRE5981RA20091009*.

3. See Lindsay, "George W. Bush, Barack Obama and the Future of US Global Leadership."

4. Barack Obama, "Renewing American Leadership," *Foreign Affairs*, Vol. 84, No. 4, July-August 2007, pp. 2-16.

5. Ryan Lizza quoted in Lindsay, "George W. Bush, Barack Obama and the Future of US Global Leadership," p. 773.

6. Fareed Zakaria, *The Post-American World*, London UK: Norton, 2009.

7. Lindsay, "George W. Bush, Barack Obama and the Future of US Global Leadership," p. 779.

8. Barry R. Posen and Andrew L. Ross, "Competing Visions for U.S. Grand Strategy," *International Security*, Vol. 21, No. 3, Winter 1996/97, pp. 5-53.

9. Lindsay, "George W. Bush, Barack Obama and the Future of US Global Leadership," p. 779.

10. Details of the 2012 KSU-SSI Symposium is available from *www.kennesaw.edu/ksussi/2012/index.php*.

11. For details of the 2011 KSU-SSI Symposium, see Volker C. Franke and Robert H. Dorff, eds., *Conflict Management and "Whole of Government": Useful Tools for U.S. National Security Strategy?* Carlisle, PA: Strategic Studies Institute, U.S. Army War College, 2012, available from *www.strategicstudiesinstitute.army.mil/pubs/display.cfm?pubID=1102*.

12. Dwight Raymond, Cliff Bernath, Don Braum, and Ken Zurcher, *Mass Atrocity Prevention and Response Options (MAPRO): A Policy Planning Handbook*, Carlisle, PA: Peacekeeping and Stability Operations Institute, U.S. Army War College, 2012, available from *pksoi.army.mil/PKM/publications/collaborative/collaborativereview.cfm?collaborativeID=11*.

CHAPTER 2

NEW THREATS; NEW THINKING

Frederick W. Smullen

The author paints a picture of a global national security landscape as he views it, what the challenges are, and what can be done, so readers can ponder what these challenges mean to citizens who care about our welfare, our security, and the safety of this country and the world at large. Therefore we should look at the global landscape to try and make sense of it and ponder what it bodes for the future. It would be easy to dismiss current events simply by saying, "We live in interesting times," as went the old Chinese proverb. The truth is, we've always lived "in interesting times." If you think about it, the challenges that face us today seem so broad and so interconnected. They increase, they evolve, but our thinking evolves as well.

Let's take a closer look at the environment and times in which we find ourselves. The world of today is a crucible of challenges. This is an era in which problems and threats have become global concerns in ways once unthinkable. As a nation, we have always known crisis and always will. But what is different, if anything, about the crises of today compared to those of the past? For one thing, most crises in the past had a beginning and an end. Although painful along the way, you knew they would not, indeed could not, last forever. Today's crises tend to defy predictability. They rise up in larger numbers, many occurring simultaneously, and they seem to persist far longer. Some are unforeseen and difficult to prepare for; others loom as threats that draw our attention. At the top of many threat lists is terrorism, something that shook our national sense of invulnerability on September 11, 2001 (9/11) and captured our call to action so as to protect the homeland from the likes of al-Qaeda, which is evolving. Our thinking needs to evolve too.

Even before the killing of Osama Bin Laden, al-Qaeda had changed. Their operational planning capabilities, including the attack on the USS *Cole*, the World Trade Center bombing, and the subsequent 9/11 attacks, bruised and rallied a nation. Once a formidable terrorist organization with a media wing, it is now more of a media organization with a terrorist wing. Yet grave threats remain: lone wolf attacks, such as the so called "underwear bomber" on Christmas Day 2009, the attempted Times Square bombing in 2010, an attempted bombing in 2011, and an attempted bombing of the U.S. capital in 2012 by a Moroccan citizen who had been living in the United States illegally for the past 12 years. These threats loom and will stay with us. There has been a rise in prominence of al-Qaeda inspired and affiliated groups, such as al-Qaeda in the Arabian Peninsula (AQAP). We cannot be lulled into thinking that these groups are only concerned with local and regional grievances. The package bomb plot emanating from Yemen in 2010 is proof that this force can be projected. We must strive to understand these groups better, and work toward the eradication of the root causes of extremism that give rise to these groups. Ironically, before his death last year, the spiritual leader of AQAP was Answar Al-Awlaqi, an American of Yemen descent, who inspired Islamic terrorists to take action against the West. Make no mistake about it, Osama Bin Laden may be dead, but his legacy lives on.

Global piracy is a swiftly moving threat. Piracy threatens and slows down commercial shipping, has a chilling effect on world trade, increases commodity prices, and contributes to regional insecurity. Pirates have thrived in recent years, maintaining a high level of attacks for the fifth straight year. In 2011, pirates attacked 439 ships and took 802 people hostage. The threat continues in 2012, as 37 attacks took place in January alone. Pirates currently hold hostage 10 ships and 159 crew members of various nationalities. Somali pirates remain the biggest threat accounting for 54 percent of all global attacks. But the dangers of piracy were brought closer to home in January 2012 when an American citizen was rescued in Somalia by U.S. Navy Seals after being held captive by pirates for 3 months. The ransoms are also growing bigger. In mid-November 2010, a South Korean supertanker anchored for months off the city of Hobyo in central Somalia fetched a $10 million ransom. Raids by South Korean and Malaysian commands in January 2012 have taught us that we need to deal differently with these pirates, and what do I mean by that? We need to take, in my view, the fight to them before they reach the high seas. We need to get them where they live, where they grow, each and every day. It is a growing problem, and one that we need to be concerned about.

Hunger and humanitarian issues do not seem as threatening but do pose problems. The humanitarian concerns of the so-called "bottom billion," those people living on less than $1 a day, and the plight of internally displaced persons and refugees, as well as those suffering from hunger, lack of clean water, and basic medical care are concerns. The nearly two billion undernourished people in the world call for urgent government action to ensure the future sustainability of the world's food supply. If you think about it, the Middle East is a classic case. A related concern is the rising price of food, which is increasingly in shorter supply. It is a historical truth that when food prices rise, conflict increases. Many of these issues create the conditions that are fertile breeding ground for dangerous ideologies.

Pandemics pose an entirely new set of challenges, and ones that evolve constantly. The threat posed by pandemics, be they naturally occurring or human caused through the use of a weaponized biological agent, is astronomical. The speed with which naturally occurring crises may be evolving may be directly related to the speed of travel and mobility of people in today's world. The severe acute respiratory syndrome (SARS) outbreak in China in 2003 illustrated that.

In this increasingly interdependent world, the effects of climate change and the persistently slow responses to it are a concern. Even if the current pace of emissions reductions continues, the earth will be at least 3 degrees Celsius (5.4 degrees Fahrenheit) warmer at the end of this century than at the start of the industrial revolution. The devastating effects of climate change do not just bring humanitarian crises to the developing world, they affect how humans live and will live in the future. Natural disasters around the world, like the powerful tsunami in Japan, the earthquakes in New Zealand, the floods in Thailand, and the hurricanes and tornadoes in America were very visible reminders, yet again, that the concerns of the world's people are often interconnected. Those global calamities in 2011 alone caused an estimated $350 billion in damage.

There will be other threats, less bellicose but threats nevertheless. Demands for highly strategic resources including energy, food, and water outstrip available supplies. Our quest to develop new sources of energy, even as we continue to exploit existing ones, is certainly not without challenges. There will be a predictable transition away from oil toward natural gas, coal, and other alternatives. Demand for food will increase as populations rise. Stable supplies of water, especially for agricultural purposes, will reach critical proportions. Will we mobilize a global economy to ensure energy sustainability through renewable resources and transition away from oil toward natural gas, coal, and other alternatives?

A crippling cyber attack on our nation's electronic infrastructure could have devastating consequences; cyber warfare and cyber espionage threaten privacy and personal security, economics, governments, and businesses. Our reliance upon these systems has grown exponentially over the years, and security must keep up with the new challenges presented every day as, increasingly, government and corporate internet sites are being hacked.

The threat posed by weapons of mass destruction (WMD), such as nuclear, chemical, and biological, is unthinkable. Nation states must work diligently and work together to decrease proliferation of these arms. The imperative is to prevent these materials from falling into the hands of nonstate actors whose irrational actions could truly jeopardize our way of life and place other international actors, ally, and adversary alike, in catastrophic situations.

PRESERVATION OF THE FORCE

Our nation's Armed Forces, the finest and bravest in the world, have seen over a decade of multiple deployments that have left our force depleted. Yes, we are no longer in Iraq and we are redeploying from Afghanistan, but care must be given to not break the force. Besides the nearly 6,200 killed and more than 47,000 wounded, thousands upon thousands have returned from these conflicts victims in other ways; missing limbs and suffering catastrophic brain injuries, post traumatic stress disorder (PTSD), and high depression and suicide rates, which hit another record high of 164 active-duty Army in 2011. There were 124 in the National Guard and Reserves nonmobilized who took their lives. Another alarming statistic is that in 2011, military divorce rates hit their highest level since 1999, with a divorce rate of 3.7 percent and nearly 30,000 marriages ended in 2011. We must ensure that these men and women receive the finest care in return for the service they have given our nation in some of our darkest hours over this past decade. In the memorable words of Winston Churchill, "Never have so many owed so much to so few." We must also ensure as the military grows smaller — and the announced reduction is 80,000 Soldiers down to 499,000 from a current strength of 570,000 by 2017 — that we do not emasculate the force.

GLOBALIZED ECONOMIC CONCERNS

One of the lessons of the global economic downturn and melt-down has been that risk, as much as and perhaps greater than reward, is globalized. The interconnected global market place is an amazing generator of wealth, but it becomes threatening when systems become unhealthy. The economic downturn has strained relations with some close allies, and care must be taken to work cooperatively to meet global economic challenges.

DISAFFECTED YOUTH

In the midst of these challenges, the youth of the world struggle to come into their own and make their way through this complex environment, often facing challenges not of their own choosing or design. The world's youth who are growing up in threatening environments are at the greatest risk of falling under the sway of dangerous ideologies. Beyond this, they are not allowed the conditions to meet their full potential and, once again, their concerns are our concerns.

Old challenges and the rise of new powers constitute potential threats that require new thinking. The world at the end of the first decade of the 21st century is a map of challenges and opportunities. Some of the players are new, and some are not new at all. Without doubt, the Arab world is an immediate challenge not only to itself but to the rest of the world as well. Given the unrest and turmoil in the Middle East, that region has become a boiling cauldron and a huge national security concern for the U.S. Government. Our strategic interests are many with friends and foes alike in that part of the world, not just in Tunisia, Libya, and Egypt, where reform movements helped depose leaders in these countries, but elsewhere as well. Clearly, the instability in the governments of Syria and Yemen remain at the top of the list of concerns at the moment. Is there still the risk of this instability creating similar rebellions in Algeria, Bahrain, Iran, Jordan, and Sudan? Should others like Kuwait, Saudi Arabia, and the United Arab Emirates be concerned about the unrest spilling across their borders? The U.S. Government needs to invest now in rigorous strategic thinking to determine how our vital national interests will be affected and how we can protect them. Whether these countries lean toward or bend away from democracies and favorable relations with America and the West can have an enormous influence on our strategic ties to nations of the region.

China, a country that currently has 115 billionaires and can erect a 15-story building in 6 days, has experienced meteoric economic growth in recent years and has seen its ability to affect and influence, both regionally and globally, increase. Some economists suggest China could become the world's largest economy by 2027, if not before. Our economies persist in requiring each other to cooperate. Meanwhile, China's military is growing stronger with time. It has constructed the world's first anti-ship ballistic missile, has developed a stealth fighter plane, and has launched its first aircraft carrier; impressive toys to accompany a new assertiveness. As China builds up its military, other nations in the region—India, Japan, South Korea, Singapore, Indonesia, and Australia—are amassing weapons of their own at a frenzied pace, causing a shift in the world's military balance and altering security concerns in the Asia Pacific region.

Russia, too, has attempted re-emergence on the world stage as evidenced by some of its actions, accompanied by the return of fierce nationalist sentiments expressed by Russia's government. As Russia enters an uncertain period of new leadership, headlined by the return of Vladimir Putin to the presidency this year, we can expect Russia to take a more hard-line position toward the United States. Problems continue in its restive border regions and could place the country on a collision course. We share with both China and Russia a mutual need for the world's resources, so we must cooperate, or compete. Can we do so responsibly?

Israel and Palestine are nagging problems. When Secretary of State Colin Powell and the author went to the State Department in 2001, the Israel-Palestine situation was at the very top of our list. We knew it had to be resolved, and we worked very hard to contribute to that resolution. Our very first trip overseas was to both Israel and the Palestinian territories to see if we could broker a dialogue and a relationship between those two forces. We failed, and we have been failing dramatically ever since. Peace in the Middle East remains an elusive dream. Ensuring security for all peoples living in this region, while preventing extremism, must continue to be a focus moving into the future. The threat of failure is simply too great.

Far to the east, North Korea just experienced a rapid change in its leadership, with Kim Jong-il unexpectedly dying of a heart attack and the reins handed to his youngest son, Kim Jong-un. New leadership can often be a time of muscle flexing and that has already begun with not totally unexpected hostile rhetoric spewing from Pyongyang. Missile tests and border altercations such as those in 2010 must not be repeated and allowed to drag this region back into conflict, nor decrease the security of our allies. Interestingly, when we sat down in Beijing with our representative to North Korea and the North Korean representatives to talk about common concerns, one of which was their need for food, we expressed our desire to have nonproliferation be a prominent way of life. This desire was not considered at that time.

The world stage has also welcomed new powers: nations such as Turkey, and Brazil, who both project influence. The privileges of this newfound power must always be balanced with responsibilities. New powers must act as agents of cooperation and prosperity, rather than increasing polarity and tension. Pakistan, at the heart of a region that has experienced so much conflict, remains a key player. Tactics used against extremist ideologies can work against our tenuous relationship. The aftermath of a recent NATO airstrike that killed 24 Pakistani soldiers and increasing efforts by Congress to decrease aid to Pakistan continue to threaten an already precarious situation. Neighboring India has grown into an economic powerhouse, yet tensions remain on the border with Pakistan. This relationship grew more tense after 2008 when Pakistani extremists attacked Mumbai with devastating results.

The world remains watchful of Iran as it continues to develop its technologies and flexes its muscles toward the West. We must keep a careful watch with respect to its nuclear agenda, its provocative actions in the straits of Hormuz, and its apparent willingness to conduct an attack against the United States. A recent assessment by James Clapper, the Director of National Intelligence, suggests the Iranians have "changed their calculus and are more willing to conduct an attack in the United States as a response to real or perceived actions that threaten the regime."[1] It further shows Iran's hostility toward the United States and its interests in this hemisphere. Questions remain about Iranian ambitions. Can international cooperation in the form of sanctions keep this situation from jeopardizing international security?

Conflicts in Iraq and Afghanistan have continued to weigh us down. For all intents and purposes, a complete redeployment of troops from Iraq took place at the end of 2011. Yet Iraq is a nation struggling to find its identity, and the 1,000-person embassy in Baghdad will be challenged. Meanwhile, our strategic attention has turned now to the situation in Afghanistan where there were 90,000 troops, although a drawdown to 68,000 by the fall of 2012 began in July 2012. Secretary of Defense Leon Panetta has declared that by mid- to late-2013, our combat mission will decline. Nation-building continues in these two laboratories. We remain committed to the mission required of the United States and the international community. The consequences of failure are too great.

Closer to home on our own border with Mexico, drug-related violence and crime continues to escalate significantly. Confronting this spillover of violence only treats the symptom. The root causes remain and must be addressed. In September 2010, when asked "What is the greatest threat or concern that keeps you up at night?" Admiral James A. Winnefed, Jr., Vice Chairman of the U.S. Joint Chiefs of Staff, replied "Drugs." We have not done a very good job with the Mexican military and the Mexican government. They blame us for demand, and we blame them for supply. Unfortunately, we have not been talking to one another. We have not been creating an atmosphere where we can solve this problem. That is a growing concern, and one that we must attack.

I have created a picture of gloom here; however, I would say there is cause for hope. Interesting times have always inspired new thinking, and we must remain dedicated to constantly challenging our assumptions to ensure that the uncertainties of the future can be met. America can and should take a lead role in projecting the kind of global thinking and leadership that garners respect. That means being ready and willing to make decisions that are courageous. America needs to stand out as a beacon of what is right in and for the world. Call it a grand plan or a grand strategy, but Obama must be always looking at the world as it exists yet have a vision of what it is likely to look like in the following years.

That starts with a coherent strategic planning process and the will to devise and follow through on a strategic plan that prioritizes challenges and responds over time to meet them successfully. Rigorous strategic planning can help avoid preventable crises. As he does the people's business, the President needs to define our vital national interests and resources available, establish our objectives, and develop a set of foreign and domestic policies that will advance America's interests and ideals.

The broadest objective of any such strategy should be to make an honest appraisal of where the world is today, and what it is likely to look like tomorrow. I call it looking beyond the horizon for potential destinations. Incumbent in this appraisal process, there needs to be a serious and vigorous national debate about the ends or the means or the exits in places of commitment like Pakistan and Afghanistan. I have been very critical of our government. Did we have this debate before we went to Afghanistan? No. Did we have this debate before we went to Iraq? No. We did not have this in Congress. We did not have it in the media. We did not have it among the American people who have, and should have, a voice.

The goal of any grand strategy should be to stabilize the current world order and create mechanisms through which change can occur. Ideally, this grand strategy would be for the greater good of America and the like-minded nations of the world by having a framework that promotes the global system and betters the prospects for trade, commerce, diplomatic contact, pluralism, and liberty. To succeed, it will need the active support and participation of many of the other 195 countries of the world and would seek involvement of others in a collaborative effort to deal effectively with a whole host of problems. One of the fundamental tenets of this grand strategy must be that the United States cannot protect every sea lane, broker every deal, or fight every terrorist group alone. The age of unilateralism is past.

The United States can do a lot but can do even more with willing partners. Speaking at the West Point graduation in May 2010, President Obama said, "America has not succeeded by stepping outside the current of international cooperation. We have succeeded by steering those currents in the direction of liberty and justice." But the United States can and should lead by example. It remains the single global super power, one that can have a unique role in this emerging world order, one that has enormous convening, agenda-setting and leadership powers. For the world, the challenges and consequences of the moment are enormous. For the United States, this moment offers the opportunity to bind the wounds to our reputation with decisions that can heal our image and strengthen our influence with like-minded nations. Doing so can responsibly contribute to making the world a better place and at the same time earn respect as a solid citizen nation of the world. It is a watershed moment that cannot be squandered.

This is a rare and unprecedented time in history. It holds unparalleled importance with respect to the opportunity to help stability, prosperity, and dignity to billions around the world by making good leadership and management decisions. The same is true for companies with respect to their research, their development, and the technologies they advance for the good of their clients and customers. They need to be willing to explore new partners and adjust to the ever changing economic climate and dynamic national security environment. If history is any indicator, which I believe it is, then perhaps the most important people, places, and events that will shape our future are things we cannot know in advance; only prepare for. In the age of exploration, a saying that described these unknown factors was inscribed at the edges of their maps: here there be monsters.

ENDNOTE - CHAPTER 2

1. James Clapper, Testimony before the U.S. Senate, February 2012.

CHAPTER 3

THE TRANSATLANTIC RELATIONSHIP: A BREAKING OR RESTORABLE PILLAR OF A NEW AMERICAN GRAND STRATEGY?

Karl-Theodor zu Guttenberg

The foreign policy community has probably heard more speeches about transatlantic relations than we have grains of sand on the shores of both sides of the Atlantic Ocean. Many of them are inspired by romantic, even nostalgic thoughts. Aside from relatively uninspired references to shared values and interests, there is still a propensity to state the unrivaled global influence of the so called "West." This tendency demonstrates an astonishing hubris.

A notable number of manuscripts still reflect on the effects of a mainly bipolar, cold war-influenced world. It is remarkable that we are still adapting to realities that have had their first turning point almost a quarter of a century ago.

Certainly, the annomination of the dates 11/9 (November 9, 1989) or 9/11 (September 11, 2001) is familiar. But they are neither synonyms nor parallels. The first date has been the rootstock of a significant global geopolitical shift. The other, as horrific as it was, serves less as a source for a new world order than as the poisonous blossom of a long-time neglected, fast growing plant that only partly has the same or similar roots. Although the significance of both dates is widely understood, many strategic answers—irrespective of whether they emerge from the United States or Europe—are still comparatively unsatisfactory, specifically regarding long-term perspectives.

Some refer to these developments as moving from a symmetric world order to a new age of asymmetry and to the consequence of seeking ad hoc solutions. Others refuse to bear the burden of a comprehensive and methodical stocktaking (or evaluation) — not only of current and forthcoming global challenges, but also of their interdependencies. Therefore, the fundament for any long-term assessments or solutions is already porous, and the basis of any pillars of so-called "Grand Strategies" that we are discussing is of limited firmness. One slogan could be: Disconnection through Connection — new, intertwined global challenges and global shifts of power imply the risk of a marginalization of traditional partnerships and multinational institutions. Or: As the world grows together, it is also growing apart.

Four major developments — global governance failures, the global shift of powers, global political awakening, and economic disparity (within and between countries) — influence the evolution of a variety of other global risks, and, ironically, a considerable number of those risks can further magnify the four overarching developments.[1]

What are the risk scenarios that have emerged or will evolve beyond the four cross-cutting global developments? We face at least five major risk clusters that are tightly connected to each other, intertwined, and often overlap into other clusters.

1. Geopolitical risks: We have been talking for years about fragile, failing, and failed states and the consequences, ranging from terrorism, proliferation of weapons of mass destruction (WMD), illicit trade, and organized crime, to piracy or corruption. Furthermore, this cluster includes all sorts of geopolitical conflicts besides classic scenarios to even such areas as space security.

2. Economic risks: As the results of fiscal crises (we have not seen the last one) or as to their reasons, one could name asset price collapses, extreme currency, and price volatilities (on energy, commodities, or consumer prices), liquidity and credit crunches, infrastructure fragility, regulatory failures, etc. Let us also not underestimate a certain retrenchment from globalization going along with these phenomena — and a resurgence of nationalism and populism. In this regard, Europe is not the only union of countries that serves as a shining example.

3. Societal risks: here we have to take into account all challenges that are linked to demographic developments and their effects like energy, food, and water security as well as chronic, infectious, and — in our hemisphere — so-called lifestyle diseases (public health expenditure in the Organization for Economic Cooperation and Development [OECD] countries has risen at twice the rate of economic growth). Western society has already undergone a dramatic change in its age structure. Some call it the "age-quake." The World Health Organization (WHO) uses the phrase "a silent social revolution." This silence echoes (yes, even silence has an echo!) political shyness and inabilities. We must not forget migration and the subsequent urban development (in the future, intercontinental migration will become increasingly important).

4. Societal risks lead us to environmental risks. I am still surprised about the degree of ignorance — or let's put it more mildly: unawareness — in high level political circles in this country when it comes to the question and aftereffects of climate change. Topics like biodiversity loss, melting of the polar ice-caps, flooding, air pollution, waste management, and a growing number of storms and cyclones also merit mention.

5. Technological risks: cyber war is as much a reality as threats from new technologies (including the invisible threat of immaterial environmental pollution, e.g., by electromagnetic radiation). All of this is no longer a "Buck Rogers" fantasy. The chances of a critical information infrastructure breakdown have not been reduced during the last couple of years (the successful cyber attack on Estonia in 2007 should have been a wakeup call). Online data and information security is a mega-topic nowadays, and so are the paradoxa that go along with the call for freedom of the Internet on one hand and the criminal misuse of the net on the other. We see the triumph of open networks—with major complexities that are almost impossible to control responsibly, for those who want to.

Indeed, this is an incomplete list, though it still shows the range of challenges we are facing today and tomorrow.

What has the transatlantic community to offer when it comes to the question of how to get a firm grip on the intertwining lines between and within the clusters? Generally, we could find quite a spectrum of possible measures, if more and explicitly coordinated efforts were to take place. But do we see anything inspiring, anything creative in the political, academic or cultural arena that aims at the challenges mentioned above? Not much, I am afraid. Nonetheless, it is necessary to assess the "epicenter" of the transatlantic relationship first, which is—it may sound simplistic—the people on both sides of the Atlantic.

However, a new generation of policymakers, scholars, and commentators shows a changed attitude and approach toward the Atlantic connection. One reason is that the background and the scope of experiences of many has changed or is at least in an evolutionary phase. In contrast to the second half of the 20th century, many young, even influential Americans have never been based or stationed in Europe. A growing number has an Asian or Latin American heritage.

Think about the students of today in Europe. Many of them were born after 1989. They have never had the existential experience of what it meant to live in a surrounding that urgently needed a functioning transatlantic partnership—imagine their upbringing and environment. A good number come from the former Eastern Europe, others are second or first generation Europeans originating from Turkey or North Africa, with different cultural roots. All this is not problematic at all—on the contrary, it is enriching and a source of inspiration—but it has to be understood and accepted when it comes to a new definition of transatlantic ties.

Second, among the younger generation, pragmatism seems to replace emotions—superficially, this finding is not a political disaster, but rather influences the value-driven approach to the relationship. Ask someone younger about these values, and you will still get the answer: democracy, human rights, rule of law, etc.—but ask the same person how these principles correspond across the Atlantic or to what extent they are implemented at home, and you may get a fascinating, wild mixture of imprecise semi-intellectual sound bites. A clear response would have to imply uncomfortable considerations like aspects of a democracy crisis now faced in certain parts of the Western world. Additionally, negative emotions seem to function quite properly across the ocean; positive sentiments are rarely expressed routinely, if at all.

The last outstanding transatlantic hope and expectation from the European side was connected to Barack Obama (but it was tied to a character and not to a traditional political and cultural construct). Today it seems that many Europeans turned their hope into disillusion. When it comes to the current President, some parts of the European foreign policy community draw the conclusion that an internationally celebrated political rockstar turned out to be a one-time Grammy, respectively Nobel prize winner, at least on the diplomatic platform.

Nevertheless, with respect to foreign affairs capacities, I do not see many auspicious alternatives right now. The range of knowledge in international matters among the remaining Republican presidential candidates is currently only beaten by the overall quality of the TV debates. It is, by the way, an exceptional experience for a European to be bashed again and again by such a spectrum of arguments. All in all, this is a very promising outlook for a flourishing transatlantic perspective.

What is left of the myth of existing transnational institutions? What is left of a creative transatlantic influence on the substance and structure of other international organizations?

First, the North Atlantic Treaty Organization (NATO) has been struggling to adapt to the new security challenges for years and has only selectively widened its scope. Cyber war or energy scarcity may serve as examples, though they have not efficiently been implemented yet. National interests perform as impressive road blocks. The Libya Operation, by the way and despite all songs of praise, is not a NATO success, if you take the decisionmaking behavior of important member states into account. NATO can never win in Afghanistan, and the remaining chance of not losing will probably be sacrificed to accommodate the mood of the voters at home. If I had to define cynicism to my children, I would start with our current Afghanistan policy.

Second, certain structures of the United Nations (UN) remind me of an iceberg drifting into waters with unpredictable warm currents, while the journey of the iceberg started in 1949. However, beneath the iceberg, a rather stable raft appears, unfortunately with only five admittedly quite comfortable seats. The only recognizable transatlantic structural attempts to expand the raft are monuments of standstill and stagnation, artistically inspired by France, the United Kingdom (UK), and the United States and knowingly attracting China and Russia as well. It is not only desperate Syrian hands that slide off the slick side planks of the raft.

Third, I do not want to elaborate in detail on the European crisis, which is worth its own conference. But the current crisis — which is not only a debt crisis or fiscal crisis, but also a crisis of understanding and therefore still a crisis of political leadership — is destabilizing the core concept of the EU as well. I am deeply concerned about the future of the achievements of the EU — achievements that too many people in Europe take for granted. Needless to say, such a crisis has spillover effects for the transatlantic partnership. It strengthens our ominous culture of mutual finger-pointing.

Finally, even organizations of more limited, though significant, scope are struggling, just to name the Organization for Security and Cooperation in Europe (OSCE) and the World Trade Organization (WTO), not to mention the Doha development round. Somehow logical, looser concepts like the G20 are gaining ground, even though the last meeting in Cannes, France, reminded me more of the Film Festivals that usually take place there. So some traditional multi- or transnational frameworks and concepts are on the verge of decay. Does the transatlantic community offer any viable answers? I doubt it. Do we understand the paradox that the circumstances that make better global governance imperative — be they conflicting interests and incentives, divergent values, or differing norms — are also the ones that make its realization so incredibly complex and often unpleasant? I doubt it as well.

Eventually, what are the consequences for Europe and the United States? Will the transatlantic relationship remain a core element of Western political influence or is it in agony because of a "Pacific and Asian 21st Century"? Can the undoubtedly growing trans-Pacific importance be an excuse at all? By no means. It may be one out of many more or less good reasons, but it is also a cheap plea.

So what to do? What are possible steps to avoid a sidelining of the Atlantic perspectives?

- Accepting a new dynamic of multipolarity may sound difficult, but is essential.
- The same is true for the understanding that global stability can be promoted and progressed only through larger scale cooperation and not through imperial behavior or domination (Zbigniew Brzezinski).[2]
- In any case, Europe has to accept trans-Pacific ambitions and should enlarge its own strategic scope. On the other hand, the United States could acknowledge the possibilities of closer responsible European-Russian relations. Both do not necessarily weaken transatlantic relations. On the contrary, they could offer opportunities

for stronger common strategic approaches and for revisions of certain, sometimes archaic, instruments or strategies (EUSS [Eastern Europe Security System]).

- In a mid- to long-term perspective, a broader cooperation between the so-called "old west" and the "new east" does not have to be a daydream any longer. We could mutually benefit from respective impulses and experiences by fostering a regional cooperative model in a multi-polar and increasingly complex geopolitical setting.
- In addition, a bold and long-term strategic vision for the transatlantic community needs to reinvigorate the transatlantic relationship by promoting a global democratic political culture (that respects specific cultural aspects). But we also have to engage in a self critical debate about the state of democracy — led by democratic countries! Existing rifts in this context are not insurmountable.
- Regarding the risk clusters described, we must confront the respective publics with the truth, and not with shimmering party and election programs.

Looking at the United States, a new grand strategy should offer more than an accumulation of unfinished diplomatic bits and pieces. I still have problems trying to figure out the overall logic behind this administration's foreign policy. Where are the connecting lines between the President's Cairo speech and the present Middle East policy? Where is the rationality besides ad hoc procedures? The same questions have to be asked with respect to the EU foreign policy approaches.

To be fair, governments will probably never resolve the dilemma between short-term thinking and the obligation to think in longer strategic terms and to firmly undergo explanatory work. They usually have to concentrate on the more immediate conflicts and disagreements. But this doesn't *exclude* the willingness to form groups and initiatives that *include* knowledge and experience, but also young ideas that range from academia to culture, and to those people who tend to see themselves in a complementary role. All this can only happen if traditions continue to develop and contribute to diversity instead of seeking a uniform global culture. I call it "the expansion of tradition."

Some thoughts that such groups or initiatives would have to cover are more than obvious for me:

- Regarding the span of the global risks and challenges, a well-informed and well-mobilized global public opinion, sharing values and norms of a "global citizenship" (but not a "uniform global culture"), would be certainly desirable, but is still closer to Utopia than to realization. Notwithstanding, in this context the modern means of digital communication could be used much more creatively.
- By accepting the differences, we need to work on our cultural ties. We tend to underestimate them, and they have significantly changed.
- Two rather banal aspects are essential. First, we need to bridge the existing uncertainty among rising powers to shoulder a greater share of global responsibilities. Second, the established powers have to surmount their reluctance to recognize the limits of their own power.
- We have to reach out way past the "old west." Engaging China, Russia, as well as Brazil, In-

dia, or South Africa and Indonesia and others is key. Some European governments still have credibility in areas where the U.S. reputation is—let's say it diplomatically—at least strained.

- Not only does the transatlantic relationship need a new narrative (as a first step toward revised concepts), but so do institutions such as the EU, NATO, UN, etc., because we will not achieve any long-lasting changes without giving our population the opportunity to understand and accept certain obvious complexities and dilemmas.

Such a transatlantic community could serve as a "pulse generator," as a "source of inspiration instead of a source for strategic despair."

To conclude, we need to show both pragmatism and emotions. Pragmatism without emotions hamstrings creativity, and, of course, uncontrolled emotions have led to historic conflicts. I propose to strive for an "emotional pragmatism." The transatlantic relationship deserves a serious endeavor to attain it.

ENDNOTES - CHAPTER 3

1. See also on some of the following risk scenarios, *Global Risks Report*, World Economic Forum, held at Davos-Klosters, Switzerland, in January 2011.

2. Zbigniew Brzezinski, *Strategic Vision: America and the Crisis of Global Power*, New York: Basic Books. 2012.

CHAPTER 4

THE NATURE AND DEMANDS OF SMART POWER

Robert Kennedy

It is often noted that the threats, potential threats, and challenges that confront and will continue to confront the United States today and in the decades ahead are far more complex than those during the Cold War. Indeed, in the decades ahead those threats and challenges will pose a severe test for American leadership in global affairs, whether they arise from the proliferation of nuclear weapons, materials, and know-how; chemical or biological weapons; terrorist organizations, transnational criminal groups, drug cartels, and individuals of malevolent intention; tribal, ethnic, or sectarian strife; or from rising regional powers, failing governments, cross border conflicts, global economic disturbances, environmental degradation, pandemics, or climate change. However, perhaps the greatest challenge of the 21st century will arise from the continued but slow relative shift from the world's predominant political, economic, diplomatic, and military superpower to *primus inter pares* in world affairs.

Following the devastation resulting from World War II, the United States emerged as an economic and military superpower.[1] Its economy was larger, and the country was richer than any other in the world. In terms of industrial strength, the United States was at an absolute and relative advantage over its allies as well as its enemies.[2] Moreover, it was sole possessor of the "bomb."[3]

Today the United States produces about 20 percent of the global economic output, with predictions that soon its economy will fall second to that of China. While the United States and Russia remain the predominant nuclear powers, there are three other so-called "declared" nuclear weapons states under the terms of the Nuclear Non-Proliferation Treaty (NPT)—China, France, and the United Kingdom (UK); three additional states that have tested nuclear weapons—India, Pakistan, and North Korea; Israel (believed to have nuclear weapons); and Iran (an NPT state) that is believed to be seeking to develop nuclear weapons.[4] Though U.S. military forces measured in total manpower remain second only to those of China, with India in a close third, economic pressures are likely to force a reduction in the overall size of U.S. Armed Forces in the years ahead. U.S. military forces can neither be everywhere all of the time nor resolve all conflicts without the assistance of others. Thus, to meet the challenges ahead, including its relative readjustment in status among nations, the United States must wisely apply the instruments of national power (political, economic, psychological, and military). This chapter addresses the nature of national power: its sources, the means by which the sources of a nation's power are transformed into preferred outcomes in the international arena, the instruments states use to do so, and what is demanded if soft and hard power are to be molded into what is now fashionably called "Smart Power."

ON POWER

In its simplest form, power is the ability to achieve what one seeks to achieve. Though there are many definitions of power,[5] in an international context power is generally considered to be the ability of a nation-state, group of states, or nonstate entities to impose its/their favored outcome on a given situation or prevent another state, group of states, or nonstate entity from doing so. It has a deliberate, active connotation. For example, French philosopher Bertrand de Jouvenel, writing over a half century ago, noted: "When Power addresses itself to a foreign state, the weight behind the words is proportional to its ability to make itself obeyed and win from that obedience the means of action."[6] It is in getting one's way, in "making" others conform to one's will, in its active, deliberate sense that power is most often understood.

Yet power has always had a much broader connotation. It is true in one sense, as de Jouvenel argued, that power "turns on obedience," and he "Who knows the reasons for that obedience knows the inner nature of power."[7] Indeed, history is marked by states employing their power to force other states to their will. However, there is more to the essence of power than can be gathered under the umbrella of obedience. Obedience, or to put it more directly, an action undertaken by Party B that is favorable to Party A is not always the result of active efforts on the part of Party A to seek obedience from Party B. A painting can have the power to produce a series of thought patterns or emotions or move the viewer to action. The picture is powerful. It has power so-to-speak. But it has not made or commanded the viewer to obey. The power it has on the viewer is often noncognitive, frequently related to the emotive aspect of a viewer's personality, though there can be cognitive, rational components based on the attitudes and/or beliefs or on the physical or psychogenic needs of the viewer. Similarly, in international affairs, for example, though an individual,

say from Nation B, may risk his life providing intelligence to Nation A because of bribe or threat, that individual may well do so for quite different reasons such
as respect for Nation A's objectives or perceptions of
shared values, a commonality of ideals, beliefs, and/
or interests. He does not obey or comply, rather he
volunteers. Of course de Jouvenel recognized this aspect of power in his exploration of the nature of obedience.[8] Moreover, it is this aspect of power, the power
of attraction or seduction (particularly in its passive
sense), that Joseph Nye, Jr., first introduced in 1990[9]
as "soft power" and further developed in 2004[10] and
2011.[11] As Nye put it in 2004 in answering the question, "What is soft power?"

> It is the ability to get what you want through attraction
> rather than coercion or payments. It arises from the at-
> tractiveness of a country's culture, political ideals, and
> policies.[12]

Nye distinguishes this so-called soft power from
hard power. Hard power "rests on inducements ("carrots") or threats ("sticks")."[13] It is "Command power . . .
the ability to get desired outcomes through coercion
and payment."[14] On the other hand, soft power is "the
ability to get preferred outcomes through co-optive
means of agenda setting, persuasion, and attraction."[15]

Soft power, in general, is based on less tangible
sources of power than is hard power. So what, then,
are the sources of a nation's power and what means
can be used to translate those sources into preferred
outcomes in the international arena?

Sources and Means of Power.

The sources on which a nation's power is based are many and varied. They include such factors as: a nation's geography; natural resources; size, nature, and health of its economy; industrial capability; quality of education; population; culture; traditions; language; history; level of technology; ability to innovate; internal organization; the quality of its diplomacy; the size, composition, training, and leadership of its military, as well as the nature and effectiveness of its weapons and equipment; its legal institutions; the efficiency and effectiveness of its government; political, economic, and social resilience; sound strategy; and national will. These are the sources or what are sometimes called the elements upon which a nation's power rests. Some of these sources can be objectively measured—e.g., landmass; population; resources; gross domestic product; external trade; and numbers of military aircraft, tanks, artillery, and manpower. Some are primarily subjective—e.g., quality of leadership, effectiveness of the diplomatic corps, morale of troops, quality of military training, and national will. However, both objective and subjective sources of power are the building blocks of a nation's soft, as well as hard, power.

Whether objective or subjective, the sources of power seldom function independently. For example, a nation may be blessed with a vast expanse of territory that might strain an invading army's logistical reinforcement to the breaking point. However, in the absence of a capable military, the defender might not be able to put up effective resistance. A nation may have an abundance of natural resources, but a weak and ineffective economy, poor governance, or corruption may inhibit or sap the ability of a nation to translate its natural resources into power. A nation with a strong economy may not be able to translate its economic strength into a tool for pressuring another state to action or inaction through the use of economic sanctions without effective diplomatic efforts to garner the support of other nations to join in sanctions. The most technologically advanced army with poor leadership or faulty strategy may fall to a less advanced army with good leadership and a sound strategy.

Success in translating the sources of power into preferred outcomes in the international arena depends in large measure on a nation's ability to influence, persuade, coerce, deter, and/or compel the actions/behavior of other international actors. Power measured in resources does not necessarily equate to power measured in preferred outcomes.[16] An understanding of these means or methods reveals essential differences between what is meant by soft and hard power.

Influence.

Influence is the ability to produce an effect without the apparent need to act, exert force, or use threats or commands. Influence is a principal aspect of "soft power." Influence depends heavily upon the perceptions of others. Influence can be indirect and passive or direct and active. Passive or indirect influence generally depends on existing relationships among nations and peoples and is the result of perceptions by others of an affinity for or attraction to such things as one's culture, traditions, language, values, institutions, or policies, or from respect by others for a nation's political, economic, or military power. For example, the

UK, with a culture, language, traditions, values, and institutions similar to those of the United States, has an influence on U.S. behavior beyond that of the UK's military or economic power. Had the UK not sided with the United States in going to war against Iraq, it is questionable whether the administration could have gained the support of Congress for that effort. Similarly, a sense of shared values and similar, if not identical, democratic institutions between most European nations and the United States affords the United States an influence in Europe beyond its military might. Of course, America's economic strength and military capabilities played a major role during the Cold War confrontation with the Soviet Union and continue to do so today. This fact, however, in no way detracts from the general affinity that affords the United States and the democratic nations of Europe influence over each other's actions.

Indirect or passive influence can also have negative effects. Where values, institutions, cultures, etc., diverge, a nation's influence in a given situation may be negative. The late Samuel P. Huntington postulated a "Clash of Civilizations: The great divisions among humankind and the dominating source of conflict will be cultural,"[17] thus signaling that differences of culture can trigger not affinity but dislike, rejection, even hatred.

Influence can also be direct or active. For example, a nation can use public diplomacy in order to promote its image. Treaties, alliances, and executive agreements also can provide a nation with direct influence on the behavior of others.

Persuasion.

Persuasion is the ability to move by argument, entreaty, or expostulation another party to a belief, viewpoint, or political position, or to undertake or not undertake (dissuade) a course of action. Persuasion involves active, intentional efforts. Like influence, its success or failure often depends on previous relationships, and like influence it is an exercise in soft power. However, persuasion depends heavily on a nation's diplomatic skill in translating knowledge of another country's interests, objectives, and concerns into effective augmentation in support of a preferred outcome. Persuasion demands actual leverage in the logic of argumentation. Thus it demands in depth knowledge of potential social, economic, political, and/or military consequences of the action contemplated, as such consequences are likely to be viewed from the target nation's perspective.

Because of the existence of multiple voices emanating from varying sectors of society that lie beyond the government's ability to control, democracies have an inherently more complex task in using a nation's diplomatic skills in attempts to persuade others to its position. Differing interpretations of events, differing evaluations of options, and different desired outcomes from different sectors of society, often from different departments or branches of government, complicate a nation's ability to speak with one voice as it articulates its position, and may reinforce uncertainties in the minds of those one is trying to persuade. Leaks of information from within the nation's bureaucracy suggesting different courses of action can further complicate the task.

Coercion.

Coercion is the ability to demand another to undertake or not undertake an action through threat, intimidation, or bribe. Coercion is active in nature. It is a deliberate attempt to pressure another party to act in ways that advance one's preferred outcomes and, as such, falls in the category of hard power. Coercion may be direct, for example, through the threat of political, economic, or military consequences the other party would find undesirable. It also may be indirect, for example, through the leaking of a memorandum or media releases provided as background or deep background[18] information, suggesting that such undesired consequences are being considered.

For coercion to be successful, actual power (political, economic, and/or military) or the perception that the coercing nation has the actual power to affect undesired consequences and the will and determination to do so are generally necessary. As with persuasion, in democracies the ability to coerce may be weakened, as parliaments or Congress debate the merits of potential threats or where parliamentary or congressional approval may be required to carry threats into force.

Deterrence.

Deterrence is the ability to discourage another from undertaking an action they might otherwise prefer to undertake. Deterrence generally falls into the category of hard power, primarily because it entails a threat to produce undesired consequences should the other fellow decide to act. It is usually understood in its passive context and generally has an effect on a state's cost versus benefit calculations under a given set of circumstances. For example, a state might be deterred from acting because of the existence of countervailing nuclear or conventional forces, as a result of potential economic or other sanctions, or because it perceives the potential loss of some promised or extant benefit, any and all of which might suggest costs in excess of benefits. Of course, the classic case of deterrence took place during the Cold War when presumably the Soviet Union was deterred from using its nuclear weapons against the United States because the United States possessed countervailing nuclear capabilities.

Deterrence also can be active, for example, by promising a desired good to another state for its inactivity. Here the line between deterrence, coercion, and persuasion becomes somewhat blurred. In one sense, it could be argued that in offering a desired good for inactivity, one is attempting to use the soft power of persuasion to convince the other party that it is in its interest to act accordingly by altering perceptions of interest. It also could be argued that one is using the promise of a benefit as a hard power bribe in order to place pressure on political decisionmakers in the target country in order to coerce them into not taking action. It perhaps could be equally argued that one state is deterring another from an action that it might otherwise take by altering their cost benefit calculations.

Like coercion, deterrence usually requires actual power, or the perception on the part of an opponent, that one has the power—political, economic, and/or military—and the will and determination to bring about the undesired consequences or to provide a desired good. Generally speaking, deterrence relies on hard power. This is not to say that deterrence per se is an exercise in hard power. Extant political, economic, or military power affects perceptions. As such, others may be deterred from acting, for example, not because Country A deployed a naval force to a region to discourage some particular activity, but because the very existence of that force in that region has structured perceptions that serve to discourage actions by others. In such a case, there is no hard power threat. The threat, if any, exists in the perceptions of others. They may perceive the existence of the deployed force as a threat, as an exercise in hard power. But the existence of military forces, per se, does not constitute an exercise in hard power. Indeed, deploying military forces for humanitarian purposes is an exercise in soft power.

Compellence.

A term usually attributed to Thomas Schelling, compellence is the ability to secure one's preferred outcome through the direct application of force — political, economic, and/or more often than not, military. It is the opposite of deterrence. It requires actual power to force an opponent to act. It is the ultimate expression of hard power. Some confuse it with coercion. For example, one definition contends: "It is compellence when the classic lawman threatens a suspect with death if he does not surrender."[19] Yet this is better understood as coercion. The suspect has not been "forced" to surrender. Rather he is encouraged to do so by virtue of threat. The suspect still has a choice. He can surrender or take his chances. On the other hand, if the lawman physically grabs the suspect or shoots him in the legs so he cannot move, there is no choice involved. He has been compelled to surrender. If Country A with a superior military force destroys Country B's advancing army, it has compelled that army to halt. If Country A threatens to destroy Country B's army if it fails to stop, it is attempting to coerce it to stop its advance. Both examples, of course, are examples of uses of hard power.

Instruments of Power.

The instruments of power are those tools — political/diplomatic, economic, psychological, and military — a nation employs to transform some, though not all, its sources of power into preferred outcomes through the use of the above noted means. However, a nation's ability to affect a particular behavior in a given situation may not depend, solely or at all, on the active use of the instruments of power. As was mentioned earlier, the ability to influence has a passive side, that of attraction and seduction, that exists prior to any attempts to induce a specific behavior on the part of another. This is the "soft power" that Nye so often trumpets. Nevertheless, though the instruments of power are active by nature, they can be employed to produce soft as well as hard power. Moreover, they often can make use of the soft power of attraction and seduction as they are employed, for example, in soft power efforts to persuade.

Political-Diplomatic.

Political-diplomatic power is the ability to achieve one's ends through reason, symbols, and/or through emotive elements of human nature. It generally resides in the land of discussions, negotiations, and demarches designed to inform, persuade, or gather information. But its reach goes well beyond the government demarche. Diplomats and their supporting elements in the various agencies of government help set the tone and tenor of relations between states and other international actors. They wallow in soft power. Their success and the success of their mission often rely on knowledge and understanding of the culture, history, traditions, norms, values, and language of their assigned country, as well as that country's political processes, players and their personalities, and the issues they are confronting. Political-diplomatic power need not be exercised directly with those who make decisions. It often functions effectively through an understanding of the milieu surrounding those making decisions and by focusing on those who exercise influence over decisionmakers in a given polity.

Success in employing the political diplomatic instrument of power also relies on a thorough understanding of the objectives and concerns of the country, countries, or other entities involved, and the capabilities those entities have to meet their objectives and alleviate or mitigate their concerns. For example, prior to Iraq's 1990 invasion of Kuwait, the George H. W. Bush administration misread, with the help of some Arab allies, Saddam Hussein's intentions and sent mixed signals to him that may have helped pave the way for Hussein's final decision to invade—an evident diplomatic failure on the part of the Bush administration. Following the invasion, the Bush administration successfully used the political-diplomatic instrument of power to build not only a supportive domestic coalition, but also an international coalition supportive and contributing to the ultimate use of hard military power to remove Iraqi forces from Kuwait. Knowledge of the predispositions of the audiences involved played an essential role. In that immediate post-Cold War environment, the Bush administration built a domestic as well as European coalition for action by equating Saddam Hussein to Hitler and evoking concerns over appeasement and further conquest. Appealing to those same audiences, as the price of a barrel of crude oil jumped nearly 50 percent during the month following the invasion, members of the administration also were quick to point out the potential economic implications should a significant amount of Middle East oil fall under the control of one man.

On the other hand, to Arabs, unlikely to be moved by the Hitler analogy, and with some perhaps happy to see higher prices for their crude oil and with many not greatly enamored by what they perceived as a generally haughty attitude on the part of Kuwaitis, the naked aggression of one Arab state against another played well.

The political-diplomatic instrument of power can also have a hard power coercive face. The withdrawal of the American diplomatic mission to Syria in February 2012, for example, was an effort to coerce the Syrian government to step down or alter its policy of killing those who oppose the rule of Bashar al-Assad. Leaks to the press, statements by policymakers, comments by diplomats, official demarches, and such that suggest the possibility of economic sanctions or military action fall under the hard power rubric of political coercion.

Political-diplomatic power originates at the highest offices of government, flowing through a variety of agencies and their representatives that deal with other nations, international organizations, and nonstate actors. As noted above, the political-diplomatic instrument is often significantly augmented by affinities that exist between the peoples and governments of the entities involved. In that sense political-diplomat power begins at home.

Economic.

When one thinks about the economic instrument of power, one frequently thinks of economic "carrots" and "sticks." Carrots and sticks are what one party uses to coerce another party to undertake an action that they might not be inclined to undertake. Carrots, for example promises of trade, economic assistance, debt forgiveness, access to technology, and the provision of resources such as military hardware, are the "sweeteners" meant to encourage a specific action. "Sweetener" is a euphemism for the word "bribe." Sticks, such as the declared intent to withdraw economic assistance, impose economic sanctions, and/or trade embargoes, are threats a state may use to elicit a certain behavior. Since carrots and sticks are unlikely to alter basic attitudes and beliefs about a given situation on the part of those to whom they are directed, they are in essence coercion instruments that reside in the realm of hard power, whether during the offer, threat, or implementation stage.

The economic instrument of power, however, should not be confused with the normal ebb and flow of trade, technology, economic aid and/or developmental assistance, and certain forms of security assistance, such as assistance provided to improve the professionalism and capabilities of police forces. The size of a nation's economy, the volume and patterns of trade, and the quality of its economic interaction in the world arena underwrite its ability to elicit the behavior of others. Such activity may provide a soft power, passive ability to influence behaviors. Economic assets and capabilities become instruments of hard power when used subtly or otherwise to deliberately bring about actions congruent with one's preferences, as, for example, is the case in U.S. efforts to get Iran to cease activities the United States and others consider are aimed at producing nuclear weapons.

Of the instruments of power, the successful use of the economic instrument has a checkered past. First, because it can have a damaging effect on a target nation's economy and thus result in the suffering of innocents, the economic instrument applied by one state can be used by the target state to unite its citizenry against those who reduce economic assistance or impose sanctions or embargoes. Another impediment to the successful employment of the economic instrument is the negative consequences it can have on the initiating country or countries and their allies. Employing the economic instrument seldom comes without pain. For example, attempting to coerce Iran into meeting its obligations under the NPT by placing an embargo on Iranian oil, if effective, is likely to result in a painful increase in the price of crude oil with potentially serious negative implications for the world economy. Despite such potential undesired consequences, the economic instrument has become an aspect of hard power that often for political and psychological effects must be employed. States need to believe that everything that could be done has been done before agreeing to the use of military force.

Psychological.

The psychological instrument of national power relies on the perceptions of others. It finds its roots in both soft and hard power, covers a wide spectrum of activities, and has a passive and active aspect. Psychological appeal is a primary ingredient of influence. Its passive aspect frequently is a byproduct of other factors and activities.[20] For example, in the aftermath of the industrial revolution, the theories of Karl Marx, two world wars, strong economic growth at home, and Soviet support internationally for those seeking to break the bonds of colonialisms, among other things, the Union of Soviet Socialist Republics (USSR) and its communist model enjoyed wide psychological appeal. The psychological impact of Soviet successes, by military or other means, certainly played a role in President Dwight Eisenhower's espousal of the "falling domino" principle.[21] Similarly, the psychology of people was on his mind in a 1955 letter to Sir Winston Churchill in which he noted that any further victories for communism would have an adverse impact on the minds of neutrals.[22]

In the post-Cold War era, the glaring success of the U.S. military in defeating in 100 hours what was then the world's fourth largest army had an enormous impact on the perceptions of America's military might. Though affecting the perceptions of others may not have been the driving force behind the U.S. use of force in the 1991 Gulf war, perceptions of a technologically dominant, militarily powerful America willing to stand up to aggression and committed to a new international cooperative system emerged. Such perceptions surely contributed to America's soft power ability to influence other players in the international arena. Today, by virtue of such factors as size, population, and expanding economy, China has affected the perceptions of others about its current and future power and its appropriate place in the world hierarchy of nations. Thus nations are becoming more deferential toward China than in years past.

On the other hand, the psychological instrument of power includes deliberate efforts to manipulate the attitudes, beliefs, and emotions of others to create favorable impressions. This is the active aspect of the psychological dimension of power. Since it relies on perceptions, it finds its roots in both hard and soft power. Thus there can be, and usually is, a psychological aspect to efforts to influence, persuade, coerce, and compel the behavior of others. For example, just before the end of the Vietnam War, the Four Party Joint Military Team, established under provisions of the January 1973 Paris peace accords, met in Hanoi. At that meeting, Colonel Harry Summers, Chief of the Negotiations Division of the U.S. Delegation, in a conversation with Colonel Tu, Chief of the North Vietnamese Delegation, remarked: "You know you never defeated us on the battlefield." Colonel Tu responded: "That may be so, but it is also irrelevant."[23] It was irrelevant because the war was fought not just at the military level, but also at the soft power psychological level. General Vo Nguyen Giap's forces may not have defeated the Americans on the Vietnamese battlefields, but they won on the psychological battlegrounds in Washington, DC, on college campuses, and in the streets of America and thus, in a sense, compelled a change in U.S. behavior.

Similarly, as Iraqi troops broke ranks, withdrew, and surrendered en masse during the 1991 Gulf War, they did so not only because they were defeated in battle, but also because of the psychological effects of America's superior technology. When in the middle of a quiet night, the tanks to left and right explode under attack from seemingly nowhere, the psychology is not to stay in your tank and fight, but to abandon the next obvious target and run. That is the ultimate in hard power battlefield coercion.

On the soft power side, the official diplomatic corps as well as a nation's public diplomacy play major roles. The diplomatic corps not only help shape perceptions of one's nation among a target nation's leaders, but also play a role in public diplomacy, the task of which is to help shape perceptions among leaders and the populace in target countries through the provision of information. Mary K. Eder, an authority in strategic communications, writes:

> All communication conducted with intent does more than merely inform. It educates, reveals, restricts, and can elicit strong emotion. Most important, information as an element of national power also influences and can powerfully inform governments, direct public opinion, affect international relations, result in military action, and build or deny support.[24]

Among the least costly and most useful instruments of public diplomacy that have been created in the post-Cold War period are the Department of Defense (DoD)-run regional centers. The George C. Marshall European Center for Security Studies, The Asia-Pacific Center for Security Studies, The Center for Hemispheric Defense Studies, The Africa Center for Strategic Studies, and the Near East South Asia Center for Strategic Studies bring together leaders from their respective regions to examine jointly many of the complex issues that confront our nations. Discussions at these centers are characterized by openness and honest attempts to understand differing points of view. Value is ascribed to individuals and their ideas irrespective of the nations from which they come. Thus, they provide a window on American society and its values and add dramatically to the reach of America's soft power.

However, both the passive and active aspects of the psychological dimension of power can be fleeting. For example, as the Soviet economy began to wane under the weight of its own contradictions in the late 1960s and early 1970s and as the repressive nature of the Soviet system became more clearly visible to others, the psychological appeal of the Soviet system diminished. Similarly, when the United States and its partners in the North Atlantic Treaty Association (NATO) attacked Yugoslavia from March to June 1999, the favorable image that many Russians had of the United States following the end of the Cold War soured. One observed a similar phenomenon in other parts of the world when the United States invaded Iraq in 2003, without United Nations (UN) authority, with a justification unsatisfying to many, and against the recommendation of many of its allies and friends. As a result, American soft power was significantly diminished.

Similarly, public diplomacy caught in a deliberate lie can raise suspicions and undermine years of efforts. To highlight the difference between truth and propaganda, Edward R. Murrow, the U.S. Information Agency (USIA) director from 1961-64 said:

> American traditions and the American ethic require us to be truthful, but the most important reason is that truth is the best propaganda and lies are the worst. To be persuasive we must be believable; to be believable we must be credible; to be credible we must be truthful. It is as simple as that.[25]

Military.

The military instrument of power is usually thought of as "hard power" — "the capacity to use violence for protection, enforcement or extension of authority."[26] It clearly operates in the realms of deterrence, coercion, and compellence. In a world of independent sovereign states, perpetually in competition for scarce resources in an environment where there is no acknowledged higher authority, military power is seen as the *Ultima Ratio Regum*.[27]

One has little difficulty understanding hard power aspects, for example, of allied military forces compelling the surrender of Nazi Germany during World War II; or the hard power value of U.S. strategic nuclear forces as deterrents to a Soviet nuclear attack on the United States during the Cold War; or, for that matter, the hard power used to evict Iraqi forces from Kuwait in 1991.

However, there are other dimensions to the military instrument of power. Today, the purely "kinetic" (a word in modern military parlance as used by Bob Woodward in his *Bush at War*) aspects of the military instrument—killing and/or destroying if you will, is often seen as increasingly less useful in solving many of the security problems nations and peoples confront.

Even during the height of the Cold War, there were those who believed that the forces amassed by the superpowers had markedly limited utility. In 1968, Harvard professor Stanley Hoffmann wrote that the superpowers:

> . . . enjoy an exceptionally high negative productivity but suffer from a low productivity of power. . . . [They are] able to prevent each other (as well as, *a fortiori*, all others) from achieving their goals sought by force . . . [however, they are unable to] fully resort to coercion in order to force another into agreement or submission.[28]

With the Cold War now more than 2 decades behind us, further questions have arisen concerning the utility of military forces. Many argue that the international environment is less dangerous today than it was during 4 1/2 decades of Soviet-American confrontation. Gone are the massive Soviet military forces threatening Western Europe. While there are significant policy differences between the United States and Russia and China, war with either seems highly unlikely. Of course, the United States does face dangers that could have devastating consequences, particularly should terrorists acquire weapons of mass destruction (WMD) or from states such as North Korea or Iran, should they acquire nuclear weapons and associated delivery systems. However, none of these dangers or their potential consequences is likely to be anywhere near the same magnitude as those that existed during the Cold War. Thus today, many question the need for large nuclear and conventional military forces. They see the primary value of nuclear weapons as resident in their utility as a deterrent. They contend that since they fail to meet just war criteria, their use, even threatened use, is not credible during lesser conflicts or confrontations. Raymond Aron once noted:

> Ballistic missiles . . . have less influence on the course of events than the English fleet sitting at anchor may have had during the 19th century. . . . They do not permit either of the great powers to dictate to their allies or clients instructing them on how they must conduct themselves. . . .[29]

This point made many years ago remains no less true today and readily applies to modern nonstate actors. Indeed, the real hard power value of military forces in the 21st century is more often likely to be inversely proportional to their destructive potential, with strategic nuclear forces as least useful and special operations conventional forces as most useful. Moreover, with such conflicts in mind as Algeria in the late 1950s, Vietnam in the 1960s and 1970s, and perhaps in such contemporary conflicts as those in Iraq and Afghanistan, those who question the utility of military power are quick to note that even a preponderance of conventional forces cannot always or easily be translated into political victory. Indeed, in ideological, ethnic, and sectarian quarrels, as well as in dealing with terrorism, the military instrument may be the least appropriate, though sometimes necessary, instrument. Ideas, it is said, cannot be defeated by force of arms.

There is much truth in such arguments. Nevertheless, the military instrument of power cannot be understood in its entirety simply as the employment of hard power. Rather, it is a multifaceted instrument that can play a role in advancing a nation's interests from soft power influence to hard power coercion and compellence. As Michael Howard, speaking about military power, noted some years ago:

> Indeed, it is not easy to see how international relations could be conducted, and international order maintained, if it were totally absent. The capacity of states to defend themselves, and their evident willingness to do so, provides the basic framework within which the business of international negotiation is carried on.[30]

Such factors as size, readiness, disposition, and perceived or demonstrated effectiveness, as well as perceptions of future capabilities can have an enormous psychological impact on friend and foe. The soft power influence of the military begins with investments in military research and development and is further nurtured by the acquisition of military systems; both of these are often seen as statements of future intent as well as capabilities. Soft power psychological aspects of military power also are often advanced by the temporary, as well as relatively long-term deployment of forces abroad. Perceptions of highly competent and effective military forces deployed to a region can help shape (influence) the views of others. For example, in December 1907 President Theodore Roosevelt dispatched an armada of 16 battleships of the U.S. Atlantic Fleet on a 14-month trip around the world. The purpose of the voyage was to showcase America's growing military power, particularly its newly acquired blue-water navy, its industrial prowess,[31] and its ability and determination to protect American interests around the globe. Belching black smoke, this steam-powered, steel armada, later dubbed the "Great White Fleet" because the ships were painted white with gilded scrollwork on their bows, traveled 43,000 miles and visited 20 ports of call. Save for a donnybrook in Rio de Janeiro, Brazil, the voyage was generally a diplomatic success, with a Chilean cruiser guiding the fleet through the Straits of Magellan, a 9-day celebration of George Washington's birthday in Callao, Peru, and with more than 250,000 people staying up all night so as not to miss the fleet's arrival in Sydney, Australia. Perhaps the most dramatic success came with the Great White Fleet's visit to Yokohama, Japan. A flimsy arch set up to honor the arrival of the Fleet caught fire. Atop the pole on the arch was mounted a Japanese flag. Before the flames could reach the flag, a U.S. Marine from the Fleet, climbed up the side of the arch that had yet to catch fire and dramatically rescued the flag. The observing Japanese crowd went wild, hoisting the Marine onto their shoulders and parading through the streets.[32]

Roosevelt also dispatched these great dread-noughts to impress upon the Japanese, who were in an expansionist mood, still chafing over their failure to get all they wanted out of the Roosevelt-mediated 1906 Treaty of Portsmouth that ended their triumphant war with Russia, and irritated over anti-Japanese riots that were sweeping California, that the United States could protect its interests in the Pacific Ocean even though the bulk of its blue-water naval assets were located in the Atlantic Ocean. Shortly after the fleet's October 18-25, 1908, visit to Yokohama, the Japanese ambassador in Washington, DC, received instructions to reach an agreement with the United States that would recognize the Pacific Ocean as an open avenue of trade, and promise equal opportunity in China. The ensuing Root-Takahira agreement was signed on November 30, 1908.[33] This was a classic exercise in the soft use of the military instrument of power to win friends and influence people. There was no threat, no bribe, and no effort to compel.

During the Cold War, the United States deployed hundreds of thousands of land, air, and sea forces to Europe. Those military deployments eased security concerns among Western Europeans and freed them to focus their efforts on post-war economic recovery. Both directly, through close military collaboration and the political collaboration that such military collaboration spawned, and indirectly, through the feeling of security U.S. military forces provided, the United States and Western European states and peoples forged close relationships. Psychologically comforted by the U.S. military presence, Europeans were often willing to let the United States take the lead on security matters, even in some cases on foreign political issues. Thus, the United States influenced the behavior of these states simply by virtue of the presence of its military forces.

Similarly, deployments in the Persian/Arabian Gulf and elsewhere provide a sense of security and stability that often serves as the glue of civil relations among states in those regions and accrues influence to the United States. Admittedly, however, in some cases one or more states (e.g., Iran in the Persian/Arabian Gulf) or nonstate actors (e.g., Somali pirates) will see such deployments as coercive in nature. Thus deployments can serve simultaneously as instruments of both the soft power of influence with friends and hard coercive power with adversaries.

Perhaps an important additional benefit to the deployment of U.S. military force abroad is the apparent direct effect on growth. A 2007 study of U.S. military presence in 94 countries from 1950 to 2000 revealed that putting U.S. forces in a country over time was associated with an increase in the per capita growth rate of that country by an extra 1.8 percentage points per year. Perhaps more interesting, the study found that military, economic, or social aid was not a good substitute. The authors found "more troops predict more growth, but more aid does not." Furthermore, the study revealed that usual explanations for this phenomenon—the multiplier effect of spending by U.S. forces on the local economy have a short-term effect, but robust long-term growth correlates more with the exemplar effect. When locals saw how the U.S. military did business, it changed the business culture and courts, with salubrious effects on commerce.[34]

The soft aspect of military forces is also evident in such activities as the U.S. training and education of foreign militaries whether in the United States or abroad, as well as other forms of security assistance, including U.S. participation in joint exercises, and U.S. involvement in peacekeeping operations, humanitarian assistance, and disaster relief. In each of these cases the U.S. military is often seen as providing a good that meets the needs of others and thus helps shape the views of those directly assisted, as well as others, about the nature of American society and its values.

The Demands of Smart Power.

Smart Power has been defined as the skillful combination of hard and soft power.[35] The Center for Strategic and International Studies Commission on Smart Power noted: "Smart power means developing an integrated strategy, resource base, and tool kit to achieve American objectives, drawing on both hard and soft power."[36] If these are the objectives of smart power, what are the essential demands of smart power that must be met if the United States is to achieve these objectives?

Vision.

The United States must have a vision of the kind of domestic environment and international order it hopes will emerge in the decades ahead. Without such a vision, it will be unable to further develop its domestic sources of power and focus the instruments of soft and hard power "smartly" in ways that support the achievement of its international vision. It will not be able to balance often competing, short, medium, and longer-term objectives, prioritizing and sacrificing what it must to achieve more important objectives and thereby encouraging movement within the international community in the desired direction.

Investing in the Sources of Power.

If the United States wishes to remain a dominant, if not always predominant, international player in the 21st century, it must further develop the sources of its soft and hard power. While it can do little to alter its geography and the provision of natural resources, the ability to develop its other sources of power is only limited by the wisdom and imagination of its national and local leaderships. For example, ensuring a healthy economy will require a wise balance between the further development of business and industry and environmental concerns such as air, water, and soil pollution that undermine the quality of working and living conditions, which add long-term, though often immediate, costs to health care, and often lower labor productivity.

In an increasingly globalized economy, U.S. success will demand stronger investments in education. To many, the current system increasingly appears to be broken. According to rankings released by the Organization for Economic Cooperation and Development (OECD) Programme for International Student Assessment, which compares the knowledge and skills of 15-year-olds in 70 countries around the world, the United States has fallen to "average." The OECD reported further noted that investment in education is paid back many times over. For example, according to the report increasing U.S. reading, math, and science scores by 25 points over the next 20 years would result in a gain of $41 trillion for the U.S. economy over the lifetime of the generation born in 2010. Bringing the United States up to the performance of the best performing education system among OECD members could result in economic gains up to as much as $103 trillion.[37] The report further notes that the quality of education depends on several factors. First, an actual rather than rhetorical commitment to education as weighed against other commitments, for example, as expressed in terms of pay versus the pay of other highly skilled workers, or as expressed in terms of how education credentials are weighed against other qualifications when people are considered for jobs. Second is "clear and ambitious standards that are shared across the system, with a focus among other things on higher-order thinking skills." Third is high quality teachers and principals—"student learning is ultimately the product of what goes on in the classroom." Last, but not least, world-class education systems deliver high-quality learning outcomes consistently across the entire education system.[38]

The United States may not be in as precipitous decline in technology and innovation as Thomas L. Friedman and Michael Mandelbaum suggested in *That Used to Be Us*. According to one recent study, it still ranks first in patents per capita. It is sixth in economic output devoted to research and development investment and seventh in scientific and engineering researchers per capita. Combining all three measures in a broad assessment of the technological and innovative capabilities of the world's leading nations, the United States ranks third. In each category, the so-called BRIC countries (Brazil, Russia, India, and China) fall far behind.[39] Nevertheless, future competitiveness in a globalized world economy demands that the United States vigorously encourage and support technological innovation. In many ways, America's technological future is highly correlated to its educational system at all levels. While the U.S. university system remains the best in the world,[40] the university product remains dependent on inputs from primary and secondary schools. According to the World Economic Forum (WEF), the United States is ranked 48th in the quality of mathematics and science education. Though there are significant questions about the validity of WEF opinion-based ratings, nevertheless, the ratings are generally in line with OECD rankings. This does not bode well for the future.

Re-examining the educational processes for U.S. diplomats and military leaders is also warranted. Once inducted into the Foreign Service, U.S. diplomats find the educational opportunities somewhat limited. There is nothing comparable to the through-career educational programs available to advance the professional skills of military officials. On the other hand, in an increasingly complex world where the demands on military personnel go well beyond battlefield skills, the military educational system has become increasingly focused on operational issues, often providing little time for education and training on issues associated with the broader aspects of national strategy, national military strategy, and the military's role in soft power projection.

Finally, when viewed from afar, what appears to many Americans as a dysfunctional political system is likely to be taken by proponents of more authoritarian models of governance as an example of the failings of democracy style government. On the other hand, other non-Americans may simply take it as the rough and tumble of democratic (republic style) politics. In either case, the long-term effects of apparently disappearing concepts of compromise within the American political system may well undermine the domestic effectiveness and efficiency of the United States and, in turn, the ability to use its soft and hard power in pursuit of American interests abroad. Political parties had yet to be formed when the *U.S. Constitution* was written and debated. However, in *Federalist Paper #10*, James Madison warned of the dangers of "faction." By faction, he meant:

> a number of citizens, whether amounting to a majority or a minority of the whole, who are united and actuated by some common impulse of passion, or of interest, adversed [sic] to the rights of other citizens, or to the permanent and aggregate interests of the community.

However, he assumed that the problem would be mitigated in a republic of vast citizenry and territory, where interest would be diffuse and the prospect for faction diminished. The republic thus would be saved from faction by compromises made to advance the broader community. Indeed, in a democratic republic, by definition there can be no absolutes. Such a system is based on finding a common way ahead. Today, in a political system where political parties are increasingly dominated by extremes, where elective politics seems to demand that the supposedly wiser representatives of the people reflect rather than inform extremes and where compromise has become a bad word, gridlock dominates to the detriment of the nation. Should this continue, America will find itself weaker in most, if not all, sources of its soft power.

Commitment to a Norms-based International Community.

The United States is unlikely to remain the only or predominant "superplayer" in the international community. If it wishes to have its interests protected and perhaps advanced in the future, it will need to continue the development of a norms-based rather than interest-based international community. As World War II was drawing to a close, the United States established itself as the preeminent advocate of a norms-based international environment, with its efforts to establish such organizations as the UN, the International Bank for Reconstruction and Development (World Bank), and the International Monetary Fund (IMF). Following the war, it played a major role in the formation of the General Agreement on Tariffs and Trade (GATT) and its successor, the World Trade Organization (WTO). In the drafting of such documents as the Universal Declaration of Human Rights, modeled in part after the U.S. Bill of Rights, the International Covenant on Civil and Political Rights, and the 1949 Geneva Conventions, and in advancing global guidelines for land use and property rights, the United States also has played a key role in advancing international law, an essential basis for a norms-based international community. Norms set by these institutions have served the United States very well. They have established mechanisms for dialogue on issues of international concern. They have provided for economic stability and development. They have advanced America's long-standing preference for free and open trade among nations, as well as concepts of human rights in peace and war.

However, for much of the first decade of the 21st century, it appeared to many that the United States, now the world's most powerful nation, was drawing back from its commitment to international norms as guides to the behavior of states. The United States failed to join such internationally favored agreements as the Kyoto Protocol on climate change, the

International Criminal Court, and the Anti-Personnel Mine Ban Convention. This, coupled with the Neoconservative harangues against the UN, multilateralism, evident preference for unilateral action, and perceived willingness to interpret international law to suit U.S. purposes regardless of commonly accepted understandings, led some to conclude that the United States had come to prefer a self-interest-based international community, where to quote Thucydides, "the strong do what they can and the weak suffer what they must."[41]

In an increasingly interdependent world, where achieving one's objective will almost always require the assistance or as a minimum the acquiescence of others, policies fundamentally guided by self-interest will win few friends, gain influence among few nations or peoples, do little to advance the nation's soft power, raise concerns about America's ultimate aims, heighten perceptions of the abuse of its power, undermine its ability to use hard power when it may be necessary, and thus be largely counterproductive. Joseph Joffe, publisher-editor of the German weekly newspaper, *Die Zeit*, writing about the United States over a decade ago, correctly noted:

> To the extent that the United States turns unilateralism into a habit . . . others will feel the sting of American power more strongly. And the incentive to discipline Mr. Big will grow.[42]

Investment in the Common Good.

U.S. successes in the post World War II Cold War era owe as much to its efforts to provide for the common good as to its military and economic clout.

Indeed, for most of the post World War II era, "the United States has acted as the foremost producer of global/regional public goods."[43] By shaping its foreign policy agenda to advance not only its own interests but also those of others, it was able to grow its soft power global influence. By holding the value of the dollar currency artificially high following the war, Americans would be encouraged to buy foreign products, helping others get their post-war economies going again. By providing them a security shield and money through the European Recovery Program (Marshall Plan), the United States freed Western European nations from the burden of heavy defense expenditures and thus allowed them to focus their limited resources on economic and social recovery. Moreover, many of the institutions the United States advanced not only helped establish norms for international behavior, but also provided for the common good. The World Bank provided loans for post-War reconstruction and development. The IMF stabilized exchange rates, making trade among nations more predictable. GATT lowered barriers, encouraging greater trade among nations and stimulating economic development. The WTO continues the processes set in motion by GATT.

Such efforts have built a better world and have contributed greatly to America's stature in the past. Continued investment in the common good is essential if the United States hopes to retain its primacy in the international community. But as Joffe has said:

> Primacy does not come cheap, and the price is measured in the currency of obligation. Leaders succeed not only because of their superior power, but also because they have a fine sense for the quirks and qualities of others--*because they act in the interest of all* [empha-

sis added]. Their labor is the source of their authority. And so a truly great power must not just prevent but pre-empt hostile coalitions—by providing essential services. Those who respect the needs of others engage in supply-side diplomacy: They create a demand for their services, and that translates into political profits, also known as "leadership."[44]

In short, investing in the common good generates gratitude among those affected, opens avenues for influence, often predisposes others to political/diplomatic overtures, and thus contributes to a nation's soft power.

Knowledge.

In the decades ahead, nothing will be more important than knowledge. Knowledge of the interests of other states and nonstate actors, their objectives and concerns, and the skillful management of a nation's public diplomacy to translate such knowledge into a favorable view of the United States will be required.

Moreover, to choose wisely among the instruments of national power and the means of their employment in any given circumstance, a thorough understanding of the individuals and/or groups of individuals a nation wishes to affect is a necessity. If the United States is to have an immediate effect on the behavior of another state or nonstate actor in the international arena, it must be able to identify those likely to be able to directly or indirectly affect the decisions to be made. This requires in-depth knowledge of the attitudes, beliefs, and predispositions of those likely to be involved in the decisionmaking process or the so-called "proximal" decisionmaking environment. It also requires an understanding of the more emotive aspects of the personalities involved. This places an enormous task on the intelligence community, not only on their ability to directly gather information needed to make appropriate judgments, but also to analyze that intelligence along with information garnered from the wide range of academics who have engaged in such efforts. Where efforts to affect the behavior of others is long-term and likely to involve the use of public diplomacy, an understanding of attitudes, beliefs, predispositions, and emotive aspects of not only the proximal, but also distal environment of the target country is required. In democracies, such a distal environment includes a wide range of groups and, of course, the public in general, upon whose consent the government often relies. In authoritarian regimes, the scope of the distal environment is likely to be more circumscribed.

Investments in education and intelligence are among the most valuable investments a nation can make if it wishes to use its soft and hard power wisely. It is the basis upon which one chooses which instrument or combinations of instruments of national power (political, psychological, economic, and/or military) to use in a given situation, as well as over time, and which means or combination of means (influence, persuasion, coercion, deterrence, and/or compellence) to employ on which international actors when and how.

Integration of the Instruments of Power.

As suggested above, smart power requires that the instruments of national power be fully integrated. The political, economic, psychological, and military instruments, deployed to influence, persuade, coerce, deter, or compel, may be used individually, in tandem, or jointly, depending on the nature of the issues to be

76

addressed. This will require cooperation and coordination across the agencies of government involved, particularly between the departments of State and Defense, but also others such as Homeland Security, Treasury, Commerce, Agriculture, and Justice. It also will require the cooperation of Congress: at minimum a Congress knowledgeable enough and determined enough to serve as a check on executive actions, while acting in an efficient, nonpartisan manner to support executive branch efforts when warranted.

More than a decade ago, the Hart–Rudman Commission signaled the need for *"strategic fusion* of all appropriate instruments of national power:"

> The nature of the future security environment appears to require advanced, integrated, collaborative planning and organized interagency responses beyond what is possible under the current interagency system.[45]

More recently, the 2009 DoD *Quadrennial Roles and Missions Review Report* also highlighted the need "to increase unity across the government for addressing common national security problems."[46]

Former Secretary of State Hillary Clinton also highlighted the need for integrative efforts:

> One of our goals coming into the administration was . . . to begin to make the case that defense, diplomacy and development were not separate entities, either in substance or process, but that indeed they had to be viewed as part of an integrated whole and that the whole of government then had to be enlisted in their pursuit."[47]

However, such integration is an enormous task. It will require addressing a wide range of issues that

I have attempted to identify elsewhere.[48] In particular, it will require the education of a wide range of government professionals, as well as diplomats to manage the processes at home and abroad. Such an education may require a Goldwater-Nichols DoD Reorganization Act of 1986 style professional education for selected nonmilitary, as well as military officials.

Invest in Public Diplomacy.

Public diplomacy is usually understood to be the means by which governments seek to advance their nations' interests through understanding, informing, and influencing the views of broader publics in foreign countries.[49] Among the principal tasks of U.S. public diplomacy are communicating American values, ideas, and policies and their rationale. It includes a wide variety of efforts, which span a spectrum from student exchanges to public media releases to the information provided by civilian and military officials of the government.

During the Cold War, it was hard to measure the benefits of such public broadcasting efforts as the Voice of America, Radio Free Europe, and Radio Liberty. We do know that those broadcasts not only shaped U.S. images but also often highlighted, by virtue of implicit example, the failings of many of the authoritarian regimes that fell to their coverage. It is equally difficult to measure the success of such programs as the Peace Corps, the Department of State-run participants programs, the various DoD-run regional education centers, as well as the Fulbright and other exchange programs. But those programs not only provide many Americans, often captive of their own insularity, an opportunity to better understand the culture, languages, and perspectives of other peoples and nations, but also advance an understanding of American culture, traditions, values, and, perhaps above all, concepts of freedom and openness to others around the globe.

Public diplomacy can be a powerful tool in advancing the interests of the nation. In the media age, with the emergence of a multiplicity of communications means, where news and entertainment are often merged and news blurred, and competing and sometimes misleading information has become increasingly common, a strong investment in public diplomacy is essential. It is in such an environment that the battle of ideas and thus the battle for the hearts and particularly the minds of others take place. If the United States is to be successful, it will need to do a better job coordinating its efforts among the various agencies of government. This neither means that all those who venture abroad on U.S. programs receive indoctrination on U.S. policies, nor does it mean that there needs to be one truth on all issues. Rather, there needs to be a greater unity of effort in communicating to foreign peoples those issues of strategic importance and sustained education of those civilian and military officials in regular contact with the media that provides them with the tools necessary to be effective communicators via the various instruments of the modern media. As Mary K. Eder has written: "At issue is the concern that America does not communicate clearly with the world. It often seems that the U.S. government sends 'mixed messages' or fails to clearly and consistently communicate policy."[50]

Humility.

During one of the presidential debates before his election as President, George W. Bush, speaking about the reactions of others to the United States, commented: "If we are an arrogant nation, they'll view us that way, but if we're a humble nation, they'll respect us."[51] This must have been sweet music to many in the world who have tired of America's claims of exceptionalism. Of course, such claims have deep roots in the American psyche, reaching back to 1630. John Winthrop, still aboard the flagship *Arabella* en route to New England, delivered a sermon to future Massachusetts Bay colonists, remarking that "the Lord will be our God and delight to dwell among us . . . wee shall be as a Citty upon a Hill."[52] The idea of American exceptionalism has often been advanced. Among others, President-Elect John F. Kennedy quoted Winthrop in a January 1961 address to the General Court of Massachusetts. President Ronald Reagan repeatedly referred to the United States as the "shining city upon a hill." Presidential candidate George W. Bush in 2000 remarked: "Our nation is chosen by God and commissioned by history to be a model to the world."[53]

The United States is exceptional in many regards. Many non-Americans see the United States as the land of freedom and opportunity. The United States has much to be admired. Nevertheless, the old adage "self-praise stinks," applies both at home and abroad, and both among individuals and between and among states. Loch Johnson has labeled arrogance as one of the seven sins of American foreign policy.[54]

America might well keep in mind that the United States is ranked fifth in world competitiveness, 16th in national infrastructure, 39th in institutions, and 42nd in health and primary education.[55] The United States also is ranked 49th in infant mortality and 50th in life expectancy, lagging behind all Western European states, except Turkey.[56] While one may take exception to one or more of the rankings, this is the way many others see us. Indeed, according to Johnson:

> there is a perception around the world that the United States has grown too big for its britches, that it has failed to live up to its noble rhetoric as a peace-loving power with lofty ideals, that it thinks its views are superior to other nations.[57]

Thus, a little humility would go a long way in advancing America's soft power and likely make applications of hard power more palatable.

Humility is demonstrated in many ways, for example, knowledge of the history, culture, traditions, language, and current issues and concerns of others; soliciting and listening to the views of others; and perhaps above all, seeing others as equals, with something to contribute to the discourse among nations and peoples. Even U.S. diplomats might benefit from further education on some of these before assignment, especially those who serve as political appointees.

Recognize the Limits of Power.

If the United States is to use wisely the instruments of national power, it must recognize that it cannot solve all of the problems all of the time. It may be able to solve some of the challenges it confronts by itself. It may be able to solve some problems with the help and/or cooperation of others. Some problems it may not be able to solve at all.

Smart power not only requires an understanding of such elementary truths, but also the knowledge needed to differentiate among the challenges and the wisdom to act only where the available resources, means, and instruments of power are likely to yield a reasonable probability of success. Humanitarians and hawks sometimes join hands advocating intervention where authoritarian regimes abuse their power and inflict gross violations of human rights on their people, recently, for example, in Libya and Syria. In such situations, if the United States is to use its power wisely, good counsel suggests caution. Quick action, without a well-thought-through plan that promises a reasonable end game and a reasonable probability of politically desirable outcomes, can spell disaster.

Furthermore, efforts to act everywhere or near everywhere are likely to be met with suspicion followed by pushback from others. There always exists within the international community the concern that the "strong are always inclined to abuse their strength. The more obvious their superiority, the more suspect they become."[58] The obvious military strength and past history of U.S. involvement makes it an especially prominent target for such suspicion.

Thus the United States must choose carefully where, when, and how it will become involved, particularly in the use of its hard power. An intemperate America wears out its own reputation and hence its ability to influence others. Moreover, efforts to act everywhere all of the time are costly in terms of a nation's economic, military, and human resources. Furthermore, if ever there was an axiom of state behavior, one that can be counted on 90+ percent of the time, it is that if one state is always ready and willing to do what is difficult and costly, other nations will let that state take care of the dirty laundry, saving themselves from the economic, military, and political costs.

Act Within the Limits of Resources.

Great powers have come and gone. One certainty is that if a nation exhausts its resources, it will face decline. It would be difficult to measure the long-term costs to the United States of its wars of choice in lives lost and the resultant drain on national treasure and the American psyche. Americans are a resilient and optimistic people. But surely the United States would be in a better position today if it had been more discrete in its choices of wars to fight. There is, of course, the argument that wars stimulate the economy through production and therefore wars, rather than a drain, can be good for the economy. This view is often supported by the argument that it was World War II that finally got the United States out of the Great Depression, not the New Deal spending of Franklin D. Roosevelt. However, I find irony in this argument that those who decry government spending often so argue. Nevertheless, if true, would not spending on domestic programs be better?

Of course, wars of choice are not the only drains on the nation's resources, spending more than you are willing to pay for can run up the national debt to levels from which recovery can only be achieved by taxing the future health and welfare of the nation. Indeed, the combined domestic and foreign spending including recent wars has run up the national debt from almost $6 trillion in 2001 to over $15 trillion today, jumping to nearly $10.7 trillion during the Bush administration and the rest during the first 3 years of the Barack Obama administration.[59] True, some of that spending was on efforts to stimulate the economy. On the other hand, engaging in two wars without raising taxes to cover costs has surely affected the U.S. resilience in recovering from the great recession and contributed to perceptions both at home and abroad of an American decline. U.S. soft power potential has been weakened, and with the economic recession its future hard power capabilities will surely be reduced.

Maintain Sufficient Military Hard Power.

Military forces equipped and trained to address the challenges of the 21st century are essential. However, smart power demands that if America's resources are to be wisely husbanded, military forces should be designed to meet the probable threats, not all possible threats. The latter is a prescription for unbounded military expenditures. Today U.S. military expenditures are about 43 percent of the world's total. By comparison, China spends about 7.3 percent, Russia about 3.6 percent, France about 3.6 percent, and the UK about 3.7 percent.[60] From an average of about $450 billion (in 2012 dollars) during the Cold War, the U.S. defense budget soared following the September 11, 2001 (9/11) attacks to over $700 billion.

Furthermore, today the United States has 11 nuclear powered aircraft carriers. In terms of size and striking power, no other country has a comparable ship. Several countries do have aircraft carriers. However, none presently has more than two, though India and Australia have three under construction.[61] The currently projected cost of the new *Gerald R. Ford* class carrier now under construction is about $13.5 billion. This does not include the cost of approximately 90 onboard aircraft, nor does it include the cost of accom-

panying forces that compose a carrier strike group —
usually one or two guided missile cruisers, at least
two destroyers and/or frigates (for example, *Zumwalt
Class* approximately $6.5 billion and the *Burke* Class
approximately $2 billion), and, on occasion, subma-
rines.[62] The United States also has:

- Ten large-deck amphibious ships that can operate as sea bases for helicopters and vertical-
  takeoff jets. No other navy has more than three,
  and all of those navies belong to U.S. allies or
  friends. The U.S. Navy can carry twice as many
  aircraft at sea as all the rest of the world combined.
- Fifty-seven nuclear-powered attack and cruise
  missile submarines. More than the rest of the
  world combined.
- Seventy-nine *Aegis*-equipped combatants that
  carry roughly 8,000 vertical-launch missile
  cells. In terms of total missile firepower, the
  United States arguably outmatches the next 20
  largest navies.
- A battle fleet displacement — a proxy for overall
  fleet capabilities — that exceeds, by one recent
  estimate, at least the next 13 navies combined,
  of which 11 are U.S. allies or partners.
- A 202,000-strong Marine Corps, which is the
  largest military force of its kind in the world
  and exceeds the size of most world armies.[63]
- Arguably the finest air forces in the world, with
  an estimated 160-200 flying hours per year for
  tactical crews, compared to 100-150 for China
  and 25-40 for Russia.
- A tactical aircraft inventory of about 2,650 Air
  Force, 900 Naval, and 371 Marine combat aircraft and including today about 140 F/A 22s

with a final purchase of 183 — one of the finest, if not the finest, aircraft in the world. It is in the process of acquiring about 2,400 F-35 aircraft as a replacement for its older aircraft at a fly-away cost of over $200 million per copy.

- The best equipped Army in the world.

All of this raises the reasonable questions of "How much is enough?" "How little is too little?" "How much is overkill?" With an over $15 trillion national debt and, as of late, annual $1 trillion federal deficits, the United States is obliged to ensure that military expenditures are still sufficient to protect America's vital interests. However, as has often been noted in the past, interests tend to expand to meet available resources. Therefore, it is useful to keep in mind as the United States sizes and equips its military forces that all interests are not vital and that military expenditures must be balanced against other expenditures that protect the homeland from attack and add to America's ability to have a favorable impact on world affairs. The United States is not deficient in offensive military striking power. Indeed, it is likely to remain superior in offensive military capabilities, even far superior to any likely military adversary for some years to come. Indeed, if there are serious weaknesses in America's security, they may well be in the ability of the U.S. to defend against crippling cyber attacks on U.S. infrastructure and in its ability to employ its military forces effectively. Such deficiencies demand significant attention.

Today the DoD Budget request for Fiscal Year (FY)2013 is about $614 billion, including $88.5 billion for overseas contingency operations, including those in Afghanistan and Iraq.[64] By way of comparison, the President's FY2013 budget for the Department of State and the U.S. Agency for International Development (USAID), including Overseas Contingency Operations to support the extraordinary and temporary costs of civilian-led programs and missions in Iraq, Afghanistan, and Pakistan is $51.6 billion.[65] That's less than 1/10 of the Defense budget. Looking to the future, among the most important military investments are those made in the research, development, testing, and evaluation (RDT&E) of military hardware, in military training, and, increasingly today and in the future, in cyber security. Investments in RDT&E permit the United States to remain technologically superior to potential adversaries. Military training and use of advanced cyber techniques are force multipliers, so-to-speak. Such force multipliers often permit the United States to operate successfully against larger militaries, as was the case in Iraq in 2003.

It is instructive to note that President Eisenhower cut the defense budget by 27 percent. However, he also doubled funding for RDT&E in order to maintain the U.S. technological edge over the Soviet Union. President Richard Nixon also reduced defense spending, but ushered in the "Total Force" concept, which gave a significant role to Reserve and National Guard forces in times of conflict.[66] This would suggest that the question of military funding in terms of smart power is what is the appropriate balance between funding for forces in being versus RDT&E. That is to say, should forces in being be sized downward while keeping the R&D base hot? It also raises questions as to how much, more or less, should be borne today by Reserve and National Guard forces? However, the larger question is: What is the proper balance of expenditures not only among the various foreign and security policy institutions, but also between expenditures on those institutions and expenditures on securing and improving U.S sources of national power?

CONCLUDING COMMENTS

The challenges of coming decades are likely to be more complex and in many ways more demanding than those the United States confronted during the Cold War. Future successes in providing for U.S. national security and advancing American interests abroad will demand the wise application of both soft and hard power. As a minimum, this will demand that the United States have a clear vision of the kind of domestic and international environment it seeks to nurture in the decades ahead. Henry Kissinger noted over 40 years ago: "We will never be able to contribute to building a stable and creative world order unless we first form some conception of it."[67] His observation remains as true today as it did in 1968 and pertains equally to the domestic as well as international environment. Indeed, success internationally will depend heavily on success at home. It also will demand that the United States invest carefully in the sources of its power both domestically and internationally.

Domestically, even more so than in the past, in an era of globalization, future American power will depend heavily on the strength of the nation's economy and, as it rebuilds its economy, on finding an appropriate balance between the further development of business and industry and environmental concerns that often have less noticed but none-the-less detrimental long-term effects on the economy. America's ability to influence events abroad also will demand that the United States vigorously encourage and support technological innovation at home, as well as invest substantially in R&D, in the education of its people in general, and in the education of its diplomats and military leaders. The latter may require a Goldwater-Nichols DoD Reorganization Act style specialized professional education for select nonmilitary, as well as military officials engaged in foreign and security policymaking. Perhaps above all, the future of U.S. power—both soft and hard—will depend on effective governance. Democracy eschews absolutes. Rather, it demands compromise among competing interests in order to achieve a consensus for advancement. A "my way or the highway" attitude among competing political factions is a prescription for decline, both at home and abroad.

Internationally, the wise application of the instruments of American power will depend, among other things, on cooperative efforts on the part of those agencies of government involved in foreign and security affairs in order to integrate effectively the instruments of American power. It will demand an unwavering investment in the intelligence community and in developing an understanding of the motivations of other international actors, a commitment to a norms-based international community, investments in the international common good and public diplomacy with a touch of humility, and a recognition of the limits of the ability of any single nation to solve all the world's problems and of the need to work with others within the limits of available resources. The application of smart power to protect U.S. interests abroad will also demand that the United States maintain sufficient military hard power to deter and, if necessary, defend its vital interests, as well as the ability to protect Homeland infrastructure and U.S. military forces from crippling cyber attacks. However, many of the challenges that lie ahead are likely to be more effectively addressed through the use of soft power than through the application of hard power. Thus America's stature in the global arena and its ability to protect and advance its interests and those of its allies and friends demands a proper balance of expenditures among the various U.S. foreign and security policy institutions, especially those that strengthen America's soft power.

Indeed, it is worth keeping in mind that it was not hard power that brought about the collapse of the Soviet empire. To be sure, hard military power played an important role. Nevertheless, Eastern European peoples did not toss the yoke of communism because of American military efforts in Asia, Africa, and Latin America. Mikhail Gorbachev didn't seek to reform the Soviet system because he had been defeated militarily or because the United States had halted the expansion of communism through the use of its military might. In fact, with the fall of South Vietnam in 1975, the United States lost the very military conflict in which it had invested most heavily during the Cold War period. Rather, it was the inability of the communist system to deliver to its peoples the promises made of a better life, juxtaposed against the success of the West. It was the inherent attractiveness of the West and America and its soft power that won the day — the strength of its economy, the attractiveness of its political system, its commitment to international institutions and international law, and its inherent vitality. Thus while hard power will remain a must, in the decades ahead, smart power demands significant investments in America's soft power.

ENDNOTES - CHAPTER 4

1. U.S. gross national product was about $200,000 million in 1940. By 1950, it was about $300,000 million (greater than half of the world's gross national product) and more than $500,000 million by 1960. See "World War II and the Post-War Boom," available from *www.nestlepurina.com/postwar.aspx*; and *The Post War Economy 1945-1960*, Washington, DC: U.S. Department of State, available from *economics.about.com/od/useconomichistory/a/post_war.htm*.

2. Christopher J. Tassava, *The American Economy during World War II*, Economic History Association, available from *EH.net at eh.net/encyclopedia/article/tassava.WWII*.

3. By 1970, U.S. GDP measured by purchasing power parity (PPP) represented about 24 percent of the world total; nominal U.S. GDP as a share of the world's total measured at official exchange rates peaked in 1985 at 32.74 percent, while remaining at about 22.5 percent at PPP; by 1997 it had shrunk to about 21 percent at PPP. See *Handbook of International Economic Statistics*, Washington, DC: Central Intelligence Agency, February 1999, p. 6 available from *permanent.access.gpo.gov/lps2917/hies.pdf*. The U.S. economic output is slightly below that level today. The global economic product in 2010 was estimated to be about $63 trillion (using official exchange rates) or 76.16 trillion (using purchasing power parity), while the U.S. was estimated to be $14.82 trillion or about 23.5 percent at official exchange rates or 19.5 percent at PPP of the global product, respectively. See *The World Factbook*, Washington, DC: Central Intelligence Agency, available from *https://www.cia. gov/library/publications/the-world-factbook/geos/us.html*. Moreover, some 2012 forecasts see China's GDP surpassing the United States by some estimates as early as 2019 and by 2025, with the United States producing about 18.3 percent of the world's output and China about 21.8 percent. See "Global Economic Outlook 2012," The Conference Board, available from *www.conference-board.org/ data/globaloutlook.cfm*.

4. Should Iran acquire nuclear weapons, there is a reasonable probability that other states in the region will seek to acquire them. Moreover, any further proliferation of nuclear weapons, materials, and know-how increases the likelihood that such capabilities will fall into the hands of terrorist or criminal groups.

5. For example, see Kenneth E. Boulding, *Three Faces of Power*, Newbury Park, CA: Sage Publications, 1989, pp. 15-18.

6. Bertrand de Jouvenel, *On Power: Its Nature and the History of Its Growth*, Boston, MA: Beacon Press, 1962, p. 17.

7. *Ibid.*

8. *Ibid.*, pp. 17-26.

9. See Joseph S. Nye, Jr., *Bound to Lead: The Changing Nature of American Power*, New York: Basic Books, 1990.

10. Joseph S. Nye, Jr., *Soft Power: The Means to Success in World Politics*, New York: Public Affairs, 2004.

11. Joseph S. Nye, Jr. *The Future of Power*, New York: Public Affairs, 2011.

12. Nye, *Soft Power, p.* x.

13. *Ibid*, p. 5.

14. Nye, *Future of Power*, p. 16.

15. *Ibid.*

16. Nye, *Future of Power*, p. 155.

17. Samuel P. Huntington, "Clash of Civilizations," *Foreign Affairs*, Summer 1993, p. 22.

18. Information provided by government officials as "background" usually refers to information that the media can provide the public, but without quoting the name of the official providing the information or the office of government he/she might represent. Information provided on "deep background" can be provided by the media to the public, but without any attribution to the government at all.

19. For example, see "Compellence" available from *en.citizendium.org/wiki/Compellence.*

20. Joseph Nye's three aspects of relational power, the ability to command change, particularly affecting other's preferences, control agendas, and establish preferences, are, in a large sense, by-products of previously established relationships that find their roots in soft and hard power, but often in soft power's ability to influence behaviors. See Nye, *The Future of Power*, pp. 10-11.

21. President Dwight Eisenhower's News Conference, April 7, 1954, *Public Papers of the Presidents*, 1954, p. 382.

22. See John Lewis Gaddis, *Strategies of Containment: A critical Appraisal of Postwar American National Security Policy*, New York: Oxford University Press, 1982, p. 131.

23. Harry G. Summers, Jr., *On Strategy: The Vietnam War in Context*, Carlisle, PA: Strategic Studies Institute, U.S. Army War College, 1981, p. 1.

24. Mary K. Eder, *Leading the Narrative: The Case for Strategic Communications*, Annapolis, MD: Naval Institute, 2011, p. xi.

25. "Public Diplomacy," available from *www.usdiplomacy.org/diplomacytoday/contemporary/public.php.*

26. Michael Howard, "Military Power and International Order," *International Affairs*, Vol. 40, No. 3, Royal Institute of International Affairs, July 1964, p. 405.

27. King Louis XIV of France (1643-1715) had the saying, *Ultima Ratio Regum* (last Argument of Kings), stamped onto the barrels of all canons that were forged during his reign.

28. Stanley Hoffmann, *Gulliver's Troubles*, New York: McGraw-Hill, 1968, p. 34.

29. Raymond Aron, "Richard Nixon and the Future of American Foreign Policy," *Daedalus*, Fall 1972, pp. 15-16.

30. Howard, "Military Power," p. 405.

31. Eleven of the 16 battleships had been constructed in U.S. shipyards between 1904 and 1907. See JO2 Mike McKinley, "The Cruise of the Great White Fleet," Washington, DC: Department of the Navy; Naval History and Heritage Command, available from *www.history.navy.mil/library/online/gwf_cruise.htm*.

32. *Ibid.*

33. Thomas Paterson, J. Garry Clifford, Shane J. Maddock, Debra Kisatsky, and Kenneth J. Hagan, *American Foreign Relations: Volume 1: A History to 1920*, 7th Ed., Boston, MA: Wadsworth, 2010, p. 255.

34. Garett Jones of George Mason University and Tim Kane of the Kansas City, MO-based Ewing Marion Kauffman Foundation undertook the study. See Amity Shlaes, "Why Obama's Pullout Push May Harm Rather Than Help," *Atlanta Journal Constitution*, February 18, 2012. Also see Garett Jones and Tim Kane, "Defense and Peace Economics," Online: Taylor and Francis, 2012.

35. "CSIS Commission on Smart Power," Center for Strategic and International Studies, Washington, DC: The CSIS Press, 2007, p. 7.

36. *CSIS Commission on Smart Power: A smarter, more secure America*, Washington, DC: The CSIS Press, 2007, p. 7.

37. Karin Zeitvogel, "US Falls to Average in Education Ranking," December 7, 2010, available from *www.google.com/hosted-news/afp/article/ALeqM5juGFSx9LiPaur6eO1KJAypB2ImVQ?docId =CNG.5337504e8f65acf16c57d5cac3cfe339.1c1*. Also see *PISA 2009 Results: What Students Know and Can Do – Student Performance in Reading, Mathematics and Science, Vol. 1*, OECD 2010, available from *www.oecd.org/dataoecd/10/61/48852548.pdf*.

38. *PISA 2009 Results*, p. 4.

39. Charlotte Mellander and Kevin Stolarick, "Creativity and Prosperity: The Global Creativity Index," Toronto, Canada: Martin Prosperity Institute, January 2011, pp. 3-7, available from *martinprosperity.org/media/GCI%20Report%20Sep%202011.pdf*.

40. See for example, "World's Best Universities: Top 400," *U.S. News*, 2011, available from *www.usnews.com/education/worlds-best-universities-rankings/top-400-universities-in-the-world*.

41. Thucydides, *The History of the Peloponnesian War*, Chicago, IL: Encyclopaedia Britannica, Inc., The Great Books, 1952, Sec 5:89, p. 505.

42. Joseph Joffe, "Who's Afraid of Mr. Big," *The National Interest*, Summer 2001, available from *findarticles.com/p/articles/mi_m2751/is_2001_Summer/ai_76560814/pg_10/?tag=content;col1*.

43. *Ibid*.

44. *Ibid*.

45. U.S. Commission on National Security/21st Century, Hart-Rudman Commission, April 15, 2001, Vol. 1, pp. xi, 4.

46. *Quadrennial Roles and Missions Review Report*, Washington, DC: U.S. Department of Defense, January 2009, p. 31.

47. Address by Secretary Hillary Clinton, Washington, DC, Brookings Institution, May 27, 2010.

48. "National Security Reform: 12 Central Questions for Responding to the Security Challenges of the 21st Century," in Robin Dorff and Volker Franke, eds., *Conflict Management and "Whole of Government:" Useful Tools for U.S. National Security Strategy?* Carlisle, PA: Strategic Studies Institute, U.S. Army War College, April 2012.

49. "Public Diplomacy."

50. Eder, p. 19.

51. Julie A. Mertus, *Bait and Switch*, New York: Routledge, 2004, p. 53, quoted in Paterson, *et al.*, *American Foreign Relations*, p. 483.

52. See John Winthrop, *City upon a Hill, 1630*, available from *www.mtholyoke.edu/acad/intrel/winthrop.htm*.

53. Important Believers & Quotes, available from *www. originofnations.org/books,%20papers/quotes%20etc/quotes.htm.*

54. Loch K. Johnson, *Seven Sins of American Foreign Policy*, New York: Pearson Longman, 2007, PP. 249-275.

55. Professor Klaus Schwab, ed., *Global Competitiveness Report 2011-2012*, Geneva, Switzerland, 2011, P. 362.

56. *World Factbook*, CIA.

57. Johnson, *Seven Sins*, p. 249.

58. Raymond Aron, *On War*, Garden City, NY: Doubleday & Company, Inc., 1958, p. 99.

59. "US National Debt by Presidential Term: Per Capita and as Percentage of Gross Domestic Product," available from *www. skymachines.com/US-National-Debt-Per-Capita-Percent-of-GDP-and-by-Presidential-Term.htm.*

60. Stockholm International Peace Research Institute (SIPRI), *Military Expenditure Database 2011*, available from *milexdata.sipri. org* displayed in Anup Shah, "World Military Spending," *Global Issues*, available from *www.globalissues.org/article/75/world-mili-tary-spending.*

61. Remarks by Secretary of Defense Robert M. Gates, available from the Gaylord Convention Center, National Harbor, MD, May 3, 2010, available from *www.defense.gov/speeches/speech. aspx?speechid=1460.*

62. For cost data, see "Analysis of the Fiscal Year 2012 Pentagon Spending Request, Feb 15, 2011," *The Cost of War.* available from *costofwar.com/en/publications/2011/analysis-fiscal-year-2012-pentagon-spending-request/.*

63. Remarks by Gates, May 3, 2010.

64. "Fiscal Year 2013 Budget Request," Washington, DC: U.S. Department of Defense, p. 1-1, available from *comptroller.defense. gov/defbudget/fy2013/FY2013_Budget_Request_Overview_Book.pdf.*

65. "State and USAID—FY 2013 Budget," Washington, DC: U.S. Department of State, available from *www.state.gov/r/pa/prs/ps/2012/02/183808.htm*.

66. For a brief historical comparison of defense budgets, see Lawrence J. Korb, Laura Conley, and Alex Rothman, "A Return to Responsibility: What President Obama and Congress Can Learn About Defense Budgets from Past Presidents," Washington, DC: Center for American Progress, July 14, 2011, available from *www.americanprogress.org/issues/2011/07/defense_budgets.html*.

67. Henry Kissinger, "Central Issues of American Foreign Policy," in Kermit Gordon, ed., *Agenda for the Nation*, Washington, DC: The Brookings Institution, 1968, p. 614, cited in Henry Kissinger, *White House Years*, Boston, MA: Little, Brown and Company, 1979, p. 66. See also Henry Kissinger, *American Foreign Policy* 3rd Ed., New York: Norton, 1977, p. 97.

CHAPTER 5

A FUTURE U.S. GRAND STRATEGY: CONFLICT MANGEMENT FOREVER WITH US, PEACEBUILDING NOT SO MUCH

Michael Lekson
Nathaniel L. Wilson

"The world is too much with us," as Wordsworth noted in a time of political and industrial revolution.[1] More than 2 centuries later, the world is still very much with us, and convulsed by a wide range of rapid changes, few of them seeming to be positive and most of them posing challenges, and sometimes direct threats, to U.S. national security. While it is never fair to require a national strategy to be sized to fit a bumper sticker or a tweet, it has rarely been harder than now to summarize the essential elements of the overarching principles underlying U.S. interactions with the wider world, along with the prioritized policies with which the U.S. will seek to manage those interactions. The times certainly call for a grand strategy. Whether or not the U.S. is likely to develop and implement one (both much easier to write about than to do), it ought to be a useful "thought experiment" to explore what such a strategy might look like. In particular, two potential elements of such a strategy—peacebulding and conflict management—have grown in importance in recent years, and it is worth considering whether this trend is likely to continue in any future strategy. The context in which these questions will be addressed is one in which the overall attitude of the American public might well be characterized by a classic country-western song: "Make the world go away."[2] At the time of this writing, with the second longest sustained overseas conflict in U.S. history still underway[3] and facing record budget shortfalls, American attitudes are decidedly not oriented outward. A January 2012 Pew Research Center poll on public priorities noted: "The public's concerns rest more with domestic policy than at any point in the past 15 years."[4] Nonetheless, the world shows no signs of going away.

This chapter first defines the terms and delineates the contours of the concepts described. The subsequent section briefly describes some of the ways in which U.S. strategy has been formally articulated. Since strategies need to be forward-looking, the problems inherent in predicting the future are explored, and the present state of affairs is described. The penultimate section argues that although American power has been the common thread tying together the global governance institutions and regimes since the end of World War II, their institutional effectiveness is fraying and the post-World-War-II security order is in unprecedented trouble. Finally, the conclusion speculates on the respective places of conflict management and peacebuilding in a future grand strategy at a time when prioritization will be a grim reality rather than a rhetorical aspiration in managing U.S. relations within a world that will continue to be very much with us.

DEFINING THE TERMS

In considering the roles of conflict management and peacebuilding in a future U.S. grand strategy, at least three terms in the preceding clause would benefit from clear definitions. This chapter is premised on somewhat broad definitions for the first two (both excerpts from the definitions in "Peace Terms" booklet produced by the United States Institute of Peace), and adopts a standard definition of the third.

Conflict Management:

> is a general term that describes efforts to prevent, limit, contain, or resolve conflicts, especially violent ones. . . . It is based on the concept that conflicts are a normal part of human interaction and are rarely completely resolved or eliminated, but they can be managed.[5]

This concept can apply either to conflicts within states or subunits thereof, or to conflicts between or among states or alliances thereof.

Peacebuilding:

> Originally conceived in the context of post-conflict recovery efforts to promote reconciliation and reconstruction, the term peacebuilding has more recently taken on a broader meaning. . . . It also includes conflict prevention in the sense of preventing the recurrence of violence, as well as conflict management and post-conflict recovery. In a larger sense, peacebuilding involves a transformation toward more manageable, peaceful relationships and governance structures.[6]

To a much greater extent than with conflict management, even in its expanded form, the term "peacebuilding" remains much more tied to the nation-building or stabilization context.

Bassani describes *Grand Strategy* as:

> An overarching concept that guides how nations employ *all of the instruments of national power* to shape world events and achieve specific national security ob-

jectives. Grand strategy provides the linkage between national goals and actions by establishing a deliberately ambiguous vision of the world as we would like it to be (ends) and the methods (ways) and resources (means) we will employ in pursuit of that vision. Effective grand strategies provide a unifying purpose and direction to national leaders, public policy makers, allies and influential citizens in the furtherance of mutual interests [emphasis added].[7]

In addition, we argue that if a strategy is truly "grand," it is not about how to solve today's problems. A grand strategy needs to be developed to deal with the future, not to provide tactical prescriptions for the present, which need to be devised within the context of whatever grand strategy was developed in the past. Let us first address the strategy question, then the issue of the future.

WHAT IS OUR STRATEGY?

In the post-World-War-II era, there have been authoritative highly-classified documents that made serious efforts to establish an overall national security strategy, most notably National Security Council (NSC)-68 during the Harry Truman administration. Whether NSC-68 was truly a "grand" strategy, the claim of its successor documents to grandness has become decreasingly plausible. The comprehensiveness implicit in the utilization of "all of the instruments of national power" has generally been achieved at the expense of coherence. Since it was mandated by the 1986 Goldwater-Nicholas Act, each U.S. President has been required to issue a *National Security Strategy of the United States*, which is the closest approximation to a U.S. grand strategy that is publicly available.[8] To the best of our knowledge and recollection (supplemented by some research), these national security strategies have not been truly strategic, but rather have tended to become laundry lists (or policy compendia, if that sounds better). While we express some uncertainty about the art of prediction, we feel fairly safe in predicting that this pattern will continue.

The 2010 U.S. *National Security Strategy* identifies four "enduring national interests": security, prosperity, values, and international order.[9] At that level of generality, there probably would not have been much dispute that our strategy sought to preserve, protect, and defend those interests during the past 30 years, or even the 30 years before that. It is tempting to predict that this consensus will continue for the next 30 years, as well, although, as will be seen, we are less confident that there will continue to be an international order to preserve.

In any case, while these post-1986 strategy documents have had varying degrees of influence over how the executive branch organizes itself and justifies budget requests, their actual strategic content is hard to pin down. The justifiable concern that security not be too narrowly defined provides entrée to almost anything for which there is a need, an argument, or a constituency to be presented as promoting national security. Bureaucratic, institutional, budgetary, and political constraints conspire to create a document that may identify a large number of goals, and a number of things to do that may have some bearing on trying to achieve each of them, but does not actually describe the way from here to there.[10] In addition, the messiness of the outside world, domestic political reality, and the interagency clearance and coordination process combine to elevate everything into a priority, even when these priorities are mutually incompatible for reasons of policy, resources, or both. In these circumstances, we should be grateful for what does ultimately emerge from this process, which is by no means without its utility, and should resist the temptation of critiquing these documents too harshly from the armchair strategist's perspective. But, on those occasions when it does appear that for a time the United States actually had a grand strategy and actually followed it, that strategy has generally been most clearly articulated in memoirs after its protagonists had left office.

THE FUTURE AIN'T WHAT IT USED TO BE

For a grand strategy to deal effectively with the future, it must be based on some idea of what that future will be, which for most mortals must be founded on extrapolating from the present and the past, drawing on both what has been personally experienced and what has been learned from history. Let us start with two inspirational texts: "That men do not learn very much from the lessons of history is the most important of all lessons that history has to teach us" (Aldous Huxley).[11] "The law of unintended consequences is the only real law of history" (Niall Ferguson).[12]

What are the threats, the challenges, and the opportunities that a grand strategy should be designed to manage? No one truly knows what the future holds. One of the most thought-provoking essays on the general subject of planning for the future is the "Overture" to *The Next 100 Years: A Forecast for the 21st Century*, by George Friedman of STRATFOR. He opens by briefly revisiting the 20th century, examining how the world looked at 20-year intervals to those in charge of strategizing. He asks what were the threats, challenges, and opportunities that they faced, and that they devised their strategies to confront. Almost invariably, what they were concerned with was either misconstrued or faded either into the background or away altogether, while problems that did not loom large, if they were noticed at all, became central to international security within the 2-decade time tranche. Of course, there were some positive surprises as well as the many negative ones.[13]

Looking even 2 decades ahead is quite a stretch for contemporary strategists. But the world may be at a point where much longer trends are about to have a decisive impact. At the conclusion of *Why the West Rules — for Now*, a 663-page analytical survey of world history from the days of the Neanderthals to the present, British archaeologist Ian Morris considers existing trends and outlines three possible futures, one mainstream and two outliers: More of the same, only with a richer China; the Singularity; or Nightfall. To expand just a little on his mainstream prediction, the methodology that Morris follows over the millennia to measure "social development" suggests that, no later than 2103 (and probably earlier), the East (especially China) will surpass the West.[14] On the simpler metric of total economic output, he cites various experts as putting the point where China surpasses the United States at 2016, 2020, 2025, 2027, and 2036. If that is, in fact, the shape of things to come, it should serve as a basis for developing and implementing a grand strategy.

However, the other two alternative futures which he presents as serious possibilities are stark contrasts, both to the mainstream projection and to each other. "The Singularity" as a term derives from the concept of gravity established in Albert Einstein's theory of general relativity; to quote Stephen Hawking, it is "a place where the classical concepts of space and time break down, as do all the known laws of physics because they are all formulated on a classical space-time background."[15]

In the analogous sense that it is used by Morris, it pertains not to fundamental physical properties of the universe, but rather to the advance of human technology. In this context, it is a concept long familiar in science fiction (it is said to have been coined by author Vernor Vinge,[16] but the underlying idea antedates him) and is perhaps most closely associated now with Ray Kurzweil,[17] a futurist whose particular vision of it sees machine-based intelligence as growing so rapidly that within a few decades, it will absorb and redefine humanity, transcending biology, and thus effectively invalidating all that we know and can project from history or the social sciences.[18]

"Nightfall" is also a science fiction reference, in this case to a story by Isaac Asimov in which, due to developments beyond its control or understanding, an advanced civilization on another planet goes mad and destroys itself.[19] While the particular trigger for night to fall in the story would not apply in our solar system, Morris devotes 15 pages to exploring some of the very down-to-earth ways that Nightfall could come about for us (including disease pandemics, famine, nuclear war, and the negative consequences of rapid climate change, among other potential catastrophes).[20]

Both Nightfall and the Singularity are presented as serious possibilities, and while we are less confident than some that the latter would be benign, we believe they should be treated as such. Nonetheless, trying to develop a grand strategy that can encompass dealing not just with the mainstream "rise of China" prospect, but also with the actual advent of these much more cosmic prospects, is not likely to produce anything that in bureaucratese, would be considered "actionable." However, serious thought needs to be given to the issues they raise, even as grand strategies are developed that assume, rightly or otherwise, that we are not headed for such discontinuous developments.

Retreating from the cataclysmic, it would still seem that any responsible grand strategy needs to take into account not just the projection of China's outpacing the United States, but also the very real possibility that China will instead fall victim to a failure to surmount its governmental, demographic, and environmental problems, or will fall short of the heights to which it now aspires for some other concatenation of not fully foreseeable factors. Whatever happens with China, the consequences for U.S. national security will be huge.

With all due respect to both Morris and Friedman, we would personally give more weight than they respectively do to contingent developments that can, albeit rarely, make a major difference (two examples important to the context of this chapter would be Adolf Hitler's decision to declare war on the United States after Pearl Harbor, and the Democrats' 1944 decision to replace Henry Wallace with Harry Truman).[21] Morris is doubtless correct that the vast majority of what we see as decisive turning points in history are more accurately understood as slight twists and turns in a river which is going to keep on running toward the sea, even if, like the mighty Mississippi, it may take the long way around.[22] But for the purposes of would-be grand strategists, as for General Ulysses Grant trying to take Vicksburg, those bends in the river are often exactly what they need to be concerned with, even while keeping the long-term direction of flow in mind. Some of these happenstance events are not the freely-made decisions of great leaders, but are intrinsically not predictable for other reasons. This is well articulated by none other than Sir Harry Flashman:

> If I had been the hero everyone thought I was, or even a half-decent soldier, Lee would have won the battle of Gettysburg and probably captured Washington. That is another story, which I shall set down in its proper place if brandy and old age don't carry me off first [unfortunately, they did], but I mention the fact here because it shows how great events are decided by trifles. . . . Scholars, of course, won't have it so.[23]

The key point is that even if one can see a trend and project from the past where history seems to be heading, human developments can, not always but sometimes, be altered by small but significant events. But taking a step back from the occasional accident (most of which do not have the kind of ramifications that resulted from whatever Flashman did or did not do at Gettysburg), there is a major problem for devising any kind of strategy, let alone a grand one: the strong tendency for human beings to *take things for granted*.[24] We are not aware of anyone, ourselves included, who is free of this trait, although levels of awareness do vary. Of course, this propensity is in effect the downside of a positive capability — the ability to generalize, to learn from experience, and to extrapolate from present perceived reality — the absence of which is certainly not going to produce a useful grand strategy, or much of anything else.

THE END OF AN ERA?

With the above in mind, we would suggest that we may be coming to the end of the post-World-War-II order. With every passing day, the ranks dwindle of those relative few who remember how nations used to interact before there was an "international community," with structures that underpin it and norms that seek to give it purpose and coherence. Anyone who was 10 years old when the United Nations (UN) Charter entered into force in 1945 would be nearing 80 today. Virtually everyone of that age and younger *takes the current international security order for granted.* But should we? We all grew up with it, so it seems the natural order of things. But is it natural and guaranteed to last, or just the temporary product of equally temporary circumstances?

This issue is most commonly addressed in terms of whether America is "declining," in either absolute or relative terms. There have been a number of books written on this subject recently. Zbigniew Brzezinski, National Security Adviser to President Carter, thinks the post-World War II structure—with the United States at the top—is uncertain in the future but for now remains:

> The more immediate risk of the ongoing dispersal of power is a potentially unstable global hierarchy. The United States is still preeminent but the legitimacy, effectiveness, and durability of its leadership is increasingly questioned worldwide because of the complexity of its internal and external challenges. Nevertheless, in every significant and tangible dimension of traditional power—military, technological, economic, and financial—America is still peerless. . . . This reality may not endure for very long, but it is still the current fact of international life.[25]

In line with this assessment, the authors of *Bending History* contend that the United States is well situated as the preeminent global power. Moreover, it can remain so even in a precarious time on the international scene:

> We believe that even though the world is undergoing rapid, sometimes tumultuous change, it is doing so in ways that are broadly compatible with the American-designed post-World War II order, and that America is well placed to manage the ongoing changes in the international system as long as it remains strong, respected, and confident. . . . Gradual, managed change that accords greater constructive roles to others as they become successful economies and polities is very much in America's national interests.[26]

This is not the place, and we are not the authors, to document how this international order developed. But it is worth noting that it started with the evolution of the UN alliance of countries that were the victors of World War II[27] into a UN organization whose mission was to keep the peace, with that mission entrusted to a security council that was given the unprecedented mandate to determine whether and when sovereign states could use force for purposes other than individual or collective self-defense (and it appears to govern and place limits even on that right [which it does recognize as inherent], although legalistic analysis and diplomatic rhetoric have far outpaced actual state practice in this regard).[28] That organization in turn grew into a truly global but increasingly feckless parliament of almost all the nations of the world. The UN provided the context for the Universal Declaration of Human Rights and many more such statements of good intentions over the years. Similarly, an unprecedented U.S. political commitment to Europe in the immediate aftermath of the war grew into an economic commitment with the Marshall Plan and a security commitment with the North Atlantic Treaty, which in turn gave rise to a real military alliance with forward-deployed American troops as part of the North Atlantic Treaty Organization (NATO). All this gave rise to a genuine feeling—at least, most of the time, among a majority of the political leadership in Europe and North America that took an interest in such matters—of a joint transatlantic community, confronting a common danger and sharing not just a common purpose but common values. This transatlantic alliance was focused on, but not limited to, the military dimension and to countering the threat posed by the Soviet Union. On neither side of the Atlantic was this in keeping with historical tradition, but by now we all think of it as normal.[29]

This chapter will also refrain from documenting the roles of the Bretton Woods System, or the World Bank and International Monetary Fund (IMF), two other global structures that have played a major role in the post-World War II order. Meanwhile, the end of (primarily European) imperialism and colonialism brought well over 100 new nations into the UN and other political, security, and economic systems and structures that had not been designed with their membership in mind. It also helped alter both the economies and aspirations of the European states themselves, which began an unprecedented continental process of unification based on free decisions rather than conquest, leading from the modest coal and steel communities to the European Union (EU), whose integrated economy is larger than that of any country in the world. A general move in the direction of increasingly open world trade and globalization has brought the "creative destruction" of free markets to all quarters of the globe, with the aggravation of those feeling the pain often much more acute than the satisfaction enjoyed by the usually greater numbers enjoying the gain. While globalization had happened before, the end of colonialism made it much more a world-wide reality than the early 20th century precedent, which was supposed to make general war impossible, but came to a bad end in 1914 and suffered further indignities following 1929.

Perhaps the single deadliest challenge emerging from World War II — the threat posed by nuclear weapons — has been handled successfully so far, though only in part by the sort of institutional arrangements outlined above. After it became clear that there was not going to be any kind of international authority managing them[30] and with the end in 1949 of the American nuclear monopoly, the solution ultimately developed was deterrence — direct deterrence for both the United States and the Union of Soviet Socialist Republics (USSR), plus extended deterrence provided by the United States for its NATO and Pacific allies. The Nonproliferation Treaty (NPT), concluded in 1968, provided a basis both for slowing the spread of nuclear weapons to other states, and for a gradual process of negotiated limits and then reductions of both American and Soviet/Russian nuclear arsenals.

One thing all these developments and more had in common was a strong American hand in bringing them about, followed by a continuing U.S. commitment to their success. One could argue that this was motivated by a combination of idealism, realpolitik, and enlightened self-interest, plus whatever other factors the reader might wish to ascribe.[31] Whatever else may be said (and much has been and will be), in the immediate period following the end of World War II, the United States dominated the world both economically and militarily—in a way that it had not before, that it has not since, and will not likely happen again—and chose to demobilize its military and to create multilateral institutions to share the task of preserving the peace. Another thing that all the institutions mentioned in the preceding three paragraphs have in common, from the UN to the NPT, is that they are in serious trouble. The difficulties are both financial and institutional; the problems that the key organizations confront include not having the ability to achieve or in some cases even define their very mission and purpose. To add a further complication, without delving deeper into economic/energy/environmental issues, the conventional view of trends on those fronts would seem to suggest a range of major challenges to world order and international security.[32]

PRESENT AT THE NONCREATION

If the current international security order is in perhaps terminal trouble, what will happen next? While nothing is certain in politics, we feel confident in predicting that it will be a long time, if ever, before a U.S. President is elected on the platform that America will be the world's policeman, let alone the world's social worker. This is not because America is necessarily doomed to decline, but because as a result of brute political and fiscal reality, neither the will nor the resources will be present, either to sustain the order, which may now be coming to an end, or to create something to replace it.

The fiscal facts speak for themselves. America's financial house is not in order. Even "smart power" is not free, and the military component that makes smart power possible comes with a price tag whose figure is more than the market will bear.

As for the political situation, judging both from historical trends and current realities, the argument being made here is that it is highly unlikely that there would be sufficient support for the kind of world role the United States has been playing even if the money to do so had not run out. There has to be a politically compelling reason for any democratic country, and certainly for the United States, to wish to play the sort of role that it has taken on since 1945. The U.S. unity of purpose of World War II was unprecedented—starting with 1776, no other foreign or domestic conflict has ever enjoyed such solid support among the American people. The international order outlined above, whose foundations were laid during World War II and which was constructed in the immediate post-war years, helped to lock in that support in a way that so conspicuously did not happen after World War I. This was possible in large measure because Americans saw themselves facing a post-war threat from a hostile and expansive Communist ideology embodied in a nuclear-armed, continent-sized superpower. The result was an acceptance of continued international commitments and engagements alien to American tradition. But even at its height, the unity of American purpose during the more than 40 years of Cold War was never comparable to that of the 4 years of World War II. It frayed badly during the Vietnam War and never fully recovered. It nonetheless proved sufficient to the task, until a confluence of underlying trends and what were called earlier in this chapter "contingent events" produced a peaceful and successful outcome of that global conflict.

The unifying theme of American foreign policy in the 1990s was to do some good in the world, political support for which was never very strong or deep once the various price tags were attached. Following September 11, 2001 (9/11), there was a brief period of unity of outrage, but there has been very little lasting unity of purpose. Whatever else they have achieved, the two major military conflicts that the United States fought in the past decade have neither strengthened a sustainable international security order nor bolstered any sense by American voters and taxpayers that they want to make any further sacrifices in pursuit of such an order. In the latter case, the result has been very much the reverse.

"Present at the Creation" moments are very rare, and usually follow the sort of destruction that is announced with a bang, not a whimper. Two of the best known such instances — the Congress of Vienna and the period from 1945 to roughly 1952 — each came at the end of a major armed struggle, with clearly defined victors and vanquished, with the former in a position to establish structures, such as the 1815 Concert of Europe and the 1945 UN Security Council, which are by no definition "fair." Following World War I, the effort at Versailles to replicate the success of Vienna a century earlier failed for a number of reasons, including in part that what seemed fair to one party did not seem so to others, and in particular that the vanquished were not resigned to that fate and that the principal victor with a vision did not stay the course — precisely because what was being called for was so alien to the U.S. sense of its role in the world.

Whether the end of the Cold War offered a lost opportunity for the establishment of yet another enduring security order is debatable but doubtful. As with Versailles, though for very different reasons, the nature of the victory was not conducive to reinventing a sustainable and effective international system. Nor (and in this case, the post-World-War-I situation is a closer analogy) was the American body politic receptive to the idea of new overseas entanglements, and neither Japan nor Europe had the means to play an appropriate role, even if on some occasions they were not without motivation. The much less ambitious idea that did emerge, of a "new world order" based on an empowered UN and an increased reliance on principled multilateralism, can hardly be said to have enjoyed more than an occasional success.

The record of effectiveness of the much less structured components of "global governance" that have grown up in the penumbra is even less impressive. The failure of global governance was taken as a given in Chapter 3 authored by Karl-Theodor zu Guttenberg in this volume. A stern but not unfair assessment of this concept is offered by Professor Randall Schweller:

> Most new treaty-making and global-governance institutions are being spearheaded not by an elite club of great powers but rather by civil-society actors and nongovernmental organizations [NGOs] working with midlevel states. Far from creating more order and predictability, this explosion of so-called global-governance institutions has increased the chaos, randomness, fragmentation, ambiguity and impenetrable complexity of international politics.[33]

There are two potentially interrelated possibilities that are worth consideration as a basis for a new international order that might have a serious prospect of meeting the challenges that appear to be overcoming the current one: that the international organizations and institutions that are depicted above as faltering and potentially on the verge of mission failure can be replaced by new ones, better attuned to current reality, or that as America does less to sustain whatever international order there is, others will do more. Neither seems likely.

As suggested above, the sort of circumstances that would offer the prospect of a serious Creation moment—on the order of 1815 or post-1945—are simply not in existence now, nor is there any reason to expect (though as noted more than once above, accidents will happen) that they will come about in the time that a new grand strategy needs to address. It is easy to argue that major changes are desperately needed. It is next to impossible to imagine how they can actually come about, at least in a positive direction. A reinvented UN would need to be established by the same countries that have failed to make the current UN work. If there is a politically feasible way to reform the UN Security Council to make it more fair, no one has found it. Making it more effective is even further out of the question.

The need to reform both the structure as well as the operational effectiveness of the UN has been recognized for decades, as documented in and demonstrated by the bipartisan 2005 UN Task Force. An excerpt from the foreword to its report (written by co-chairs Newt Gingrich and George Mitchell) sets the tone:

As it approaches its sixtieth anniversary, the United Nations needs reform and reinvigoration. Otherwise, the organization risks declining credibility, and its own future will be at risk.[34]

The Task Force cited a long string of reports calling for reforms in UN management dating back to the late 1940s, but achieving little or nothing, being bogged down under the weight of the institution's enormous inertia, a record that reinforces the point that real reform is not going to happen. The values that underlay the UN charter were not universally shared at the time that it was written, nor are they today. "Responsibility to Protect" may have found its high-water mark in Libya, along with the overall concept of "brother's keeper" internationalism as an actual practice rather than a noble aspiration. The very role of the UN, the importance of the P-5 (the five veto-wielding permanent members of the UN Security Council), and the unique standing of the Security Council in legitimizing force or other hostile actions against recalcitrant states are all part of the post-World War II order. This is not the way that international conflict was managed at any time before 1945. The UN is not working effectively for its primary purpose. For varying reasons, those in a position to make it less ineffective by paying the bills and providing the other resources (including but not limited to military ones) appear by their actions to have concluded that it costs more than they are willing or able to provide. In some cases, they feel that they are being asked and expected to pay at a level that ought to but does not grant them the corresponding status in the structure that they believe they merit. It would be surprising if the UN itself does not continue, but its ability to be a practical rather than symbolic center of an international security order, which never really took hold in the Cold War years, has continued to deteriorate following a brief period of better times in the early 1990s. It would be even more surprising if that trend does not continue.

Like the UNSC, the NPT is the product of the situation at the time of its creation (the NPT came into being when there were five nuclear-weapons states, which happened to be the same as the UN Security Council's P-5 victors of World War II). Both the UN Security Council and the NPT can be logically portrayed as intrinsically unfair. But, as with the UN Security Council, the same countries that find fault with the NPT, whether members or not, will be the ones that have to create any plausible amended or successor treaty regime, which will also need to be satisfactory to those who are not unhappy with the current arrangements. While it is not difficult for experts to imagine a revised or replaced NPT regime that would be both fairer and more effective, it is virtually impossible, for us at least, to imagine how to reach universal agreement to any change that would actually strengthen it.

One assumption implicit in all of the above is the continuing centrality of the nation-state. Despite the importance of issues that regularly cross borders (which is one of the major reasons for having multilateral organizations in the first place), and of transnational belief systems, both religious and ideological, which can inspire both states and nonstate actors, the fundamental security structures continue to be states, and, in some special cases (NATO being the most prominent and most successful), assemblages thereof that scrupulously respect their members' sovereignty. For a time, there was a feeling that an ever deeper EU might invalidate this observation. The Euro crisis is a strong counterargument. Whether nation-states are here to stay, they will retain their central role in international security for at least as long as any new grand strategy remains relevant, and probably much longer. It is more difficult to predict the nature of the structures in which states will aggregate themselves in quest of security. Survival is a core interest. Thus, over a finite period of time, in the presence of a clearly defined threat or threats, a collective security arrangement can continue, if the cost is not too high. In the case of NATO and the EU, among others, shared values also have strengthened the bonds among their founding states and thus of the organizations themselves, and the accession process has fortified those values in many of the states that sought to join both organizations over the years. But both have now reached the point where further expansion is decreasingly plausible, and the bruised feelings of unsuccessful aspirants to membership will be reflected in new geopolitical fault lines.

Although NATO and the EU have never been immune to a similar failing, the UN's concept of universal membership soon made it impossible to conceal the disjunction between noble aspirations and frequently ignoble reality, especially as related to the conduct, both internal and external, of member states. Moreover, while actually acting on the basis of shared values can in many circumstances increase the attractiveness of such organizations, both the costs and risks of doing so, the many incomplete successes, and the painful reality that good deeds are rarely done consistently can undercut internal cohesiveness, especially with respect to perceived "free riders," including those in positions of authority. Institutional inertia and clever efforts at reinvention can keep organizations going much longer than many might have predicted, but such measures can sometimes conceal the fact that the organizations themselves are hollowing out. The League of Nations did not formally disband until 1946, but beginning with the Japanese invasion of Manchuria in 1931, it had ceased to be a serious part of the security landscape.

Looking forward, global power is realigning itself, and not in a peacebuilding-friendly way. Even more than was the case in the 1990s, neither Europe nor Japan has the resources or the domestic political base to take on additional international burdens, either to maintain or reinvent the international security order. None of the newly aspiring powers of the 21st century, even China, is going to achieve the level of global dominance that, combined with an attractive set of political, economic, and cultural ideas, made possible America's post-1945 creation moment and sustained it thereafter. Even in the unlikely event that some partial, and probably fragile, successor order were to emerge, anyone expecting that it would be based on the values that have underlain the post-World War II order as described above should examine the reasons for making such an assumption.

QUO VADIMUS?

Following this rather melancholy overview of the origins, present state, and prospects of the international security order, any who have read this far might well wonder what this all portends for peacebuilding and conflict management as part of a future American grand strategy, even keeping in mind the difficulties of political prediction.

Referring back to the way those terms were defined at the outset of this chapter, "peacebuilding" — in the sense of outsiders moving into a troubled nation-state to end its conflicts, stabilize its society, build its institutions, and set it on a secure path to democracy and prosperity — is likely to play a very much decreased part of such a strategy, and an even smaller part in actual practice. Peacebuilding in this sense is simply not an endeavor which there is any good reason to expect that the American body politic can be persuaded is a good investment of scarce discretionary resources. With the possible exception of Bosnia, popular support for serious and sustained efforts in this regard has come about only when they have been seen as an element of the active conduct of a specific kind of armed conflict (primarily Vietnam, Iraq, Afghanistan) — the sort of conflict for which popular support can be guaranteed to wane over time, with a consequent collapse of support for the peacebuilding supplement to the military mission. But in the coming years, this sort of peacebuilding is not likely even to be given a chance to have the rug pulled out from underneath it, since for political, economic, and military reasons — and in the expected absence of anything comparable to the Cold War "containment of Communist expansion" argument that underlay Vietnam, or the 9/11-related rationales for Iraq and Afghanistan — the political and economic barriers to American entry to another conflict of that sort are now so high as to be almost insurmountable, and are likely to remain so for the life of any potential new grand strategy.

Nonetheless, peacebuilding will remain an active and important component of international relations. This is particularly true with regard to work done by NGOs around the world. A wide range of organizations specialize in different facets of peacebuilding. Much of their funding comes from U.S. agencies, or counterparts from other developed countries, as well as from various parts of the UN family. This will likely continue, although probably at reduced levels. There is a vibrant peacebuilding community, which has developed increasing and impressive coherence and patterns of collaboration.[35] This kind of peacebuilding work will continue to be noted in future National Security Strategies of the United States, along with many other important endeavors. But to the extent that these documents actually reflect a governmentally crafted and executed grand strategy to which major government resources are devoted, peacebuilding is not likely to be a central element of it.

Humanitarian relief (as distinct from humanitarian intervention) will continue to enjoy popular support, to a much greater extent than traditional development efforts. However, for either relief or development, both the executive and especially the legislative branches are likely to be increasingly tight-fisted with funding, and ever vigilant against being drawn down the slippery slope into stabilization, let alone counterinsurgency. This will almost certainly mean that many dangerous situations threatening American interests will not be directly addressed, and that the hard-learned lessons of how to do these jobs right will not get a chance to be applied. Failed, failing, and fragile states are not conducive to international stability, but from a cost-benefit standpoint, Americans (or Europeans, Japanese, Australians, or Canadians) are not likely to devote much beyond token resources to trying to address this problem. To put it mildly, peacebuilding success stories are scarce, at least on a strategic scale, and money is even more scarce. When it comes to peacebuilding, we should thus expect to see a lot less of the same.

"Conflict management," however, was defined in a broader way. Conflict itself is not going away, and there will be an abiding U.S. concern to protect, and if possible advance, its own interests and equities. For reasons of self-interest (enlightened or otherwise), it will wish to try to help keep such conflicts from turning violent, particularly (perhaps almost exclusively) between and among states. Conflicts of particular concern as of this writing would include the nuclear proliferation-generated standoff between Israel and Iran, the perennial enmity between India and Pakistan, and Beijing's growing assertiveness in the South China Sea. More could be added to the list even now, and if the argument outlined above about the potential end of the post-World-War-II security order is valid, other sources of conflict, including some problems long thought resolved or even forgotten, could well join the list in coming years. Economic and resource conflicts — not always violent, though often having that potential, but in any case directly threatening domestic prosperity in the United States and elsewhere — also loom on the horizon.

The need to manage such conflicts is likely to be much more compelling, and the prospects of success to appear at least somewhat less unpromising, than on-the-ground peacebuilding. Not long after the fall of the Berlin Wall, one of the few American diplomats who foresaw that development told one of us that the coming years would bring a return to traditional diplomacy, by which he meant a much more complex set of international interactions than those which had been governed by the structure that the East/West divide had provided during the Cold War. For those who experienced it, the Cold War was complex enough, and the risks of getting it wrong were sometimes quite high. It took a bit longer than the diplomat anticipated for what he predicted to come about, with much of one decade taken up with efforts at what was referred to above as "brother's keeper" internationalism, and much of another focused on trying to solve problems in and emerging from the Islamic world. Neither of these two attempts at a unifying principle has proved a satisfactory basis for an international security order, and neither is likely to provide a central principle for any U.S. grand strategy.

What we are likely to see instead is the need for even more conflict management, if this is understood as a mix of at least two of the three D's (defense and diplomacy — as indicated above, we are less sanguine about the role of development). Recalling the concerns explored above both about the dangers of taking trends for granted and the possibilities of contingent events having disproportionate consequences, both the diplomats and the military will have to place a premium on flexibility.[36] They will also need to practice selective engagement, since the threats and challenges will be multifold and all elements of national power are going to be on tight rations for some time to come. "Doing more with less" is a fine phrase, but as a guide to policy, it is too often used as a pretext to avoid prioritization.

While keeping in mind the precursors to the "Nightfall" threats noted above, as well as the rise of China (see Chapter 12 by Liselotte Odgaard in this volume) and, the decline and possible fall of the post-World War II security order, challenges that a U.S. grand strategy will need to address include aggressive nonstate actors of all kinds (including, but by no means limited to, terrorists); the possible end of the taboo on the actual use of nuclear weapons, which, paradoxically coupled with the extended deterrence of the U.S. nuclear guarantee, has been a key element of the post-World War II order; revolutionary developments in technology; the vulnerability of Information Technology (IT)-centric infrastructure; and continuing uncertainty over whether economic growth can be restored, sustained, and made more widespread, as well as how to manage access to vital and sometimes scarce natural resources. (The reasons why a would-be grand strategy becomes just another policy compendium are all too apparent.) Recalling the comments earlier in this chapter about the difficulties of prediction, there will be many developments that in retrospect may appear obvious, but which to those who have to discern them looking forward are not obvious at all. In short, there will be no shortage of conflicts to manage, and we will all need to keep getting better at it if we want this story to have a happy ending.

ENDNOTES - CHAPTER 5

1. The title of a sonnet by English poet William Wordsworth, first published in 1807. It is readily accessible in print and online.

2. Written by Hank Cochran, sung by artists ranging from Elvis to Ray Price to Dean Martin and, of course, Willie Nelson; Eddy Arnold took it to #1 in 1965. Available from *en.wikipedia.org/wiki/Make_the_World_Go_Away*.

3. While Vietnam still holds the distinction of being the longest war in American history, the overall context in which Americans confront the issues addressed in this chapter needs to be appreciated. In his presentation at the XXIII Annual Strategy Conference held at the U.S. Army War College on April 10-12, 2012, Under Secretary of the Navy Robert Work distributed a chart that compared the war-to-peace ratio of the Cold War and post-Cold-War periods. For the 506 months of Cold War (starting in 1950, and including both Korea and Vietnam), the United States was "at war" for 138 months. For the 271 months looking back from April 2012, the United States had been at war for 130 months "and still counting." The Cold War ratio was thus 1 month at war for every 2.67 months at peace. What the chart called the post-1990 "Forever War" ratio was 1 month at war for every 1.08 month at peace. By April 2013, that latter ratio of war-to-peace was greater than 1:1. The full set of slides for Under Secretary Work's presentation is available from *www.strategicstudiesinstitute.army.mil/files/2012-strat-conf-work.pdf*.

4. The report is available from *www.people-press.org/2012/01/23/public-priorities-deficit-rising-terrorism-slipping/*.

5. Dan Snodderly, ed., *Peace Terms: Glossary of Terms for Conflict Management and Peacebuilding*, Washington, DC: Academy for International Conflict Management and Peacebuilding, United States Institute of Peace, 2011, p. 15.

6. *Ibid.*, pp. 40-41.

7. Joe Bassani, Jr., "Saving the World for Democracy: An Historical Analysis of America's Grand Strategy in the 21st Century," Thesis, Norfolk, VA: Joint Forces Staff College, Joint Advanced Warfighting School, 2005, p. 2, available from *www.au.af.mil/au/awc/awcgate/ndu/bassani_jaws_american_grand_strategy.pdf*.

8. James Locher, "Are We Strategically Inept?" speech, XXIII Conference, "The Future of U.S. Grand Strategy in an Age of Austerity: Challenges and Opportunities," Strategic Studies Institute, U.S. Army War College, Carlisle, PA, April 11, 2012; John K. Bartolotto, "The Origin and Developmental Process of the National Security Strategy," Strategy Research Project, Carlisle, PA: U.S. Army War College, May 3, 2004, *p.* 1. In particular, this and the next two paragraphs draw extensively on the Bartolotto paper.

9. Barack Obama, *The National Security Strategy of the United States*, Washington, DC: The White House, May 2010, p. 17, available from *www.whitehouse.gov/sites/default/files/rss_viewer/national_security_strategy.pdf*.

10. A paraphrase of Locher.

11. Andrew Roberts, ed., *What Might Have Been: Leading Historians on Twelve 'What Ifs' of History*, London, UK: Phoenix, 2005, p. 8. Roberts takes the quote from "a framed letter written by Aldous Huxley in 1959" which he has "by my desk at home."

12. Niall Ferguson, "Europe's Lehman Brothers Moment," *Newsweek*, June 18, 2012, pp. 34-37. Quote is from p. 37.

13. George Friedman, *The Next 100 Years: A Forecast for the 21st Century*, London, UK: Allison & Busby, 2010, pp. 1-13. In pp. 1-3, Friedman looks back at the 20th century. The remaining 10 pages of the "overture" look forward.

14. Ian Morris, *Why the West Rules – For Now: The Patterns of History, and What They Reveal About the Future*, New York: Farrar, Straus, and Giroux, 2010, pp. 582-583. His "social development" metrics are explained in an appendix, pp. 623-645. See also pp. 591 and 608.

15. Stephen Hawking, "Breakdown of Predictability in Gravitational Collapse," *Physical Review D*, Vol. 14, No. 10, 1976, p. 2460, doi: 10.1103/PhysRevD.14.2460; Hawking deals with this concept in a way more accessible to the general reader in *A Brief History of Time: The Updated and Expanded Tenth Anniversary Edition*, New York: Bantam Books, 1998.

16. Vernor Vinge, "The Coming Technological Singularity," presentation, VISION-21 Symposium, NASA Lewis Research Center and the Ohio Aerospace Institute, Westlake, OH, March 30-31, 1993, available from *www-rohan.sdsu.edu/faculty/vinge/misc/singularity.html*; James Gardner, "The Intelligent Universe," Steven J. Dick and Mark L. Lupisella, eds., *Cosmos & Culture*, Washington, DC: National Aeronautics and Space Administration, 2009, p. 366.

17. Morris, p. 593 et seq.

18. Ray Kurzweil describes the Singularity thus:

> It's a future period during which the pace of technological change will be so rapid, its impact so deep, that human life will be irreversibly transformed. Although neither utopian nor dystopian, this epoch will transform the concepts that we rely on to give meaning to our lives, from our business models to the cycle of human life, including death itself. Understanding the Singularity will alter our perspective on the significance of our past and the ramifications for our future. To truly understand it inherently changes one's view of life in general and one's own particular life.

See also Ray Kurzweil, *The Singularity Is Near: When Humans Transcend Biology*, New York: Viking Penguin, 2005, p. 7.

19. "Nightfall," first published in 1941, can be found in a number of science fiction anthologies, as well as in Asimov's own collections. The Science Fiction Writers of America (SFWA)

professional association voted it "the best science fiction story of all time," where "story" means short story and "all time" means 1929-64, following which the SFWA began making annual awards. Together with the other stories that were selected, "Nightfall" can thus be found in Robert Silverberg, ed., *The Science Fiction Hall of Fame, Vol. I*, New York: Tor Books, 2003 [orig. 1970]). Morris's bibliography cites Isaac Asimov, *The Complete Short Stories I*, New York: Bantam, 1990).

20. Morris, pp. 598-613.

21. Since, as will be seen, the central importance of the legacy of World War II is one of the premises of this chapter's analysis, two further "what if's" are noted from Roberts, p. 3, citing Conrad Russell:

> If we [the British] had not invented, during the winter of 1938/39, a new alloy and a new furnace to make it which hardened the propeller casing of the Spitfire, and made it 50 m.p.h. faster than the Messerschmitt instead of 50 m.p.h. slower, it is surely likely that Hitler would have won the war.

He also cites, pp. 11-12:

> . . . what so nearly happened on Thursday 16 October 1941, a date that some historians . . . see as the most important date of the twentieth century. For it was on that day that Stalin decided not to take the special train that he had made ready to get him out of Moscow to beyond the Urals, but instead to stick it out in the capital, come what may.

22. Morris, p. 29. Morris draws on the fields of biology, sociology, and geography, broadly defined to include human/economic as well as physical geography, to explain humanity's development paths.

23. George MacDonald Fraser, ed., *Royal Flash: from the Flashman Papers, 1842-3 and 1847-8*, New York: Alfred A. Knopf, 1970, p. 3.

24. Aldous Huxley, "Maine de Biran: The Philosopher in History," *Collected Essays*, New York: Harper & Brothers Publishers, 1959, p. 226.

Most human beings have an almost infinite capacity for taking things for granted. By the mere fact of having come into existence, the most amazing novelty becomes in a few months, even a few days, a familiar and, as it were, self-evident part of the environment.

25. Zbigniew Brezezinski, *Strategic Vision: America and the Crisis of Global Power*, New York: Basic Books, 2012, pp. 21-22.

26. Martin S. Indyk, Kenneth G. Lieberthal, and Michael E. O'Hanlon, *Bending History*, Washington, DC: Brookings Institution Press, 2012, p. 279.

27. "Declaration by the United Nations," *The American Journal of International Law*, Vol. 36, No. 3, Supplemental: Official Documents, July, 1942, pp. 191-192, available from *www.jstor.org/stable/2213575*. One lesson that President Roosevelt appears to have learned from President Wilson's ill-fated League of Nations was to use the same name for the wartime alliance that would also be used for the peacetime collective security arrangement.

28. Mark P. Popiel, "Redrafting the Right of Self-Defense in Response to International Terrorism," *Gonzaga Journal of International Law*, Vol. 6, No. 3, 2002, pp. 7-9, available from *www.gonzagajil.org/pdf/volume6/Popiel/Popiel.pdf*, see especially pp. 4-12. Chapter 5: The Security Council, Article 23, *Charter of the United Nations*, June 26, 1945, available from *www.un.org/en/documents/charter/chapter5.shtml*.

29. For an interesting history of transatlanticism, see Kenneth Weisbrode, *The Atlantic Century*, Cambridge, MA: Da Capo Press, 2009. Whether or not we are in the early years of a possible "Pacific Century," it is very hard to imagine the circumstances which would generate a "transpacific community" or an awkwardly pronounceable "transpacificism." This is at least partially due to the geographic factors ("it was maps, not chaps") that Morris (Chap. 8) identifies as the primary reason, in contrast to culture, the actions of individual leaders, and happenstance for the fact that Europe rather than China reached, conquered, and colonized the Americas, helping ensure the subsequent 500-year ascendance of "the West."

30. Accounts of the efforts to put atomic energy and associated weaponry under international control include John H. Barton and Lawrence D. Weiler, eds., *International Arms Control: Issues and Agreements*, Stanford: Stanford University Press, 1976, p. 70; United Nations Department of Political and Security Council Affairs, *The United Nations and Disarmament: 1945-1970*, New York: United Nations, 1970; Dean Acheson, *Present at the Creation: My Years in the State Department*, New York: W. W. Norton & Company, 1969, pp. 149-156.

31. For a provocative discussion on this topic, see Michael Mandelbaum, *The Case for Goliath*, New York: Public Affairs, 2005. There is no shortage of books, articles, studies, and the like to support any perspective that appeals to the reader.

32. While rendering no judgment on the pros and cons of "peak oil" or other such arguments, it should be noted that there are a number of nongeological reasons why counting on cheap oil (or any kind of cheap energy) is a risky proposition. It is worth citing a recent judgment in *The Economist*: "Just as the industrial revolution was built on coal, the post-second-world-war economy was built on cheap oil. There will surely be a significant impact if it has gone for good." "Feeling Peaky," *The Economist's Buttonwood's Notebook Blog*, April 21, 2012, available from *www.economist.com/node/21553034*. On the other hand, a more upbeat look at our energy future is now beginning to gain some prominence; as of this writing, the most interesting thinking of its implications for international security that we have seen has been done by Walter Russell Mead, "Energy Revolution 3: The New American Century," available from *blogs.the-american-interest.com/wrm/2012/07/18/the-energy-revolution-3-the-new-american-century/*. As noted, energy issues, although highly important, are beyond the scope of this chapter, as reflected in their being addressed only in a footnote. Mead notes, as do others writing about tar sands, shale oil, and the like, that "it is too soon to tell just how much of this potential can be unlocked," and that there are environmental issues that will need to be addressed. From the standpoint of this chapter, and on first consideration, there does not appear to be any intrinsic reason why Mead's vision of the United States as an energy superpower would entail its adopting what he might call a "Wilsonian" approach to multilateralism, rather than a "Hamiltonian"

commitment to open markets. Our initial assessment is that while there are many reasons to welcome a possible future of U.S. "energy abundance," in and of itself such a development is not likely to remedy our economic woes, nor to turn back the receding tide of political support for maintaining the post-World War II international security order as described below. In any case, even the cursory treatment of this footnote illustrates the importance of carefully considering what one is taking for granted when thinking about the future.

33. Randall L. Schweller, "Ennui Becomes Us," *The National Interest*, December 16, 2009, January-February 2010, available from *nationalinterest.org/article/ennui-becomes-us-3330*.

34. Task Force on the United Nations, *American Interests and UN Reform: Report of the Task Force on the United Nations*, Washington, DC: The United States Institute of Peace, 2005, esp. pp. 41-61. This quote is from p. vi; those in the following sentence are from p. 43. The report is available from *www.usip.org/files/file/usip_un_report.pdf*. Further information about the UN Task Force is available from *www.usip.org/node/3690*.

35. For example, see Steven Ruder, "Peacebuilding Expands Across Disciplines, Study Shows," available from *www.usip.org/publications/peacebuilding-expands-across-disciplines-study-shows*.

36. In this regard, it is worth exploring the emergent phenomenon of "collective conflict management" characterized as

> a relatively new pattern of cooperation in international affairs with no organizational center or universal rules of the road. . . . A defining feature of these relatively cooperative ventures is that they span global, regional, and local levels in terms of their institutional membership or actor composition.

Quote is from Chester A. Crocker, Fen Osler Hampson, and Pamela Aall, eds., *Rewiring Regional Security in a Fragmented World*, Washington, DC; The United States Institute of Peace Press, 2011, p. 545.

CHAPTER 6

THE ROLE OF PEACEBUILDING AND CONFLICT MANAGEMENT IN A FUTURE AMERICAN GRAND STRATEGY: TIME FOR AN "OFF SHORE" APPROACH?

Charles J. Dunlap, Jr.

INTRODUCTION

As the post-September 11, 2001 (9/11) wars in Iraq and Afghanistan wind down, it is the right time to examine the role of peacebuilding and conflict management in a future American grand strategy. With the enormous cost in blood and money these efforts have tallied, it seems clear that nations, to include especially the United States, need to consider alternative approaches to accomplish their strategic goals. As unpopular as the recent conflicts have become in the American body politic, it seems inevitable that circumstances arise where peacebuilding and conflict management operations are needed.

Accordingly, it is incumbent upon the Armed Forces to develop methodologies to accomplish these missions, and to do so in a way that is supportable by the public. The purpose of this chapter is to examine what that approach might be and how it might address the existing deficiencies in peacebuilding and conflict management techniques, and to do so in the context of an American grand strategy. It will propose an "off shore" approach, one that leverages American asymmetric capabilities, while realistically assessing the difficulties occasioned by manpower-intensive approaches that are extant. The chapter begins with a discussion of the threshold questions, the ones that will provide the necessary context for the proposal: What is grand strategy? Does America have one?

WHAT IS GRAND STRATEGY?

Answering this question presents a daunting challenge, as there are so many respected authorities who believe that America does not have a grand strategy now, and has little prospect of formulating one that is suitable for planning purposes in the near future.[1] Yet definitions for grand strategy exist. For example, the American Grand Strategy Program at Duke University defines grand strategy as a "quintessentially interdisciplinary concept, approach, and field of study."[2] It goes on to say that:

- Grand strategy is the art of reconciling ends and means. It involves purposive action — what leaders think and want.
- It operates in peacetime and wartime, incorporating military and nonmilitary tools and aggregating subsidiary tactics, operations, and policies.
- Grand strategy begins with theory: leaders' ideas about how the world is, or ought to be, and their states' roles in that world. Yet it is embodied in policy and practice: government action and reaction in response to real (or perceived) threats and opportunities.
- It lends itself to vigorous interpretive academic debates, yet it is so realistic that practitioners can and must contribute for it to be properly understood.[3]

With that understood, the Duke program defines *American* grand strategy as:

the collection of plans and policies by which the leadership of the United States mobilizes and deploys the country's resources and capabilities, both military and nonmilitary, to achieve its national goals.[4]

One might say, then, that American grand strategy simply seeks to create an environment where American values can flourish, to include especially the free enterprise system as well as a liberal democratic polity. This is not intended to be yet another expression of American exceptionalism, but rather a manifestation of the idea that these two principles offer the best hope of realistically harnessing human nature for not just American interests, but for the global common good writ large.

This is not to advocate unbridled free enterprise. Free enterprise that is exploitive of individuals, especially those in a society who—for any number of reasons—feel themselves dispossessed or unable to access the means of upward mobility, can be the source of societal discontent and disorder. Additionally, free enterprise that is indifferent to the environment in a world increasingly aware of the global consequences of environmental mismanagement can generate hostility across a range of actors from individuals to non-governmental groups to nation-states and even to consortiums of nation-states.

Democracy, *qua* democracy, can itself be the source of alienation if it is permitted to devolve into majoritarian tyranny. *Liberal* democracy, with its respect for individual rights and the rule of law, has an architecture that includes freedom of the press, an independent judiciary, and other attributes that help to avoid the kinds of pressures that can manifest themselves in violence when individuals and groups feel hopelessly subjugated by governments who simplistically cater to an undifferentiated version of "popular" will.

Yet it is nevertheless true that these concepts — free enterprise and liberal democracy — when tempered by the considerations just discussed, provide the best hope of reconciling mankind's inherent impulse to act in its own best interests, with a parallel need to act collaboratively in a complex and interconnected world. Certainly these values have imperfect characteristics, but overall, they have proven superior to other concepts of human organization.

AMERICAN GRAND STRATEGY AND CONFLICT

Quite obviously, the values of an American grand strategy so defined thrive best in a conflict-free environment. Historically — and, indeed, to this day — the primary purpose of the state is to create that environment. The means of doing so frequently was — and, it seems, still *is* — to organize the means of violence on behalf of the state — or collection of states — and to apply it whenever the condition of peace was disturbed or threatened. In a perfect world, individuals and states inclined to disrupt peace would be deterred from doing so by the prospect of conflict that, as a matter of logic, would be an inefficient and cost-prohibitive means of resolving disputes.

It is not, of course, a perfect world. Some individuals and states have perceived, and likely will continue to perceive, a security asymmetry that can be exploited to their benefit. What is more, for a variety of reasons —

religion, ideology, cultural identity, and more—they can rationalize a sense of entitlement of superiority for themselves. Such perceptions can translate—however illogically—into a belief that those so disposed possess the power to achieve their ends by force. Efforts to dissuade such conclusions can be effective, but have their limits simply because intransigence can also be a feature of the human mind, and one that can contaminate the thinking of entire societies, to include those who are otherwise cosmopolitan and even generally pacific.

Plato reportedly adroitly observed that "only the dead have seen the end of war." Thus, we must accept that the nature of the human condition is such that for the foreseeable future—irrespective of *any* grand strategy—the vagaries of the human condition—not to mention humanity's aggressive impulses—will continue to challenge the success of an American grand strategy as I defined it.

Yet the inevitability of human conflict does not mean we should abandon efforts to avoid it. Every instance of success represents lives saved and futures preserved. Even where violence cannot be avoided, efforts to ameliorate and limit its effects are patently worthy endeavors because they readily encourage a minimization of human suffering, as well as help create a space, so to speak, for liberal democracy and free enterprise to take root and prosper.

The question then is how best to create those spaces in an era of the ever present risk of violence? In an interesting article in the March/April 2012 issue of *Foreign Affairs* entitled "A Clear and Present Safety," the authors Micha Zenko and Michael A. Cohen assert that America is safer and more secure than ever before, and faces no great power rival and no serious threats.[5] According to Zenko and Cohen, the United States needs a foreign policy that reflects that reality.

The article also contends that:

> because of the chronic exaggeration of the threats facing the United States, Washington overemphasizes military approaches to problems (including many that could best be solved by nonmilitary means).[6]

It goes on to insist that:

> although U.S. military strength has occasionally contributed to creating a conducive environment for positive change, those improvements were achieved mostly through the work of civilian agencies and nongovernmental actors in the private and nonprofit sectors.[7]

Zenko and Cohen are not alone in their views. In his recent book, *Winning the War on War*, Joshua Goldstein made a similar claim, arguing that, "in fact, the world is becoming more peaceful."[8] Goldstein gives great credit not to the United States, but to the United Nations (UN) for its peacekeeping and other operations that he argues could be even more successful were they better funded and supported.

While there is much to commend about Zenko and Cohen's essay (as well as the Goldstein book), the problem with the thesis that both propound is the insufficient appreciation of what the world will be like if U.S. military power is perceived as compromised. If that were to become the case, there is the extraordinarily dangerous prospect that opportunistic nations will destabilize the world if they get the impression that U.S. military power is on the wane, let alone being deliberately diminished. Some around the globe may cheer but, unfortunately, many are not necessarily the friends of peace.

The real value of U.S. military power is that its mere existence in many instances permits — and gives gravitas to — the very civilian/nongovernmental organization (NGO) soft power concepts Zenko *et al.* endorse. To be sure, it is quite true that many successes in the past were the product of diplomatic, humanitarian, economic, and other distinctly nonmilitary efforts, but they were accomplished in a world where enormous American military power was always lurking in the background. The reality, as uncomfortable as it may be for many, is that the U.S. military is the irreplaceable peace enabler in today's world.

There is little reason to assume that the same kind of soft-power victories that Zenko and others celebrate would be possible if the military equation is altered in a serious way. Should the overwhelming U.S. conventional — and unconventional — capability recede, adversaries may see opportunity, perhaps not today, but in the foreseeable future. Once a capability is dismantled — as has been done by the United States with the F-22 manufacturing line[9] — it is very difficult, if not impossible, to resurrect it. We must never forget that U.S. military power takes the military option off the table for many competitors. Economic, social, political, etc., competitions remain, but creating an environment where the military option becomes conceivable is hardly a desirable outcome.

To be clear, one might rightly agree that U.S. military spending must come down to some degree in order to help get our economic house in order, and that the nonmilitary elements of American power need to be better brought to bear in the execution of American grand strategy in the years to come. Yet, some still believe that U.S. *military* might must remain the fundamental — if not central — element of American grand strategy for as long as we can imagine.

PEACEBUILDING AND CONFLICT MANAGEMENT: THE LESSONS LEARNED

Of course, devising a fresh approach to peacebuilding and conflict management requires an unvarnished examination of the operations of the past decade, and there are certainly many lessons to be learned from the conflicts in Iraq and Afghanistan. The effort to reorient entire societies in Iraq and Afghanistan via a strategy that was manpower-intensive and ground-centric has proven to be flawed.

Certainly, the American Soldier, given enough time and enough resources, can accomplish almost anything, to include the remaking of entire countries. The problem is that doing so first requires the application of military force to the existing ruling cadre and its instruments of power so sternly and persistently as to imprint upon the society a sense of defeat so complete that the environment is created where a completely new and — it is to be hoped — more peaceful and democratic society can emerge and the likelihood of resistance is markedly diminished.

Norman Friedman suggests this in his 2004 article *Is Modern War Too Precise?*[10] In it, he indicates that for all its faults and shortcomings, the devastating World War II aerial bombardment of Germany may not have won many "hearts and minds" among the German people "but it did help preclude any post-surrender violence like what is now being seen in Iraq."[11] Regrettably, in Iraq, an ill-considered "race to Baghdad" in 2003 stretched logistic lines and enabled Saddam's Fedayeen to achieve some tactical success against support troops poorly prepared for infantry combat. This became something of a "proof of concept" for Iraqi insurgents that U.S. troops were, in fact, vulnerable.

It would have been far better to have exercised more patience and allowed American air and artillery to progressively devastate Iraq's elite military formations. Instead, they were allowed to melt away and form the core of the insurgency, which was never really crushed in nearly a decade of occupation. The Iraqi people — to include especially those who became the resistance — never internalized the shattering sense of defeat that enabled the Germans and Japanese at the end of World War II to abandon their deeply embedded militaristic, racist, and totalitarian ideologies.

Despite the experience with Japan and Germany, American leaders do not seem to fully comprehend what it takes to truly transform entire societies in a timeline shorter than several generations. Curiously, Chairman of the Joint Chiefs of Staff General Martin Dempsey admitted that the aim of purging Afghanistan of the Taliban could have been achieved militarily, since the United States:

> could have started at one end of Afghanistan and fundamentally overrun it, destroyed it, created a situation where we would make it a near certainty that the Taliban couldn't come back, because there wouldn't be anything to come back to. . . .[12]

General Dempsey hastened to add that such a forceful effort was "not who we are."[13] There are, of course, several observations to be made here, starting with the idea that American values extant during World War II are not necessarily ones to be abandoned. More specifically, if the suggestion is that focusing

141

on the destruction of the enemy—the Taliban in this instance—invariably involves the wholesale obliteration of civilians and their property, he underestimates the revolutionary capabilities of a technological revolution that allows force to be applied in a discrete way that is fully lawful and moral. That technological revolution has, according to retired General Barry R. McCaffrey, "fundamentally changed the nature of warfare" by allowing the rise of persistent, long-term reconnaissance and precision strikes.[14]

It is becoming increasingly clear that force—particularly in counterinsurgency (COIN) situations—is the *proven* solution, especially when rapid results are needed. As Professor Anna Simons of the Naval Postgraduate School contends:

> Not only does COIN's own history reflect the need for a stunning amount of brutality, but the fact that in campaign after campaign, commanders have found themselves desperate to be able to apply decisive force reveals what every generation ends up (re)discovering the hard way: soft approaches don't impel enough people to change their ways fast enough.[15]

Her conclusion fits with that of an ever-widening range of experts. Jill Hazelton of Harvard's Belfer Center contends, contrary to popular wisdom, that

> [s]uccess in COIN does not require the protection of the populace, good governance, economic development, or winning the allegiance or the loyalty of the great majority of the population.

Importantly, she says it "does not require building up all of the institutions of the state."[16] The grim realities of which she speaks should give pause to

142

COIN theorists who disparage the efficacy of force. In April 2011, the *Washington Post* reported that in Afghanistan, the:

> security improvements have been the result of intense fighting and the use of high-impact weapons systems *not normally associated with the protect-the-population counterinsurgency mission.*[17]

Nevertheless, because the U.S. military establishment was dominated by ground-centric thinkers, the "solution" to the challenge of peacebuilding and conflict management necessarily had to involve ground forces, and lots of them. In the case of COIN, that solution doctrinally eschewed force. Such was the nature of *Field Manual* (FM) 3-24,[18] published in 2006. It was, as one pundit put it, "warfare for northeastern graduate students" and other "people who would never own a gun."[19] Among other things, it called for enormous numbers of counterinsurgents (to comprise about 5 percent of the populations), with each Soldier prepared, as the FM said, to become "a social worker, a civil engineer, a school teacher, a nurse, a boy scout."[20] Nation building quite obviously was a critical element of the doctrine.

Executing the doctrine espoused in FM 3-24 justified huge increases in the size of American ground forces. Unfortunately, it ignored some key history about COIN operations and the presence of a large number of foreign troops. COIN expert William R. Polk insists that the "fundamental motivation" for insurgents is an "aim primarily to protect the integrity of the native group from foreigners."[21] Likewise, in 2008, former Army Chief of Staff General John Wickham warned that "[l]arge military forces alienate local populations, succeed less and cost more."[22] More recently, John Brennan, Assistant to the President for Homeland Security and Counterterrorism, pointed out:

> Countries typically don't want foreign soldiers in their cities and towns. In fact, large, intrusive military deployments risk playing into al-Qa'ida's strategy of trying to draw us into long, costly wars that drain us financially, inflame anti-American resentment and inspire the next generation of terrorists.[23]

THE FUTURE: "OFF SHORE" PEACEBUILDING AND CONFLICT MANAGEMENT

So what does all this mean for the future of peacebuilding and conflict management, given the grand strategy I have outlined? At the outset, it is essential to understand that it does *not* mean that the United States should abandon peacebuilding and conflict management efforts. Nor does it mean that it is utterly inconceivable that the United States might again conduct a large-footprint operation *à la* Iraq or Afghanistan. What it does mean, however, is that large-footprint operations for peacebuilding and conflict management missions need to undergo fundamental rethinking.

Part of this requires the acceptance, however unwanted, of certain cold political realities, which include the fact that public support for the large-footprint war in Afghanistan is collapsing. Not only do 78 percent of Americans favor withdrawing troops,[24] 66 percent believe that the war has not been "worth fighting."[25] With respect to the latter, beyond the human cost, our present strategy is extremely costly. The expense of deploying one American Soldier to Afghanistan for 1 year has ballooned to $1.2 million,[26] a figure to which planners must be especially sensitive now that the U.S. public is supporting substantial cuts in defense spending.[27]

While it does seem that it might be cheaper to deploy civilians to accomplish many of the nation-building tasks currently performed by the military, the viability of that option is suspect.[28] As a Congressional Research Service report dated February 2, 2012, entitled *Building Civilian Interagency Capacity for Missions Abroad: Key Proposals and Issues for Congress*, reveals, the U.S. Government's ability to conduct such missions remains deeply flawed, if not in disarray.[29] In any event, there is a tyranny of numbers involved, as even the most optimistic assessments do not contemplate many more than 2,000 experts would be involved, even if resources outside of government were tapped.[30]

Just as problematic is the sheer difficulty of peace-building and conflict management in deeply flawed societies under circumstances where, as indicated above, the political decision has been made not to use force to the extent that has proven successful in past situations, even if it can be applied in a way that is fully lawful and moral. Still, in conflict management situations, force will necessarily have to be employed, but likely not via large numbers of American ground forces. The models for the future are more likely to be along the lines of the Kosovo intervention of the late 1990s and Libya in 2011. As the *New York Times* put it:

> Libya proved that the leaders of some medium-size powers can be overthrown from a distance, without putting American boots on the ground, by using weap-

ons fired from sea and air with the heaviest load carried by partner nations — in the case of Libya, European allies and even some Arab states.[31]

In essence, this might be called "offshore conflict management." This is not an especially new concept, and has been suggested for a number of scenarios of potential conflict. Retired Marine Colonel Thomas X. Hammes has, for example, developed a proposal he calls "Offshore Control" aimed at leveraging U.S. technical advantages as a means of addressing the security challenge of China without necessarily putting a large mass of American troops on the Chinese mainland.[32]

In a sense, options for conflict management that avoid large troop deployments seem consonant with the Barack Obama administration's emphasis on counterterrorism operations aimed at key enemy leaders conducted by drones and special operations forces. In fact, the President recently explicitly stated that in Afghanistan, his "goal is not to build a country in America's image" but rather "to destroy [al-Qaeda]."[33] To the extent this involves drone attacks against al-Qaeda leadership, it has enormous support from the American people, with 83 percent approving of their use.[34]

Of course, not all conflict management can be accomplished by drones, or even special operation ground strikes like that which eliminated Osama bin Laden. That does require American ground forces, but with rare exceptions, the face of such operations ought to be indigenous personnel. In order to build the kind of capacity that host nations need, on-site trainers and mentors may be required, as is currently being done in Afghanistan. On-site mentorship does, however, carry an increased risk of a rogue killing a foreign trainer. As of this writing, the North Atlantic Treaty Organization (NATO) lost 19 soldiers to such attacks in 2012 alone.[35]

A FRESH ENVIRONMENT

How, then, to do it? Perhaps what is needed is a *massive* program to take people out of their environment — to include even to the United States — so they can focus on the kind of transformative training, indeed, *thinking* that is essential to truly reforming and remaking the societies of failed or failing states. Doing so can also facilitate access to the necessary training personnel and resources. This would be as applicable for building expertise in the civilian sector — government administrators as well as people from private enterprises — as it would be for the security services.

There is strong rationale for such an approach. Now retired Army Colonel-turned-university professor Peter Mansoor noted in a 2005 interview that training Iraqi forces outside of Iraq had its benefits:

> The great advantage is the security is much better. You don't have to guard the installation to the degree you have to in Iraq. . . . Another advantage is if it's staffed by foreign officers, they don't have to come into Iraq and become targets in order to teach. Also, existing facilities can be used that don't require a lot of renovation or rebuilding, as is the case with many buildings in Iraq.[36]

Obviously, a similar approach elsewhere would not eliminate the risks. But the chance of a rogue arising in such an environment can be minimized with careful vetting. The advantages are, in any event, manifold. For example, the difficulties of recruiting and deploying skilled and experienced civilians to remote and dangerous locales would be markedly eased, especially if facilities could be located in the United States. Importantly, there are models already existing in the U.S. military of such programs working successfully. For example, the U.S. Air Force operates the Inter-American Air Forces Academy at Lackland Air Force base in San Antonio, Texas, where technical courses are taught, "in Spanish and in English, to students from more than 22 countries every year."[37]

To be successful, the scope of such schools and other educational facilities must be large and diverse. Even for a country the size of Afghanistan, this could involve tens of thousands of individuals each year. While certainly costly, it can hardly compare with the $1 million plus cost of sending a U.S. person to Afghanistan for a peacebuilding operation. Creating such a structure within the United States (or, perhaps, another country) may not be practical, but it may be possible to build a dedicated program within the existing American educational structure. For example, a program for advanced education might be constructed under the aegis of Kennesaw State's Program in International Conflict Management, where international students are given the opportunity to learn in the relative safety and security of an authentic American setting — and evaluate for themselves the potential application to their native country.

An important element of such an "off shore" approach would be the availability of training and education in the native language of the students, while at the same time making English-language instruction available. Further, opportunities could be crafted for the students to learn about American culture and values. This is, emphatically, *not* intended to displace the culture and values of the students' home countries, but rather to help dispel the misperceptions of the United States that can arise in nations needing peacebuilding and conflict management.

This educational process can be supplemented by in-country and online programs (in the indigenous language) by means of equipment and facilities supplied by the United States but manned by local nationals. Moreover, mentoring relationships can be built and maintained through daily interactions via Skype or similar technologies, to include social media formats. Again, the physical presence of some U.S. personnel cannot (and, likely, should not) be eliminated, but the numbers could be reduced to the level that realistically can be accommodated by programs such as the Civilian Response Corps.

CONCLUSION

The proposal this chapter advocates is certainly not a perfect one and will not satisfy every stakeholder. Unquestionably, for example, this kind of "off shore" proposal can be rightly criticized as a too lengthy, costly, and political capital-consuming methodology. Yet this back-to-basics approach may be the only way to realistically create the environment for genuine change, a process that can well take several generations. The "quick fixes" (e.g., build a school, equip a clinic, or grade a road) so attractive to the American mindset just do not work as effectively as one might hope.

Consider the work of researchers Daron Acemoglu and James A. Robinson. Although not focused on peacebuilding *qua* peacebuilding, their research leads them to the relevant observation that nations fail "when they have extractive economic institutions, supported by extractive political institutions that impede and even block economic growth."[38] This cannot be offset merely by digging wells, building clinics, or even economic development projects; it may necessitate dramatic changes in attitudes among leadership and other elites. Indeed, without appropriate institutional leaders, any physical assets provided become yet one more cause for conflict as corrupt power brokers scramble for control of anything of value.

It is a mistake to underestimate the difficulty of rooting out venality writ large in less than a generation. This is one reason our efforts in Afghanistan remain stymied. As General David Petraeus said in 2010, "there's no question that corruption has been, for however long this country has probably been in existence, been part of the–literally the culture,"[39] a point reiterated recently by former Secretary of Defense Leon Panetta.[40] Indeed, "too much corruption," along with "too many Afghan deserters" and "too few NATO trainers," has been reported as a key obstacle to training Afghans to take over security duties once NATO departs.[41]

Even those disposed to be optimistic about the outcome in Afghanistan have no illusions about the depth of this societal flaw and what it will take to overcome it. Major General H. R. McMaster, who led a task force to root out corruption, was recently reported as saying that:

> [T]he root of Afghanistan's corruption problem goes deeper, to three decades of 'trauma that it's been through, the legacy of the 1990s civil war . . . [and] the effects of the narcotics trade.' Add to that the unintended consequences of sudden Western attention starting in 2001: 'We did exacerbate the problem with lack of transparency and accountability built into the

large influx of international assistance that came into a government that lacked mature institutions.'[42]

While it may not necessarily take decades to excise the corruption endemic to Afghan society, it is clearly a long-term task. Selected uses of force employing off-shore and light-footprint capabilities for conflict management can help buy time for nonmilitary processes to work if, and only if, a major effort is made to grow the next generation of political, military, and economic leaders with a sophisticated understanding of the damaging effects of corruption on Afghanistan's future. Much the same can be said for other — and future — "Afghanistans" around the globe.

There are many unique factors about Afghanistan that make it an imperfect example of the kind of peace-building and conflict management issues that will arise in the coming years as the United States grapples with building an approach that meets the needs of U.S. grand strategy, yet is one that is sound in the political reality of an austere funding environment. To be politically viable, we must develop options that are less demanding in blood and money.

Off-shore peacebuilding and conflict management will not work in every instance, but the basics of it — that is, the idea of a light footprint approach that leverages America's asymmetric advantages in high technology[43] — might perhaps be a useful starting point when the next such challenge arises, as it inevitably will. At the end of the day, the approach must be grounded in the idea that notwithstanding whatever assistance any outside entity can provide, the ultimate responsibility is upon the people themselves, and developing *their* capabilities (as opposed to ours, *per se*) is the central task of peacebuilding and conflict management as we look ahead.

ENDNOTES - CHAPTER 6

1. See, for example, Rosa Brooks, *Obama Needs a Grand Strategy, Foreign Policy,* January 23, 2012, p. 1, available from *www.foreignpolicy.com/articles/2012/01/23/obama_needs_a_grand_strategy?page=0.*

2. *What is Grand Strategy?* Durham, NC: Duke University Program in American Grand Strategy, available from *www.duke.edu/web/agsp/index.html#grandstrategy.*

3. *Ibid.*

4. *Duke American Grand Strategy,* Durham, NC: Duke University Program in American Grand Strategy, available from *www.duke.edu/web/agsp/index.html.*

5. Micha Zenko and Michael A. Cohen, "A Clear and Present Safety," *Foreign Affairs,* March/April 2012, p. 79.

6. *Ibid.,* p. 81.

7. *Ibid.,* p. 91.

8. Joshua S. Goldstein, *Winning the War on War: The Decline of Armed Conflict Worldwide,* Boston, MA: Dutton/Plume (Penquin), 2011.

9. John Tirpak, "The F-22 and Clout Deficit," *Air Force Magazine,* July 23, 2012, available from *www.airforce-magazine.com/DRArchive/Pages/2012/July%202012/July%2023%202012/TheF-22andCloutDeficit.aspx,* quoting Air Force Chief of Staff Norton Schwartz as saying there is "no chance" of restarting the F-22 manufacturing line.

10. Norman Friedman, "Is Modern War Too Precise?" *U.S. Naval Institute Proceedings,* December 2004, p. 4.

11. *Ibid.*

12. *A Conversation with General Martin Dempsey*, Washington, DC: Carnegie Endowment for International Peace, May 1, 2012, available from *carnegieendowment.org/files/050112_transcript_dempsey.pdf*.

13. *Ibid.*

14. As General Barry McCaffrey, USA (Ret.) has observed:

We have already made a 100 year war-fighting leap-ahead with MQ-1 Predator, MQ-9 Reaper, and Global Hawk. Now we have loiter times in excess of 24 hours, persistent eyes on target, micro-kill with Hellfire and 500 lb. JDAM bombs, synthetic aperture radar, and a host of ISR [intelligence, surveillance, and reconnaissance] sensors and communications potential that have fundamentally changed the nature of warfare.

General Barry R. McCaffrey, *Memorandum for Colonel Mike Meese, United States Military Academy, Subject: After Action Report*, October 15, 2007, p. 5 (italics added), available from *www.mccaffreyassociates.com/pages/documents/AirForceAAR-101207.pdf*.

15. Anna Simons, "Soft War + Smart War? Think Again," *E-Notes*, Philadelphia, PA: Foreign Policy Research Institute, April 2012, available from *www.fpri.org/enotes/2012/201204.simons.soft-war-smart-war.html*.

16. Jacqueline L. Hazelton, "The Hearts-and-Minds Approach Versus The High-Force Low Accommodation Approach," *Compellence and Accommodation in Counterinsurgency Warfare*, September 2010 (unpublished manuscript on file with author) (Italics added).

17. Rajiv Chandrasekaren, "In Afghanistan's South, Signs of Progress in Three Districts Signal a Shift," *Washington Post*, April 16, 2011, available from *www.washingtonpost.com/world/in-afghanistans-south-signs-of-progress-in-three-districts-signal-a-shift/2011/04/14/AF7gBwqD_story.html* (Italics added).

18. *Field Manual 3-24, Counterinsurgency*, U.S. Department of the Army, December 15, 2006, p. D-8 (hereafter FM 3-24), also des-

ignated by Headquarters Marine Corps Development Command, Department of the Navy, as *Marine Corps Warfighting Publication No. 3-33.5, Counterinsurgency,* December 15, 2006, p. 1, available from *www.scribd.com/doc/9137276/US-Army-Field-Manual-FM-324-Counterinsurgency.*

19. The full paragraph stated:

[The COIN Manual's] reception reflected Petraeus's considerable media networking skills as well as the appeal of counter-insurgency doctrine among sections of the country's liberal-minded intelligentsia. This was warfare for northeastern graduate students—complex, blended with politics, designed to build countries rather than destroy them, and fashioned to minimize violence. It was a doctrine with particular appeal to people who would never own a gun. The field manual illustrated its themes with case-study vignettes whose titles suggested the authors' ethical ambitions: "Defusing a Confrontation," "Lose Moral Legitimacy, Lose the War."

See Steve Coll, "The General's Dilemma," *The New Yorker,* September 8, 2008, available from *www.newyorker.com/ reporting/2008/09/08/080908fa_fact_coll?currentPage=all.*

20. FM 3-24, note 18, para 2-42.

21. William R. Polk, *Violent Politics: A History of Insurgency, Terrorism & Guerrilla War, from the American Revolution to Iraq,* New York: Harper, 2007, pp. xiv-xv.

22. John A. Wickham, "Why a Smaller Footprint is Good," *Arizona Daily Star,* November 9, 2008, available from *gunnyg.word-press.com/2008/11/15/large-military-forces-alienate-local-populations-succeed-less-and-cost-moreby-john-adams-wickham/.*

23. Remarks of John O. Brennan, Assistant to the President for Homeland Security and Counterterrorism, *The Ethics and Efficacy of the President's Counterterrorism Strategy,* Washington, DC: The Wilson Center, April 30, 2012, available from *www.wilsoncenter. org/event/the-efficacy-and-ethics-us-counterterrorism-strategy.*

24. Fox News Poll (conducted by Anderson Robbins Research (D) and Shaw & Company Research, April 22-24, 2012, available from *www.pollingreport.com/afghan.htm*.

25. ABC News/*Washington Post* Poll, April 5-8, 2012, available from *www.pollingreport.com/afghan.htm*.

26. Todd Harrison, *Analysis of the 2012 Defense Budget*, Washington, DC: Center for Strategic and Budgetary Analysis, July 15, 2011, p. 7, available from *www.csbaonline.org/wp-content/uploads/2011/07/2011.07.16-FY-2012-Defense-Budget.pdf*.

27. R. Jeffrey Smith, "To Trim the Deficit, Americans Favor Much Deeper Reductions at the Pentagon than Their Leaders Do," iWatch News, Washington, DC: Center for Public Integrity, May 10, 2012, available from *www.iwatchnews.org/2012/05/10/8856/public-overwhelmingly-supports-large-defense-spending-cuts*.

28. Yochi Dreazen, "Afghanistan's Civilian Surge Comes with Enormous Price Tag and Uncertain Results," *The National Journal*, September 8, 2011, available from *www.nationaljournal.com/nationalsecurity/afghanistan-s-civilian-surge-comes-with-enormous-price-tag-and-uncertain-results-20110908*.

29. Nina M. Serafino, Catherine Dale, and Pat Towells, *Building Civilian Interagency Capacity for Missions Abroad: Key Proposals and Issues for Congress*, Washington, DC: Congressional Research Service, January 23, 2012, available from *fpc.state.gov/documents/organization/183725.pdf*.

30. Nina M. Serafino, *Peacekeeping/Stabilization and Conflict Transitions: Background and Congressional Action on the Civilian Response/Reserve Corps and other Civilian Stabilization and Reconstruction Capabilities*, Washington, DC: Congressional Research Service, January 12, 2012, available from *www.fas.org/sgp/crs/natsec/RL32862.pdf*.

31. Thom Shanker and Eric Schmitt, "Seeing Limits to 'New' Kind of War in Libya," *New York Times*, October 21, 2011, available from *www.nytimes.com/2011/10/22/world/africa/nato-war-in-libya-shows-united-states-was-vital-to-toppling-qaddafi.html*.

32. Thomas X. Hammes, "Offshore Control: A Proposed Strategy," *Infinity Magazine*, Spring 2012, p. 10, available from *www.infinityjournal.com/article/53/Offshore_Control_A_Proposed_Strategy*.

33. Transcript of President Barack Obama's speech from Bagram Air Base, Afghanistan, May 2, 2012, available from *worldnews.msnbc.msn.com/_news/2012/05/01/11492424-transcript-of-president-barack-obamas-speech-from-bagram-air-base-may-2?lite* (Italics added.)

34. Scott Wilson and Jon Cohen, "Poll Finds Broad Support for Obama's Counterterrorism Policies," *Washington Post*, February 8, 2012, available from *www.washingtonpost.com/politics/poll-finds-broad-support-for-obamas-counterterrorism-policies/2012/02/07/gIQAFrSEyQ_story.html*.

35. "NATO Soldier Killed in Afghan Shooting," *Aljazeera*, May 6, 2012, available from *www.aljazeera.com/news/asia/2012/05/201256131119330234.html*.

36. Lionel Beehner, Interview with Colonel Peter Mansoor on Training Iraqi Forces, New York: Council on Foreign Relations, October 6, 2005, available from *www.cfr.org/publication/8984/interview_with_colonel_peter_mansoor_on_training_iraqi_forces.html*.

37. See Inter-American Air Forces Academy, U.S. Air Force, Lackland AFB, TX, available from *www.lackland.af.mil/iaafa/index.asp*.

38. Warren Bass, Book Review of *Why Nations Fail*, by Daron Acemoglu and James A. Robinson, *Washington Post*, April 20, 2012, available from *www.washingtonpost.com/entertainment/books/book-review-why-nations-fail-by-daron-acemoglu-and-james-a-robinson/2012/04/20/gIQAcHs8VT_story.html* (quoting the authors).

39. Kate McCarthy, "Petraeus Denies Resignation Threat; Backs President Karzai," ABC News, December 5, 2010, available from *abcnews.go.com/blogs/politics/2010/12/exclusive-gen-david-petraeus-denies-resignation-threat-backs-president-karzai/*.

40. Secretary Panetta Interview with Judy Woodruff at the Pentagon, Washington, DC: U.S. Department of Defense, May

3, 2012, available from *www.defense.gov/transcripts/transcript. aspx?transcriptid=5025*:

> Corruption, you know, has been part of that culture, just as it was in Iraq, just as it is in other areas of the Middle East. It's one of the things you've got to deal with. If you eventually want to develop a stable, governing operation there that provides stability, they're going to have to do a better job in trying to control the level of corruption that's there.

41. Julie Cavanaugh, "Why It's So Hard for NATO to Train Afghan Forces, *Christian Science Monitor*, April 22, 2012, available from *www.csmonitor.com/World/Asia-South-Central/2010/1202/ Why-it-s-so-hard-for-NATO-to-train-Afghan-forces.*

42. David Feith, "H. R. McMaster: The Warrior's-Eye View of Afghanistan," *Wall Street Journal*, May 11, 2012, available from *online.wsj.com/article/SB100014240527023044511045773922811468 7 1796.html?mod=WSJ_Opinion_LEADTop#printMode.*

43. See, for example, General Douglas M. Fraser, USAF and Major Wendell S. Holmes, "Haiti Relief: An International Effort Enabled through Air, Space, and Cyberspace," *Air & Space Power Journal*, Winter 2010, p. 5, available from *www.airpower.au.af.mil/ airchronicles/apj/apj10/win10/2010_4_03_fraser.pdf.*

CHAPTER 7

ALWAYS AN OUTSIDER:
U.S. MILITARY ROLE
IN INTERNATIONAL PEACEBUILDING

William Flavin

The U.S. military has been involved in peacebuilding for most of its history. The U.S. military developed the Western United States, supported Reconstruction in the Southern United States after the Civil War, supervised the Civilian Conservation Corps in the 1930s and assisted with other depression era programs. However, these activities inside the United States in support of the building of the U.S. nation differ from what was called for in the overseas adventures in Mexico, the Philippines, Central America, Cuba, Japan, Germany, South Korea, Africa, the Balkans, Iraq, and Afghanistan where the U.S. military action was transitory and alien to the culture and society. This chapter will look at the challenges and opportunities that the military must face when attempting to support international peacebuilding enterprises.

International peacebuilding, at its heart, is a national (host-nation) challenge and responsibility, and national factors will shape its pace and sequencing. Even though the international community will be directly engaged in assisting a country, local political processes will be fundamental for success and will include extensive political mediations and compromises.

The U.S. military will always remain an outsider to this peacebuilding process and the country it is trying to assist. It can never have sufficient knowledge about the host country and the other international actors because of its institutional processes and the temporary nature of its involvement. The military will be asked to undertake a wide variety of tasks beyond its basic combat skills because of its ability to plan, organize, respond, and mobilize resources. It is an institution noted for seizing the initiative, taking action, and getting results. Those are the qualities that will be most needed initially in stabilizing a situation and allowing peacebuilding to proceed.

This chapter will consider just what can be known by the U.S. military about another society, its structural issues, its resilience, its long-term grievances, and its vision for the future. What can the military realistically be expected to understand about the other international and regional actors? By its actions, the military will have an effect on the host nation but is it capable of understanding and controlling what that effect will be? How much is the military self-aware of the consequences of its actions in supporting peacebuilding? Does the military have institutional inhibitors that proscribe what it can reasonably be expected to do? It is an organization whose main focus is on finding, fixing, fighting, and finishing an enemy. How does this institutional bias advance or retard peacebuilding? Does the military's culture prevent that level of collaboration that is needed within the whole of U.S. Government and with the nongovernmental organization (NGO) and international government organization (IGO) community to support successful peacebuilding missions?

In many instances the military will be necessary, so the chapter will propose a way ahead, building upon the strengths of the military institution. It will look at the knowledge, skills, and abilities that the military can and should possess and how to address the gaps that will exist.

UNKNOWN UNKNOWNS

Understanding the problem is always the best place to start. Any number of frameworks, assessment tools, and methodologies has been developed to determine drivers of conflict and long-standing structural grievances of the host nation. Yet even with all of these tools, there is a limit to what can be understood by military units and acted upon.[1]

The Type of Intelligence that the Military Traditionally Collects Does Not Support Peacebuilding.

Military intelligence has traditionally been focused on the "threat" rather than on the environment. Even though the doctrine on stability and counterinsurgency stresses the need to look deeply into the people among whom the military is operating, the institutional default position is threat based. The most recent description of these shortfalls was identified by Major General Michael Flynn, the Chief of CJ2, International Security Assistance Force, and CJ2, U.S. Forces–Afghanistan, in his paper titled *Fixing Intel*:

> Eight years into the war in Afghanistan, the U.S. intelligence community is only marginally relevant to our overall strategy. Having focused the overwhelming majority of our collection efforts and analytical brainpower on insurgent groups, our vast intelligence apparatus still finds itself unable to answer fundamental questions about the environment in which we operate and the people we are trying to persuade. Ignorant of

161

local economics and landowners, hazy about who the powerbrokers are and how we might influence them, incurious about the correlations between various development projects and the levels of cooperation of villagers, and disengaged from people in the best position to find answers—whether aid workers or Afghan soldiers—U.S. intelligence officers and analysts can do little but shrug in response to high level decision-makers seeking the knowledge, analysis, and information they need to wage a successful counterinsurgency[2]

Any number of frameworks and approaches has been tried, from the Interagency Conflict Assessment Framework to the District Stability Framework. All of these tools are great innovations trying to get at the essence of determining what is driving the conflict, but they require understanding, finesse, collaboration, and time. Their value is enhanced if the analyst possesses linguistic and cultural skills and direct knowledge of the piece of the earth in question. Those who can successfully implement such tools are few and far between and are difficult to recruit and retain. The U.S. military has tried to obtain such knowledge by developing ad hoc organizations such as the "Human Terrain Teams," a program employing personnel from the social science disciplines such as anthropology, sociology, political science, regional studies, and linguistics to provide military commanders and staff with an understanding of the local population and the environment. The results of this initiative have been mixed, but the commanders have gotten some benefit out of the attempt. These tools have their limitations, depending upon the willingness of the various peoples and factions in the host nation to cooperate.

Visitors Are Only Told What the Host Wants Them to Know.

The military force engaged in peacebuilding that attempts to transform conflict will always be an outsider, a temporary visitor in the country. The military personnel may only be in the country for a few months or a few years. At best, they can acquire an incomplete knowledge of the host government and its people. The knowledge they do acquire will be influenced by the source of information. In the fractured society in which the military will be required to operate, there will be many competing elements trying to fill the gaps and exploit the opportunities created in the wake of major conflict. Each will be providing the military key bits of information designed to enhance their position. The United Kingdom (UK) *Doctrinal Manual on Military Support to Stabilization* discusses this very challenge. It identifies at least three major groups with which the military must deal: the government, elites, and the general population. All of these groups have objectives they will be trying to pursue and will be trying to see how they can leverage the military forces on their behalf. The military will be trying to leverage these groups, while at the same time trying to understand what is going on. This tension will always be a problem for the outsider.[3]

The U.S. military occupation force that landed in Korea in 1945 was ignorant of even the basic information on Korea. Thousands of soldiers had been trained to understand Japanese customs and organization by the U.S. Army Military Government School, but policy prohibited the study of Korea in Army Schools. There was no adequate intelligence, so the XXIV Corps, fresh from the fighting in Okinawa, arrived hungry for information. The source of their information was to be the former Japanese occupiers, Koreans who had collaborated with the Japanese, and Korean elite who possessed an excellent grasp of English. Each of these groups had an agenda, and the military force was not able to clearly understand to what extent they were being manipulated. The U.S. military government formed their initial ideas about Korea during the first months of occupation on the 350 separate memoranda drafted by Japanese officials. Based on this biased input, the U.S. occupational command looked upon Korea as "hopeless as a society," and this informed future planning and decisions. Many of the crises and problems faced by the United States during the occupation, and their approaches to those problems, were based on questionable local sources of information, each of which had an agenda.[4]

There are symbols, rituals, behavior models, and linguistic practices that take many years to master, and the military just does not have the time to develop such an understanding. Additionally, the military must depend on sources that may be hostile to military forces in general. Many times, external sources must be relied upon that may not be telling the complete story. It is also in the host nation's interest to maintain the initiative so that the outcomes can be shaped in accordance with its agenda and therefore will shape the information provided. The host nation knows that the U.S. military will not be there forever and therefore must continually shape its environment for life when the U.S. military departs.

Policymakers Develop Goals Based on this Inadequate Understanding and Wishful Thinking.

Richard Millet's study of the U.S. engagements between the Spanish American War and World War II in nation building and constabulary development makes the point that reality on the ground at times does not get in the way of policy in Washington. When assessing the U.S. Policy toward Cuba, the Philippines, Nicaragua, Haiti, and the Dominican Republic, Millett makes the following observation:

> But, when polices were being formulated, no American official, civilian or military, appears to have asked if replacing such forces with a better trained and equipped constabulary would change their relation to the rest of society or in any way alter the traditional political equation which made force the final arbiter. Nor does there appear to have been any questioning of how nationalist sentiments would react to a foreign-created security force, or how that force, itself, would react once foreign control was ended. . . . Instead of asking such questions, policymakers seem to have assumed that a constabulary created with American instructors and under American-imposed regulations would behave like an American military force. There was no understanding.[5]

There have been many studies on the lack of knowledge and invalid assumptions that framed the U.S. approach to both Iraq and Afghanistan and the subsequent struggle to gain situational understanding. Many times, the policymakers will assume that the U.S. systems and procedures are superior to those of the host nation, and therefore all that needs to be done is to introduce the locals to the U.S. systems and procedures.[6] In her article in *Prism*, Laura Cleary makes this point as she examines what is and is not possible in exporting the U.S. model of civil military interaction to another country. There are differing cultural reference points between the U.S. military trainers trying to impart a concept of a military in a democratic society to another country that has a different historical perspective. It will not be enough just to professionalize the host nation's military force. Millet has recorded how the United States professionalized several militaries in Central America, only to see them impose military rule.[7]

The Military Force Will Have an Incomplete Knowledge of the U.S. Government and the International Community.

Ever since the 1994 engagement in Haiti, the U.S. Government has attempted to develop a whole-of-government approach to coordinate its actions and share knowledge among the agencies of government. Various presidential directives and proposed congressional legislation have been developed to encourage the agencies of government to cooperate with each other. There have been a number of initiatives designed to increase the knowledge, understanding, and coordination for the whole of the U.S. Government. Still, there is a challenge among all agencies to understand what each is about. The U.S. Government was designed to ensure that power would not be consolidated in the hands of the few in order to protect the liberty and freedom of the many. There are obstacles embedded in the U.S. governmental system that work against coordination and understanding. Overcoming these obstacles requires a significant political price; one that most are unwilling to pay. This presents a challenge, as institutions are chartered as stovepipes and provided requisite authorities and funding that reinforce separation. Over time, the U.S. bureaucracy has grown into a maze of overlapping, redundant, and conflicting structures that has compounded the challenge. A study of complex contingency operations found that:

> a key lesson learned has been that personnel in the various agencies and military services involved do not possess an adequate knowledge of the function, organization, capabilities, and limitations of the other entities with which they are expected to coordinate their activities.

A study by the joint staff revealed that 35 percent of Joint Staff officers were working directly with the interagency for the first time; 70 percent of them said that they had received no formal training in joint, multinational, or interagency activities. Seventy-six percent of senior leaders said that their staff officers required improved skills in supervising interagency personnel.[8]

Military Forces Are Not Aware of the Impact of Their Actions.

Additionally, the military force itself is not self-aware. It most often does a poor job at understanding what effect its presence is having on the situation.

In support of the 1994 Unified Task Force (UNITAF) deployment to Somalia, the United States established its support function in Mogadishu with no assessment on how this would affect the local social and economic situation in the country. Young Somali males were encouraged by the prospects of U.S. employment and moved into the city. Few of them were hired. But the result was that they left their traditional clan areas and the influence of the clan elders and became the unemployed, shiftless, and desperate elements in the city. Here, war lords such as Mohammad Farah Aidid could prey upon them. The U.S. military force was unaware that the presence of their support base was destabilizing the social contract within Somali society and that the lure of filling contracts was having a destabilizing social impact.[9]

The problems can be even more subtle and can influence ideas and attitudes and affect the legitimacy of the operation. In both Iraq and Afghanistan, rumors were started at various times that the U.S. command was contracting local men to work in the dining facilities, forcing these devout Muslims to handle pork. Many of the workers that were actually employed were third country nationals, some of whom were indeed Muslim. Additionally, many Muslim contractor employees who were secretaries and support staff ate at these dining facilities where forbidden fare was served. The "All American Food" served at the dining facilities by the contractor not only provided fare for the propagandist, but also failed to build the local capacity that the mission was all about.

None of the succulent tomatoes or the crisp cucumbers grown in Iraq made it into the salad bar. U.S. government regulations dictated that everything, even the water in which hot dogs were boiled, was to be shipped in from approved suppliers in other nations. Milk and bread were trucked in from Kuwait, as were tinned peas and carrots. The breakfast cereal was flown in from the United States, made in the USA. Fruit Loops and Frosted Flakes at the breakfast table helped boost morale.[10]

In both Iraq and Afghanistan, the U.S. military is substantially engaged in development activities enabled by a significant funding tool, the Commanders Emergency Response Program (CERP). Over 60 percent of the U.S. funds supporting reconstruction in Afghanistan are allocated via the Department of Defense (DoD). The effects of this funding on Afghanistan are significant. Yet by all accounts, in both Iraq and Afghanistan, there has been an inability to determine just what effect this spending has had in the long term on accomplishing the overall U.S. objectives. The Special Inspector General for Iraq Reconstruction (SIGIR) has conducted over 370 audits and inspections, five lessons learned reports, and hundreds of investigations, and has had problems connecting programs with outcomes. There have been repeated calls to better monitor these programs so as to understand the connections between the actions of the U.S. military, who are addressing the drivers of conflict, and others, who are building the appropriate local capacity to reach sustainable peace.[11]

Military Tends to Stereotype New and Unfamiliar Environments.

Prejudices and stereotypes are always there and hinder peacebuilding. The effect of stereotyping can lead not only to a failure of programs and long-term success, but also to violence, discontent, and the loss of legitimacy for the mission. There are many examples from the early engagements in Latin America and the Philippines. Post-September 11, 2001 (9/11), the military has come with the stereotypical approach to the Arab world that is shared on main street America, and that a number of cultural awareness programs have attempted to address. Sebastian Junger, in his book "War," records these stereotypes, prejudices, and the effects they have on the relationships with the people and the ability to gain valuable information from the people. This also relates to the ability to use the language. Again, the need for interpreters also isolates the Soldier. The interpreter creates his own reality, manipulating both sides of the engagement, either intentionally or unintentionally. There are many examples of this happening. The U.S. military has attempted to deal with this issue by arranging training sessions with interpreters, but usually only for staff and commanders and not for the infantryman who is in contact with the locals.[12]

Members of the U.S. military will come with an understandable cultural bias about how a military force should be organized and the relationship of that force to the democratic organs of government. That bias will inform their approach toward the security force assistance mission. The recipient military may come from an entirely different tradition with an entirely different outlook. Unless that bias can be overcome and a workable solution reached, skills can be transferred, but transformation will not be achieved.[13]

INSTITUTIONAL REALITY

The military is a "can do" positive organization that is oriented toward results. Inadequate information is not a deterrent for action. Militaries abhor vacuums and disorder. Militaries will impose order first and ask questions later.

The Military Is Used as a Stop Gap Because of Its Response and Resources.

The military has been called upon to make the trains run in Kosovo, run the banking system in the Dominican Republic, and conduct agricultural extension services in Afghanistan. None of these are core competencies of the military but, because of the wide range of expertise that can be resident in the military and the can do attitude in dealing with any demand, the military fills in when civil expertise is either not available or inadequate. This may be better than letting situations disintegrate, but all of the studies and after action reports clearly state that early transfer from the military to a whole-of-government approach is the only hope for balanced development. The United States Institute of Peace (USIP)/U.S. Army War College Peacekeeping and Stability Operations Institute (PKSOI) *Guidelines for Stabilization and Reconstruction* is clear that a comprehensive approach is the only way to attain a viable peace. When the military is left to run projects other than training military forces or when even the training of military forces is not part of a comprehensive security sector reform, the results have not been encouraging. Historians of the U.S. military interventions in Latin America have concluded: "Efforts to change a society by altering one institution never produce the desired effect and inevitably bring undesired effects."[14]

Military Designs Measurements to Meet Its Needs and End States.

Because the engagement of the military is temporary and the units themselves rotate throughout this engagement, this tends to drive the various units toward achieving objectives in the short term. The military must achieve results on the watch of the current commander. The commander and unit will get graded on their performance, and therefore they will be results oriented. Therefore, the military will seek metrics that can demonstrate success not just for the organization, but also for the leaders whose careers depend upon such success. The tendency is to focus on measures of progress rather than effectiveness, given that the latter have an incubation period longer than individual unit deployments. Peacebuilding is a long-term venture the time horizon of which does not fit the military deployment schedule. Therefore, units tend to look at high visibility projects that can have immediate impact. The initial focus of projects in Afghanistan in 2002 was to search for quick impact programs that would provide the most visibility for the limited funds available and "win the hearts and minds" of the people in support of the United States. It was not focused on performing surveys and establishing long-term projects in coordination with the U.S. Agency for International Development (USAID). Over time, this mind set shifted. Still, by 2007, commanders were still being evaluated for committing all of their commander's emergency response program monies and starting more projects than the previous unit.[15]

Military Focus Is on Short-Term Security as the *Sine-Qua-Non*, and Peacebuilding Is Secondary, Supporting, and of Lesser Importance.

This is reflected in the organization and orientation of the military. For example, the development of police forces in Afghanistan under military lead resembles auxiliary infantry to fight insurgents rather than community police. This tendency was also present in the development of constabularies in the Philippines, Nicaragua, and Haiti earlier in the century. Because of the lack of civil affairs structure, the military assigned civil military duties to other branches. For example, in Afghanistan, artillery officers would be assigned the duty of negotiating with local authorities to establish the conditions for peaceful conflict transformation. They were provided with money and instructions but little or no training for this most sensitive and strategically significant job. They often had no experience dealing with interpreters, other governmental agencies, and local political situations. Obviously, these jobs were considered less important than combat-related jobs because the military would never have taken a civil affairs officer and placed him in an artillery position without extensive training. Yet, they thought nothing of taking anyone and placing them into a civil military position.[16]

The Center for Complex Operations (CCO) in its survey of Provincial Reconstruction Teams (PRT) observed that the structure of the units facilitated a kinetic maneuver approach to security first and the rest of the peacebuilding activities secondary. Although the Diplomacy, Defense, Development (3D) approach was the overall objective of the International Security Assistance Force (ISAF) commander, his civil/military

173

plan was not being implemented properly because structurally and procedurally units are optimized for combat. The S-3 Operations section focused on security, and other parts of the civil/military approach were run out of the civil military operations (CMO) section that was separated from the operational section. In traditional military staffs, the S-3 runs the operation and has primacy, so naturally, security in a military sense takes priority. How a unit organizes and assigns responsibilities for security and peace-building functions does not reflect current Army doctrine as found in *Field Manual* (FM) *3-07, Stability*, or FM 3-24, *Counterinsurgency*, but reflects the structures that were developed post-World War II where CMO became a separate but subordinate staff section.[17]

The military focus on the security sector tends to force the other sectors to a secondary status, and this can influence other actors' approaches with unfortunate long-term results. Javid Ahmad and Lousie Langeby of the German Marshall Fund make this very observation about Afghanistan. They conclude that the focus on security has placed economic development secondary, and the development that was done was based around the international security presence.[18]

Similarly, reports from some members of the Human Terrain Teams support the observation that, institutionally, military forces focus on short-term stability rather than long-term peace building. Mathew Schehl, who ran a Tactical Human Intelligence Team in Central Iraq during 2003-05, wrote in his blog that commanders he dealt with were focused on the immediate, and not the long-term, transformational aspects of the mission:

"Success" is defined in the short term . . . specific objectives are pursued without necessary regard for long-term implications.

Information produced will tend toward a narrow conception of culture and social systems, i.e., that information which is only as relevant as its immediate utility to the field commander, fostering a simplified ideation of "good guy, bad guy," without regard to social or historic contexts and processes. . . .

The utilization of such information is subject to the whims and spot decisions of the field commander.[19]

Military Excels at Transferring Technical Skills but Transferring Values is Difficult.

Military forces have demonstrated that they can transfer technical skills quite well to other countries. Many of the forces in Asia and Latin America have been recipients of this technical training. But how well are values and understandings transmitted and internalized? How well are they taken on board? How long do those values last beyond the engagement period? Without a long-term commitment, such as the extensive program of in-country engagement and training of officers in the United States extended to the Korean army for over 30 years, it is difficult to affect values in a short-term post-conflict environment.

Military and Community Police Frameworks Clash.

The military framework is to organize the world into friends, enemies, and others. The approach is to find, fix, fight, and finish the enemy. Collateral civilian damage and death is considered a risk that can be accepted to finish the enemy and is sanctioned under international law. Police framework is to protect civilians and property, while bringing violators of the law into the justice system. Collateral damage is not acceptable, and the focus is not on finishing an enemy, but arresting a suspect and allowing a rule of law system to process that suspect.

Information is handled differently in each system. In the military, intelligence is developed to find and fix the enemy so that enemy can be defeated. In the justice system, information is gathered to prosecute a suspect. That information must meet the criteria of the rule of law system to be admissible.

The military has often been required not only to perform police duties, but also to train and equip police. This is caused either by a lack of civil police assistance or frustration of the military with the progress of police development. The results have not always been successful. Based on the frameworks above, police trained by the military tend to resemble mini-infantry units. In Afghanistan, they were designed to supplement the counterinsurgency (COIN) fight. Police trained solely by the military, and not as part of a comprehensive security sector reform package, tended not to be responsive to local controls, and they exhibited centralized control outside of state controls. Order and security often trumped justice and the development of a rule of law system. It sought to increase the power of the central government to provide security but ended up supporting nondemocratic processes.[20]

Reality of Long-Term Development Clashes with Short-Term Reality of Military Engagement.

There are many stories of locals taking advantage of the short-term focus of the military force. The Office of the Special Inspector General for Reconstruction (SIGIR) in Iraq has recorded many such incidents. For example, three separate commanders of three different units that replaced each other spent Commander's Emergency Response Program (CERP) monies for a local generator that was never purchased. No one was in one place long enough to follow through. That, coupled with inadequate records, lack of good metrics for evaluating peacebuilding activities, lack of a whole of U.S. Government oversight, and a short-term time horizon for each military unit, has allowed such situations to develop.[21]

TIME AND RESOURCES

There will not be enough time or resources to do the job the way it should be done. Therefore, there will always be pressure to hurry up, when hurry up is often the wrong approach.

Goals Established Do Not Match Realistic Time Frames Nor Resources.

The time needed to transform a post-conflict country though peacebuilding methods is often underestimated. It is not realistic that broken societies and dysfunctional systems of governance can be altered in a few years. Often, the goals laid down are unrealistic, and the influence of outsiders exaggerated. These issues were demonstrated with the building of the Afghanistan and Iraq armies. The initial approach was a quick fix to get into the field forces capable of handling the insurgent threat. Both programs went through growing pains requiring restarting the programs with more realistic objectives and longer lead times.

When the Coalition Provisional Authority (CPA) for Iraq was established in 2003, it had neither the time nor the resources to plan and execute effectively. The CPA was asked to provide results immediately but reality overcame the enterprise, and the largest rebuilding program in history grew far beyond what was envisioned. Between May and July 2003, planned U.S. expenditures had increased nine-fold over what was anticipated. The story of the mismatch between goals, time, and resources in both Afghanistan and Iraq has been described by many SIGIR reports and in other books and journals.[22]

Rotation of Forces Limit What Is Possible.

The force generation of the military rotates forces and individuals from 2 to 6 to 12 months and occasionally 24 months. Given the long time needed to transform post-conflict societies, this rotation places constraints on what is possible. Each unit must demonstrate progress and let the command know that it has done better than the previous unit. This has led to new programs being started and existing programs being modified. The story of the generator noted above is emblematic of a deeper problem and a source of tension between the military and the development community. Time horizons between what the military would like to see to stabilize a situation and what the development community needs to prove to be successful are a constant source of friction. The implementa-

178

tion and expectations of programs that are, in essence, development programs take many years to be proven successful.[23]

Political Pressure to Withdraw Trumps All.

Once the national policy starts to shift, and over time it will, then the pressure to get out will overwhelm all of the concerns. Vietnamization was a case study. The goals were to:

> expand, equip, and train South Vietnam's forces and assign to them an ever-increasing combat role, at the same time steadily reducing the number of U.S. combat troops.

The first was:

> strengthening the armed force of the South Vietnamese in numbers, equipment, leadership and combat skills. The second component is the extension of the pacification program in South Vietnam.

The first was achievable, but it would take time. For the United States, it was trivial to have a U.S. helicopter pilot fly in support, but helicopter operations were too much part of ground operations to involve U.S. personnel. As observed by Lieutenant General David Palmer, to qualify an Army of the Republic of Vietnam (ARVN) candidate for U.S. helicopter school, he first needed months of English language training to be able to follow the months-long training, and then additional field time to become proficient. In other words, adding new capabilities to the ARVN would often take 2 or more years. Palmer did not disagree that the first component, given time and resources, was achievable.

Pacification, the second component, presented the real challenge . . . it was benevolent government action in areas where the government should always have been benevolently active . . . doing both was necessary if Vietnamization were to work.

But the U.S. domestic shift away from support for the war was translated down to the troops on the ground as pass and run. End date rather than end state became the reality.[24] Such pressure has already been applied to Iraq and Afghanistan.

WHAT IS POSSIBLE

Knowing the Unknowns.

As discussed above, although it will not be possible to understand all the nuances involved in dealing with a host nation, there are some steps that can be taken that will reduce the level of uncertainty. Working toward an agreed whole-of-government assessment tool, improving education and training in the areas of stability concepts and doctrine, broadening assignment opportunities with other U.S. agencies, increasing engagement with other countries and cultures, enhancing the whole-of-government scenarios and training opportunities at military training centers, incorporating cultural and social aspects into appropriate training venues, and seeking every opportunity to expand the intellectual horizon of the military will go a long way toward nurturing understanding of what is possible and what is not possible when engaged in supporting peacebuilding.

The last attempt to create a whole-of-government assessment tool was in 2008 with the Interagency

Conflict Assessment Framework (ICAF). It was based on USAID's conflict assessment framework that borrowed from the World Bank's tools. It was the basis for the Tactical Conflict Assessment Framework (TCAF) and the subsequent District Stability Framework used in Afghanistan. Its purpose was to develop a common understanding among all agencies of government of the dynamics driving and mitigating violent conflict. Although approved by the Deputies Committee and written into the stability doctrine of the military, it has not found universal application. It has been used in support of embassies over 35 times since its inception, but there is neither systemic application nor training in the U.S. military on its application. This initiative needs to be continued and improved.[25]

Leader education is key and essential to understanding. The Center for New American Security's February 2010 report, *Keeping The Edge: Revitalizing America's Military Officer Corps*, concludes that the education for officers is inadequate to address the current and emerging security concerns, and an overhaul of the education programs is essential.[26]

> There is substantial tension in officer training programs between cultivating excellence in tactical and technical competencies and developing the qualities needed for operating in complex environments in concert with multiple partners. A more holistic officer development program is required to counteract a disproportionate focus on tactical training over strategic education. Strategy and warfighting are integrative tasks, requiring not only the ability to operate specialized equipment or to command a tactical unit, but also an understanding of how different pieces fit together to ensure the achievement of national objectives.[27]

There are other calls for action along with several recent articles to institutionalize proper education at all levels of military officers that address full spectrum operations. The Winter 2009-10 issue of *Parameters*, U.S. Army War College, devoted a major section toward developing the strategic leader. The articles have identified the challenge in the past in institutionalizing such subjects as cross-cultural understanding that are critical for full spectrum operations and recommending solutions. Additionally, the *House of Representatives Report on Professional Military Education* examined to what extent the U.S. military services are incorporating irregular warfare and stability into their curricula. It concluded that although there has been some progress, it is not enough. It stated that the:

> Officer Professional Military Education Policy (OP-MEP) has no distinct Learning Area for stability operations, despite those operations being recognized as a core military mission comparable to combat operations since 1995 by Departmental policy, which directed that stability operations be 'explicitly addressed and integrated across all DOD activities,' including those involved in education."[28]

To fight stereotyping, there are a number of cultural tools and courses that have been developed as a result of the U.S. engagement in Operation IRAQI FREEDOM (OIF) and Operation ENDURING FREEDOM (OEF). Centers such as the Air Force Cultural and Language Center have many products and outreach to deal with stereotyping and help the military understand the environment.

How can the military know itself? This is the most difficult problem, but, again, there are tools. Knowing yourself is part of the standard doctrine for deception.

That doctrine stresses the need to understand how your unit and its actions appear to the enemy before you can hope to manipulate the enemy's perceptions. The same concept of understanding yourself and the consequences of your actions should be applied concerning peacebuilding. The most basic question should be asked: What are the indirect effects of conducting operations like running a fire base? Just the presence of a large logistical military footprint in a country can alter the operational environment. If the command has not completed an in-depth assessment as the framework requires, then it will be operating in the blind and executing support contracts that will counteract what the comprehensive development programs are trying to achieve. Displacement of local capacity or alteration of the social economic factors needs to be considered when building a large U.S. footprint in a country. This understanding of the force must include contract support. Direct contracting affects the host government, the elites, and the people of the country and therefore can have immediate and long-term impact. The purpose of this contracting is to interact directly with the locals to produce an effect that supports mission accomplishment. Examples are training, educating, and advising host nation military, paramilitary, and police forces; training, educating, and advising all ministries of the government, both national and local, on conducting security sector reform that includes reform of penal, judicial, and legal codes as well as disarming, demobilizing, and reintegrating into civil society; assisting in intelligence operations to include interrogations, providing security forces, both static and mobile, in support of the movement and delivery of people and goods; and establishing and managing command, control, and communication centers. These are the contractors that are most likely to be armed and the most likely to use deadly force. All of these activities directly advance the U.S. mission in theater. This effort must focus foremost on building effective, legitimate, and resilient states. The ultimate responsibility for the stabilization and reconstruction process belongs to the host nation. This means all efforts of both the U.S. Government and their contractors must assist the host nation government and civil society to ensure that they lead and participate in both planning and implementation. Utilization of host nation processes and structures, both formal and informal, builds ownership. The key issue is how to meet immediate needs, yet also build long-term capacity. There is a tradeoff between relying on private contractors or U.S. governmental agencies to meet the immediate needs of the population and thereby reduce the risk of instability; while laying the more time-consuming groundwork for state institutions to deliver essential services and strengthen the legitimacy and effectiveness of a nascent democracy. The other concern is determining what tasks should be contracted and what tasks need to remain in the hands of U.S. governmental agencies. The tendency in Iraq and Afghanistan has been to use the United States or third country nations as an immediate solution to obtain stability. As of June 2009, nearly 88 percent of the contractors in Iraq and Afghanistan were third country nationals, only 8 percent were local, and the rest were US nationals. What are the implications of using third country nationals?[29]

The division between what should be a U.S. Government face versus a contractor face must be determined by the outcomes. The U.S. objective is to instill a concept of democratic governance that is responsive to the needs of the people. A U.S. governmental face in key advisory positions sends a different message from a contractor face, even if that contactor is a subject matter expert. There must be a collaborative approach and a determination as to what messages need to be sent to achieve the effect desired. A combination of current federal employees and contracted personnel providing expert assistance can work well to instill the ideas of democratic control. It becomes difficult to convince local governors, chiefs of police, and politicians in Afghanistan not to hire their own illegal and unlicensed private military companies (PMCs) when the United States leads by example in its dependence on such organizations. Dennis Keller made the following evaluation of the U.S. role in foreign police training:

> Simply using a contracting mechanism to conduct police training does not create the kind of institutional capacity in the USG that is required for a consistently effective approach to enable local police to establish and maintain a safe and secure environment in a recovering state. Contracted police trainers often cannot or will not operate in non-permissive environments, thus confining their training to the capital city or secure areas, leaving unsecured remoter areas of a country without desperately needed police trainers and mentors, as is often the case in Iraq and Afghanistan today. If a particular contracted police trainer/mentor is identified as having superior ability to impart police skills and values in a foreign environment, there is no mechanism to keep that person on at DoS INL [Department of State, Bureau of International Narcotics and Law Enforcement Affairs] or elsewhere in the USG to help establish institutional knowledge and long-term capacity to manage and conduct foreign police training.

While DoS INL seems to be most involved in foreign police training, with Department of Justice's ICITAP

[International Criminal Investigative Training Assistance Program] somewhere behind it in this arena, neither of these offices nor any other USG agency has assumed a definitive lead role for foreign law enforcement assistance to coordinate the diverse, multi-agency array of foreign police training that has slowly grown as a result of institutional creep to fill a police training void created by the U.S. Congressional cutoff of USAID police training activities in 1974. The lack of a lead agency with overall responsibility for foreign police training, similar to DoD's responsibility for foreign military training, carries with it a number of consequences. The USG has no International Military Education and Training (IMET) Program-equivalent to systematically bring police officers to the U.S. for training, such as DoD has for foreign military officers. The USG does not have a comprehensive assessment program, though one is in development, to identify the state of law enforcement and police in a foreign country. The USG has not developed what the military would call "doctrine," or agreed upon procedures and principles, to integrate State INL's emphasis on the enforcement aspect of police training, with USAID's community policing and overall justice sector and ministerial reform programs.[30]

CONCLUSION: UNDERSTANDING AND DEALING WITH INSTITUTIONAL REALITY

Understanding what the institutional constraints and restraints are and understanding what is possible and not possible is a starting point. Efforts to change a society just through the military changing its security force or providing a temporary safe and secure environment never produces the desired effect. Using the comprehensive approach always works better as the USIP's *Guidelines for Stabilization and Reconstruction* have amply illustrated. The United Nations (UN) capstone doctrine states under the Peacebuilding Activities section:

> While the deployment of a multi-dimensional United Nations peacekeeping operation may help to stem violence in the short-term, it is unlikely to result in a sustainable peace unless accompanied by programmes designed to prevent the recurrence of conflict.[31]

No matter what the military will try to do to shape the outcome, the host nation has its own objectives and its own ideas, and over time as the influence of the military force wanes, local imperatives take over. Host Nation ownership is a key principle in both the U.S. and UN doctrine, and the military must be comfortable with that concept. What the military builds will, over time, evolve into something else. Korea is the case in point. At the end of the day, Korea exerted its national agenda. But the United States maintained a long-term relationship with Korea, and that helped shape the outcome.

Primum non nocere is a Latin phrase that means "First, do no harm." This is one of the key tenets of physicians and first responders, and should be considered when dealing with the military contribution to peacebuilding. There is no standard approach nor formulas that can apply in each situation. The military must not only try to understand local conditions, but also their own institution and what effects it is having on the environment. Great attention should be paid to unintended consequences of actions that may affect power relationships, societal dynamics, and even policymaking in capitals. This concept needs to be considered in the doctrine, planning, and training of military forces and will require an adjustment. This "do no harm" approach should also be in collaboration with the whole of the U.S. governmental approach and the host nation itself so that at the end of the day, the host nation will have ownership with the ability to deal with drivers of instability.

ENDNOTES - CHAPTER 7

1. Some examples of assessment tools are the Interagency Conflict Assessment Framework developed by USAID, the District Stability Framework developed by ISAF in Afghanistan, Measuring Progress In Conflict Environments by USIP, and the Conflict Assessment Framework by the World Bank.

2. Major General Michael Flynn, Captain Matt Pottinger, and Paul Batchelor, *Fixing Intelligence: A Blue Print for Making Intelligence Relevant in Afghanistan*, Afghanistan: ISAF, January 10, 2010, p. 1.

3. United Kingdom (UK) Ministry of Defense, *Joint Doctrine Publication 3-40, Security and Stabilization: The Military Contribution*, Shrivenham, Wiltshire, UK: The Development Concepts and Doctrine Center, November 2009, pp. 2-24 and Chap. 3.

4. Ronald H. Spector, *In the Ruins of Empire: The Japanese Surrender and the Battle for Post War Asia*, New York: Random House, 2007, pp. 150-153.

5. Richard L. Millett, *Searching for Stability: The U.S. Development of Constabulary Forces in Latin America and the Philippines*, Occasional Paper 30, Fort Leavenworth, KS: Combat Studies Institute Press, 2010, p. 124.

6. Author's experience as a Special Forces Staff officer in U.S. Central Command (CENTCOM). In 1983, after the attempted coup by the Kenyan Air Force, a Special Forces advisor team was sent to the country. The Chief of Special Operations for CENTCOM, without any knowledge of Kenyan society or the structure of the Kenyan armed forces, presented a plan for the restructuring of the Kenyan armed forces. When the author asked how he could do that without any local understanding, he stated that the U.S. model was the best in the world, so there was no need to

188

understand local issues. If the Kenyans would just adopt the U.S. model, all would be OK. Kenya rejected this recommendation.

7. Laura R. Cleary, "Lost in Translation, The Challenge of Exporting Models of Civil-Military Relations," *Prism*, Vol. 3, No. 2, March 2012, pp. 25, 33.

8. Joint Staff J-7, *Joint Staff Officer Study: Preliminary Findings*, PowerPoint Presentation, Washington, DC: U.S. Department of Defense, March 10, 2008; Center for Law and Military Operations, *U.S. Government Interagency Complex Contingency Operations Organizational and Legal Handbook*, February 24, 2004; William J Olson, "Interagency Coordination: The Normal Accident or the Essence of Indecision," Gabriel Marcella, ed., *Affairs of State: The Interagency and National Security*, Carlisle, PA: Strategic Studies Institute, U.S. Army War College, December 2008, p. 223; Nora Bensahel and Anne M. Moisan, "Repairing the Interagency Process," *Joint Force Quarterly*, Vol. 44, 2007, pp. 106–108.

9. Walter Clarke, Deputy Chief of Mission, U.S. Embassy, Somalia, during Operation RESTORE HOPE, and Mark Walsh, District Administrator in Baidoa, Somalia, for the UN Office for the Coordination of Humanitarian Affairs (UNOCHA), interviewed by the author at PKSOI in 2000, where all three were employed.

10. Rajiv Chandrasekaran, "Excerpt: Imperial Life in the Emerald City: Inside Iraq's Green Zone," October 10, 2007, linked from Media Bistro Home page available from *www.mediabistro. com/articles/cache/a8798.asp*.

11. Cleary, p. 95; Stuart W. Bowen, "No More Adhocracies; Reforming the Management of Stabilization and Reconstruction Operations," *Prism*, Vol. 3, No. 2, March 2012, p. 4.

12. Sebastian Junger, *War*, New York: Hachett Book Company, 2011.

13. Cleary, p. 25.

14. Richard L. Millett, "Limits of Influence, Creating Security Forces in Latin America," *Joint Force Quarterly*, Vol. 42, 3rd Quarter, 2006, p. 15.

15. William Flavin, *Civil Military Operations: Afghanistan*, Carlisle, PA: Peacekeeping Stability Operations Institute, March 23, 2004, pp. 20-21; Captain Devin Flavin, artillery office, 173rd Afghanistan, 2007, interview by author in Carlisle, PA, 2010.

16. Flavin, interview with author.

17. Dale Erickson, "Civmil in the U.S. Sector Afghanistan," briefing to PKSOI by the Center for Complex Operations, National Defense University (NDU) at PKSOI, Carlisle, PA, June 15, 2011.

18. Javid Ahmad and Louse Langeby, "Can the Afghan Economy be saved?" *Foreign Policy*, February 3, 2012, e mail message to author dated February 5, 2012.

19. Roberto J. Gonzalez, *American Counterinsurgency: Human Science and the Human Terrain*, Chicago, IL: Prickly Paradigm Press, 2009, p. 69.

20. Dennis E. Keller, *U.S. Military Forces And Police Assistance In Stability Operations: The Least Worst Option To Fill The U.S. Capacity Gap*, Carlisle, PA: Peacekeeping and Stability Operations Institute, U.S. Army War College, April 2010, p. 18. These institutional shortfalls in U.S. capacity for police training were identified by a State Department official at the Conference for Building Capacity in Stability Operations: Security Sector Reform, Governance, and Economics, jointly sponsored by the Association of the United States Army (AUSA), Center for Naval Analyses (CNA), and PKSOI, Washington, DC, April 6, 2009.

21. Cleary, p. 95.

22. *Ibid*; Bowen, p. 6.

23. Major Gregory Johnson, Vijaya Ramachandran, Julie Walz, "CERP in Afghanistan; Refining Military Capabilities in Development Activities," *Prism*, Vol. 3, No. 2, March 2012, p. 85.

24. David Palmer, *Summons of the Trumpet*, Novato, CA: Presidio Press, 1978 , pp. 219-220.

25. Caroline Earle, "Taking Stock: Interagency Integration in Stability Operations," *Prism*, Vol. 3, No. 2, March 2012, pp. 41-42.

26. Dr. John A. Nagl and Brian M. Burton, ed., *Keeping The Edge: Revitalizing America's Military Officer Corps*, Washington DC: Center for a New American Security, February 2010.

27. *Ibid.*, p. 6.

28. Allison Abbe and Stanley M. Halpin, "The Cultural Imperative for Professional Military Education and Leader Development," *Parameters*, Vol. 39, No 4, Winter 2009-10, p. 29; U.S. House of Representatives Committee on Armed Services Subcommittee on Oversight and Investigations, *Another Crossroads? Professional Military Education Two Decades after the Goldwater-Nichols*, Washington, DC: April 2010, p. 73.

29. Joint Forces Command, *Handbook for Private Security Contractors in Contingency Operations*, III; Moshe Schwartz, *Department of Defense Contractors in Iraq and Afghanistan: Background and Analysis*, Washington, DC: Congressional Research Service, December 14, 2009, p. 11; Moshe Schwartz, *The Department of Defense's Use of Private Security Contractors in Iraq and Afghanistan: Background, Analysis, and Options for Congress*, Washington, DC: Congressional Research Service, December 19, 2010, p. 8.

30. Dennis E. Keller, *U.S. Military Forces And Police Assistance In Stability Operations: The Least Worst Option To Fill The U.S. Capacity Gap*, Carlisle, PA: PKSOI, U.S. Army War College, April 2010, p. 18. These institutional shortfalls in U.S. capacity for police training were identified by a State Department official at the Conference for Building Capacity in Stability Operations: Security Sector Reform, Governance, and Economics, jointly sponsored by AUSA, CNA, and PKSOI, Washington, DC, April 6, 2009.

31. Department of Peacekeeping Operations, *United Nations Peacekeeping Operations: Principles and Guidelines*, New York: United Nations, Department of Field Support, 2008, p. 25.

CHAPTER 8

THINKING GLOBALLY, ACTING LOCALLY: A GRAND STRATEGIC APPROACH TO CIVIL-MILITARY COORDINATION IN THE 21ST CENTURY

Christopher Holshek

Thank God we're a great country. We can stand a lot of this nonsense. But let's not test it too closely.

General Andrew Goodpaster

Given the grand strategic imperatives of the 21st century, the civil-military nexus of conflict management and peacebuilding is more relevant to international engagements and American grand strategy than ever. However, the U.S. civil-military approach to foreign policy and national security needs overhauling because it remains largely based on an outdated national security paradigm, itself predicated on an imbalanced interpretation of the fundamental civil-military relationship in American society that was forged under the exigencies of the Cold War era and revitalized since September 11, 2001 (9/11). There is plenty of evidence for this growing incongruity as of late, given the tremendous difficulties, for example, in post-conflict Iraq, in stabilizing Afghanistan, in counterterrorism operations in Africa, and in the military's strained relations with many nongovernmental organizations (NGOs).[1] Given the constraints and restraints of the emerging strategic and operational environments, however, the full potential of the civil-military nexus in international engagements cannot come to bear unless: first, civil-military coordination is seen as strategic rather than merely operational or tactical; and second, that civil-military coordination must essentially be the application of the democratic civil-military relationship—and thus military action is through, and in support of, civilian organizations and local government entities. This is in the best interest of all stakeholders, especially the military. To attain such economies of effort, cost, and risk at all levels, the actions of uniformed state instrumentalities must be consonant with their own societal values. In policy and practice, civil-military coordination has to walk the talk.

This is actually good news for the United States, for no other nation is better suited to lead this transformation, given its dynamic, multicultural civil society and its democratic national values and tremendous social capital, as well as the U.S. military's extensive institutional experience in civil-military coordination— if, of course, the United States makes the necessary adjustments.

This strategic opportunity requires exploring: first, how the grand strategic context for civil-military coordination has changed between the 20th and 21st centuries; second, the U.S. civil-military relationship over this time; third, understanding civil-military coordination strategically—i.e., "thinking globally"; and fourth, understanding civil-military coordination in application—i.e., "acting locally."

A TALE OF TWO CENTURIES

The global context for civil-military coordination[2] has changed. Top-down, power-driven Western notions of national sovereignty and security of the 20th century are less relevant than the emerging, values-based, bottom-up human security actualities gaining ascendency in a now hyper-connected, globalized world—in other words, the referent for security is increasingly the individual or community rather than the state.[3] The constraints of this transformed international environment, along with the restraints of growing resource scarcity and capital shortages for the United States, other Western countries, the United Nations (UN), and the wider donor community form the two grand strategic imperatives of our times. These have correspondingly transformed the functioning paradigm for security, humanitarian relief, and development across the full range of conflict prevention and management as well as for peace operations, with associated changes in the approach to the civil-military nexus as a whole.

From a broader perspective, the fundamental shift in the international order between the 20th and 21st centuries has been more inflective than intrinsic, particularly in the balance and interplay between what has been called "soft" (coercive) and "hard" (persuasive) power. National power in both its source and application is characterized by an industrial-era, state-centric, top-down, zero-sum, empirical, and calculable game of war and peace played largely by diplomats and soldiers, interest-driven, and manifested mostly in hard currency and armies. It reached its zenith in the 20th century. What is now beginning to hold greater sway is influence, derived from national, societal, and organizational strengths, rather than state-centric power—post-industrial, bottom-up, and values-based involving myriad nonstate and intrastate actors across an ambiguous spectrum (or cycle) of conflict and peace and associated complexities. In this new "ecosystem,"

Napoleon's observation that "in war, the moral is to the physical as three is to one" takes on an even more appropriate meaning.

Concentrated military, financial, and other forms of coercive power are the ultimate expression of a state-centric international order. But what now increasingly characterizes that order is the warp and woof of a struggle for sociopolitical and economic organization in the spaces beyond and between states, amplified and accelerated by the 24/7 media and social networks that make "the narrative" predominant. In the 21st century, coercive power is losing both its dominance and appropriateness. Hard power is more threats-based, resource-intensive, zero-sum, reactive, and short-term (i.e., tactical). It is, however, faster-acting, more controllable, and more measurable. Soft power, in turn, is more suitable to collaborative, human security settings. It is community-based, largely resident in civil society and the private sector, and is more adaptable, economical, renewable, engaging, synergistic, and durable (i.e., strategic). It is normally slower to take effect across a broad, unpredictable front, although social networking technologies as of late have had accelerating and amplifying effects.

This is not to say that hard power is obsolete—just no longer as overriding. In truth, this rebalancing is a return to a historical American grand strategic equilibrium predating the Cold War. Despite National Security Council (NSC)-68's emphasis on diplomacy's continued lead in American grand strategy and George F. Kennan's refrain to "first use moral authority," the "militarization" of applied American power in the latter half of the 20th century had soft power (in policies, programs, and budgets) functioning more as a "combat multiplier." In form as well as function, the face of

U.S. foreign policy has been a military one. In truth, what brought down the Berlin Wall was the tipping point of rising expectations of Eastern Europeans (not unlike the social unrest seen in many places today), while allied military power contained the Soviets. In other words, hard power was the holding—or containing—action, while soft power was the offensive dynamic. The North Atlantic Treaty Organization's (NATO) vast arsenals enabled what NSC-68 called the "corrosive power of freedom" to go to work on the self-contradictions of the Soviet state over time. Self-determination, an ideal first socialized on an international scale by President Woodrow Wilson in the wake of World War I, became a prime security mover. With the collapse of that order, the recontextualization and rebalancing that should have taken place as far back as 1989 is now more obvious a quarter-century later.

This epochal reality is truer for the United States than any other country, as the world's only global power for the last generation. But its national strategic style goes much further back in history. Since the Civil War, the United States has looked to win its wars, deter its adversaries, and assure its allies through overwhelming industrial and technological superiority predicated on an abundance of cheap resources, cheap labor, cheap energy, and cheap capital—it could afford a wasteful, surplus mentality. Since 1945, it had been the dominant power in the world—it could afford its own interpretation of "exceptionalism," while everyone else was internationalizing.

Of equal importance to the grand strategic imperative of environment constraints are resource restraints. For the first time in centuries, the United States is entering a newfound era of relative strategic scarcity. It can no longer take an abundance of resources for granted. The economic and financial basis of traditional state-centric power is diminishing through a globalization process that the United States itself has largely set in motion. Beyond reducing America's throw-weight in general, it is translating into an end of unilateral freedom of action. "Asymmetric" threats and the rise of regional powers have already been mitigating long-standing U.S. advantages, while global competitors can now better bankroll their own agendas. Perhaps most importantly, information and social networking technologies and low-cost socio-cultural enterprises now present inexpensive equalizers to older, more costly, and more centralized industrial-era forms of power. The moral, or psychological, is now plainly overtaking the physical.

In the 21st century, there is no dominant power as seen in the prior century. Although the United States will remain the premier world power for decades to come, its ability to wield especially more traditional forms of power will be much more constrained and restrained by factors less and less within its span of control. Indeed, the heyday of state-centric power *per se* in the new international arena is diminishing. Power is dissipating into more distributed forms. As the upheavals in the Middle East and North Africa are demonstrating, the dynamic is now more about the strength, influence, and reach of ideas, globally archetypical but community-based. More importantly, it is about how these ideas communicate and work in people's lives—in a word: innovation. In fact, the power of nation-states alone is becoming less relevant than the influence of people and organizations networked outside of and within governments. These are almost entirely civilian.

In the much more chaotic, unpredictable, and uncontrollable international order of the 21st century, the United States no longer dominates. It can still lead, albeit with a more strategic, rather than tactical, leadership style. You can use a more coercive and directive style when you dominate; but when you do not, you have to lead more persuasively—from behind as well as the front—as will be explained later.

Along with the changed context for national and international power is the changed nature of security. Security has become more than globalized; it has also become more humanized, civilianized, and democratized. Waves of popular unrest in response to everything from jobs, food prices, public pensions, poor educational and job opportunities, wealth disparities, and energy and the environment evince a groundswell of discontent with the inability of elites to deliver on socioeconomic fundamentals and essential public services. Security, prosperity, and social welfare are increasingly intertwined, making it everybody's business. In the American psyche, security was something someone else in a uniform did somewhere "over there." But in an intricate, hyper-connected global ecosystem where minor disturbances can have worldwide ripple effects in a matter of hours, this is all changing.

In Africa, for example, home to the bulk of security, development, and civil-military challenges for decades, "human security"—termed "civilian security" by the U.S. State Department in predictably exceptionalist fashion—and civil society problems such as poverty and food security, rule of law and justice, governance, economic development and job creation, and public health have long defined the security problem,[4] calling for approaches going well beyond "whole of government" to "whole of society."[5] Comprehensive and collaborative approaches to conflict prevention and post-conflict operations in multilateral, human security settings are everyday for civil society organizations working there and elsewhere. They stress the long-term, legitimacy, and relationship-building characteristics of development. In this more normative paradigm, development, appropriately done, is therefore not a component of security, it *is* security. This is vital to understanding the difference from security in the 21st century not as simply an expansion of the state-centric national security paradigm into social disciplines — which seems to be the current interpretation in the United States government. Rather, U.S. development policy is seen more as an instrument of foreign policy, serving national (security) interests and aimed at the proliferation of the American model of political order.

Given the growing limitations of hard power commensurate with the rise of soft power, increasing interconnectivity of global communities, the integration of security and development, and burgeoning resource restraints — all driving more comprehensive, collaborative, and coordinated approaches, the recontextualization, rebalancing, and proper alignment of the civil-military nexus remains at the locus of international intervention, whether for humanitarian, development, or reasons of state interest.

Yet, the instrumentalities featured in the American approach to the world — indeed, the entire foreign policy and national security apparatus of the United States — remain predicated on a 20th century paradigm for which "national security" concerns have trumped all other prerequisites. This national security paradigm, which has pervaded practically all aspects of applied U.S. foreign and national security policy, is itself predicated on an interpretation of the fundamental civil-military relationship in American society that was forged under the exigencies of the Cold War era and revitalized since 9/11. (The last major overhaul of the organization of U.S. national security was the National Security Act of 1947.) It should therefore be no wonder that most U.S. civil-military approaches to applied foreign and national security policy are correspondingly out of synch.

Beyond Eisenhower's prescient warning about the "military-industrial complex," Americans are now accustomed to a vast national security state that, with the war on terrorism, permeates life at home and not just in policies abroad:

> Since September 11, 2001, the U.S. government has created or reconfigured at least 263 organizations to tackle some aspect of the war on terror. Thirty-three new building complexes have been built for the intelligence bureaucracies alone, occupying 17 million square feet—the equivalent of 22 U.S. Capitols or three Pentagons. The largest bureaucracy after the Pentagon and the Department of Veterans Affairs is now the Department of Homeland Security, which has a workforce of 230,000 people. The rise of this national security state has entailed a vast expansion in the government's powers that now touch every aspect of American life, even when seemingly unrelated to terrorism. Some 30,000 people, for example, are now employed exclusively to listen in on phone conversations and other communications within the United States. In the past, the U.S. government has built up for wars, assumed emergency authority and sometimes abused that power, yet always demobilized after the war. But this is, of course, a war without end.[6]

The biggest reason for this has been in how U.S. grand strategy since World War II has been threat-based, fear-driven, and enemy-centric, embedded in American culture:

> Since the end of the Cold War, America has been on a relentless search for enemies. I don't mean a search in the sense of ferreting them out and defeating them. I mean that America seems to have a visceral need for them. Many in the United States have a rampant, untreated case of enemy dependency. Politicians love enemies because bashing them helps stir up public sentiment and distract attention from problems at home. The defense industry loves enemies because enemies help them make money. Pundits and their publications love enemies because enemies sell papers and lead eyeballs to cable-news food fights.[7]

THE FAULT LIES NOT IN OUR STARS . . .

Most scholars and commentators on the subject of the civil-military relationship in the United States turn first to Samuel Huntington's seminal work, *The Soldier and the State*, to begin discussion. It is more fitting, however, to go back nearly two more centuries to the Constitution of the United States, whose division of powers and authority, along with its system of checks and balances, "has succeeded not only in defending the nation against all enemies foreign and domestic, but in upholding the liberty it was meant to preserve."[8] The American way of the civil-military relationship is thus fundamental not only to the profession of arms; rather, it is fundamental to American civil society:

> Civil-military relations in a democracy are a special application of representative democracy with the unique concern that designated political agents control designated military agents. Acceptance of civilian supremacy and control by an obedient military has been the core

202

principle of the American tradition of civil-military relations. U.S. military officers take an oath to uphold the democratic institutions that form the very fabric of the American way of life. Their client is American [civil] society, which has entrusted the officer corps with the mission of preserving the nation's values and national purpose. Ultimately, every act of the American military professional is connected to these realities [that] he or she is in service to the citizens of a democratic state who bestow their trust and treasure with the primary expectation that their state and its democratic nature will be preserved.[9]

This was, by and large, the civil-military consensus in the United States until after World War II. Until then, the typical pattern was to maintain a small, professional force, which could be augmented in the event of national emergency through the militia (today's Reserves), thus placating the general distrust of the military among the American public (reflected, arguably, in the Second Amendment). In the wake of World War II—for the first time in U.S. history—a large, standing (and eventually professional) peacetime military force has persisted. Huntington's book appeared in 1957, the same year as Sputnik, when, also for the first time in its history, the United States was faced with the clear and present danger of nuclear Armageddon.

Given this historic departure and the existential exigencies of the Cold War, Huntington's interpretation of the civil-military relationship is understandable. Paradoxically, Huntington concluded that to preserve democracy, society should grant the military substantial autonomy in managing international violence, in exchange for submission to civilian direction. For his theories, critics excoriated Huntington as overly militant, students staged protests during lectures, and Harvard fired him.[10] Huntington's model, which suspended the traditional consensus and balance of the American civil-military relationship, made more sense under the conditions of the Cold War and the international order it maintained. Once those conditions changed and that order began to break down, however, first with the fall of the Berlin Wall and then resuming with the difficulties of applied American power in the post-9/11 years (as explained above), the inherent flaws of Huntington's model became increasingly obvious: "the most significant shortcoming of Huntington's construct was its failure to recognize that a separation between political and military affairs is not possible—particularly at the highest levels of policymaking."[11] In other words:

> Huntington's claim that an autonomous military profession should . . . develop its expertise free from outside involvement is also problematic. For one thing, it underestimates the impact of service culture and service parochialism. Left to their own devices, the services may focus on the capabilities they would like to have rather than the capabilities the country needs. Even beyond this concern, an emphasis on autonomy heightens the risk of creating a military unable to meet the requirements set out in the U.S. military's own doctrine, which talks of the need to integrate all instruments of national power (diplomatic, informational, military and economic) to further U.S. national interests. . . . Effective partnerships in war are likely to require collaborative education, training, planning and capabilities. . . . This applies to foreign partners — military and civilian — as well as American. . . . This logic led Huntington to the extraordinary argument in his concluding chapter that the solution was for American society to become less liberal and more like the military in its culture and values. This proposed solution is extraordinary because it is a clear reversal of ends–means logic: instead of the military serving to protect Ameri-

can values, American society should change its values to serve the interest of military effectiveness. Only the existence of an existential threat would seem to justify such a proposition.[12]

This idea of the military as social role model is not as arcane as one might think. President Barack Obama expressed similar ideas in his 2012 State of the Union address. After beginning his speech by lauding the achievements of the U.S. Armed Forces, he said:

> At a time when too many of our institutions have let us down, they exceed all expectations. They're not consumed with personal ambition. They don't obsess over their differences. They focus on the mission at hand. They work together. Imagine what we could accomplish if we followed their example.[13]

With the popularity of the military in American society at an all-time high and that of politicians at an all-time low, the civil-military societal imbalance that began with World War II is now over 70 years old:

> The veneration and outright hero-worship, now at a crescendo, is an unhealthy distortion of our time-honored yet taken-for-granted civil-military relationship, for a number of reasons . . . over time, it has also lent to a psychology of greater readiness to call upon the military in the pursuit of our national interests abroad, or to perform tasks, such as humanitarian or disaster relief or nation-building—contributing to the 'militarization' of our foreign policy and the 'securitization' of foreign assistance. We have even seen a greater presence of the National Guard in our relief responses at home, despite the intent of the *Posse Comitatus* Act of 1878. Another is the perpetuation of a military industrial complex that is now a detriment to our prosperity and which we can less afford.[14]

This decoupling and distortion of the traditional American democratic civil-military relationship is not only manifest in the horizontal dysfunctions of inter-agency and civil-military coordination, it has also contributed to a vertical imbalance with an overemphasis on operations and tactics, leading to what strategist Colin S. Gray has called "a persistent strategy deficit" in the United States, pointing out that:

> If you do not really function strategically, it does not much matter how competent you are at regular, or ir-regular, warfare—you are not going to collect the po-litical rewards that American blood and money have paid for.[15]

Interestingly, Gray points out that the "awesome" tactical power and performance of the U.S. military, in contrast to its strategic retardation, is similar to that seen by Germany during World War II—of course, a nightmarish case of civil-military "co-ordination" (Gleichschaltung)[16] that proved catastrophic. James R. Locher III, principal architect of the Goldwater-Nichols Act of 1986 and President of the now-defunct Project on National Security Reform, further notes that, in addition to having no grand strategy since the Cold War, the United States has had no national security strategy, either:

> Yes, we have had a document that we call the 'National Security Strategy.' But it is a collection of goals and objectives without any actual plans for achieving them. The 2010 *National Security Strategy* is more of the same. It is a strategic-communications document—not a strategy. It was even written by the Strategic Communications Directorate of the National Security Staff, not the Strategy Directorate.[17]

The vertical disparity between policy and operations is thus very real, underscoring the connection between the global and the local, between the strategic and the tactical:

> As military organizations expand their work into civil governance areas, it is not only the distinction between soldiers and civilians that blurs. It is also the social coding that military and nonmilitary agents use to describe the military organization and its particular ethos and rationality. As a result, it become unclear what kind of organization the military is and what it could and should be used for. It becomes difficult to communicate in an exact manner about military affairs.[18]

THINKING GLOBALLY: UNDERSTANDING THE CIVIL-MILITARY NEXUS AS FUNDAMENTALLY STRATEGIC

In truth, the alignment of civil and military inflections of power and influence has always been the central challenge to anyone and everyone involved in trying to prevent, mitigate, or manage conflict and enforce, keep, or build peace. Given the grand strategic imperatives of the 21st century, however, this locus has only grown in significance. Context being what it is, if there is to be a paradigm shift in civil-military approaches — viewed from both sides — more in line with the emerging *Zeitgeist*, then two fundamental realities must be appreciated. First, civil-military coordination (cooperation and operations) is inherently thinking globally (or strategically). Second, to be both effective and credible, civil-military coordination must be an application of the democratic civil-military relationship that is morally consistent and symmetric — as above, so below.

With respect to the first insight, when looking from the more global, human security vantage point of the 21st century, a more comprehensive and collaborative understanding of civil-military engagement becomes possible. As such, context takes precedence over content, partnership more than predominance, strategy more than operations and tactics, and human more than organizational enterprises. In the information age, legitimacy and credibility—expressed through and conveyed in "the narrative"—preponderates.

This is no doubt especially true in the culturally charged Muslim world, where the United States, having broken the eggs of autocracy in Iraq, can perhaps help Arab civil society make the omelet of self-governance, albeit in a more indirect and limited way. Ironically, a good example of the moral over the physical is how the United States is currently paying for its less than credible image on the Arab Street earned over the years, especially in its inability to be an agent of change in Egypt. In this sense, therefore, the most important lesson of the war in Iraq is not that better planning, operational approaches, and tactics may have changed its outcome. "Instead, the real solution is re-thinking American grand strategy."[19] This insight may be leading the Obama administration, for example, to shift delivery of aid and technical assistance through international civil society organizations, the UN, and other partners rather than directly from U.S. Government run programs—in a sense, "leading from behind" in fostering peace as it did in supporting the war in Libya. The Middle East and North Africa Incentive Fund proposed for Fiscal Year 2013 will also work much this way.

It is also true, as the United States shifts its global geopolitical priorities away from its near-obsession with the Middle East and Central Asia to East Asia and the Pacific: "When the only global power becomes obsessed with a single region, the entire world is unbalanced. Imbalance remains the defining characteristic of the global system today."[20] The growing competition between American and Chinese models in Asia-Pacific societies and bodies politic will define the real, ongoing challenge there, as opposed to the latent contingency of some kind of great showdown between U.S. and Chinese forces. In fact, civil-military coordination as a "strategic enabler" for the U.S. Pacific Command took place more than a half-dozen years before the Obama administration. Within the context of its theater engagement strategy, the Pacific Command has long been conducting "civil affairs projects" to help secure basing rights and, conversely, deny them to potential adversaries such as China.[21]

The relevance of human security is most apparent in the weak and fragile states of Africa — more important than a lower-level U.S.-Chinese competition than in the Asia-Pacific region. Africa, where the nation-state is hardly the established operating organizing principle of governance (and in some places may never be), is where the majority of conflicts, fragile and failing states are concentrated globally.[22] Particularly in Africa, security is as much a socio-psychological issue as it is a power political issue:

> Most of today's African fighters are not rebels with a cause; they're predators. That's why we see stunning atrocities like eastern Congo's rape epidemic, where armed groups in recent years have sexually assaulted hundreds of thousands of women, often so sadistically that the victims are left incontinent for life. . . . Child soldiers are an inextricable part of these movements. The LRA, for example, never seized territory; it seized

children. Its ranks are filled with brainwashed boys and girls who ransack villages and pound newborn babies to death in wooden mortars. In Congo, as many as one-third of all combatants are under 18. Since the new predatory style of African warfare is motivated and financed by crime, popular support is irrelevant to these rebels. The downside to not caring about winning hearts and minds, though, is that you don't win many recruits. So abducting and manipulating children becomes the only way to sustain the organized banditry. And children have turned out to be ideal weapons: easily brainwashed, intensely loyal, fearless, and, most importantly, in endless supply.[23]

While the kind of human security challenges such as youth and gender-based violence in Africa may characterize the greatest threats to international security, they simultaneously present the greatest opportunities for influence and partnering on many levels and in many ways. The development community's greater attention to and collaboration on these two issues is one evidence of this.

Despite numerous advances in policy and doctrine, the "paradigm shift" in U.S. international security approaches has yet to occur. Not until changes in policy and doctrine are reflected in programs and budgets: Dollars continue to flow overwhelmingly to defense over diplomacy and development — throughout American involvement in Afghanistan, "the vast majority of aid went to the Afghan security forces and not development."[24] The military, for quite understandable reasons, has espoused many tasks civilian agencies have been either slow or incapable of taking up. The truth of the matter is that, while commentators argue that a deeper merging of civil and military objectives and capabilities has taken place, evidence from the ground informs us that the sophisticated wording of academics and policymakers (such as concerted action, integrated approach, '3D', holistic approach, security-development nexus) seldom find their way into the concrete conduct of applied civil-military relations — or civil-military coordination.[25]

The problem with the "militarization of foreign policy" and the "securitization of aid," of course, is that the U.S. military's chief focus is security, so its relief and development activities emphasize winning the 'hearts and minds' of a population, not the human-itarian imperative of saving lives, doing no harm, and ensuring local ownership of reconstruction efforts.[26]

This largely explains the rub with humanitarian organizations. Yet, size or assignment should not mat-ter — with the possible exception of major combat op-erations, the Department of Defense (DoD) is not (nor should ever be) the lead agency. Even then, beyond Carl von Clausewitz's famous dictum that "war is merely an extension of policy by other means," strate-gist B. H. Liddell Hart reminds us that "the aim in war is to achieve a better peace."

Yet, "bad-guy baiting" has long been the way for congressional appropriation of national security driven security assistance or foreign aid funding. U.S. operations abroad thus remain threats-based and command-and-control managed. They are primarily operational and tactical in their focus, and rarely rep-resentative of regional let alone grand strategy. It is not only that such "legacy" approaches to security and civil-military coordination are less and less effective — witness the growing realization of the inefficacy and ephemeral effects of "winning hearts and minds" — they are no longer affordable.[27] Civil-military coordi-nation and other engines of 21st century collaboration must be more strategic from the outset. In fact, Sol-diers themselves must become "post-modern."[28]

The potentialities and economies of effort, cost, and risk at all levels of the central civil-military nexus of international engagements cannot, therefore, reach fulfillment unless this nexus is understood from a fundamentally strategic perspective:

- Civil-military coordination is inherently comprehensive and collaborative. Like strategy itself, it is holistic, cumulative, and convergent in ends, ways, and means. It is best suited to manage the seams of power and the gaps between organizations and processes.

- Civil-military coordination inherently bridges (state centric) whole of government with the whole-of-society/community. It leverages all forms of power and inflections of influence at all levels in order to create conditions for a transition to greater civilian lead and control and promote self-sustained civil society. In doing so, it keeps hard power more implied than applied at best; or at worst, minimizes or mitigates its costs and risks when it must be applied.

- Civil-military coordination is inherently informational—a human search engine that evaluates and offers a coping mechanism for uncertainty and complexity. As such, it helps minimize fog and frictions existing in seams, gaps, and transitions, as well as facilitates collaborative decision cycles—a key strategic and operational advantage over competing entities.

- It is synergistic, innovative, and persuasive— enabling, moderating, and balancing. It promotes unity of purpose and economy of effort while managing change, risk, and expectations. Like "Generation Flux," it draws together disparate players across "stovepipes" toward a medium of cooperation and crowd wisdom largely through brainstorming and co-creation—but for which information transparency and sharing is absolutely vital.

- Civil-military coordination is inherently sociocultural. Because it is a human enterprise, it is in essence about relationship-building, which is how things get done in human security environments. Because it involves engagement of the local populace, it demands cultural awareness, helping the credibility and legitimacy of the whole effort.
- By enabling a more proactive use of civilian and soft power, it elicits the military principle of offense. By enabling more effective leveraging of less costly and more sustainable civilian power over more costly and risk-laden hard power, it evokes the military principle of economy-of-force (or economy of effort, cost, and risk).
- Civil-military coordination is inherently anticipatory (and less reactive) due to the need to collaborate in advance in order to reach desired common objectives or manage disparate interests. It calls for an approach more like Hall of Famer Wayne Gretzky, who observed: "A good hockey player plays where the puck is. A great hockey player plays where the puck is going to be." In other words, it induces its practitioners to think and act with greater foresight.
- Applied civil-military coordination involves a strategic, enabling style of leadership, invoking persuasion, political bargaining, collaboration, consensus and relationship-building. Another way to describe the strategic leadership style

is "leading from behind" — creating conditions for the success of others so the full menu of options may be brought to bear (and blood and money spared). Moreover, it should emphasize managing expectations all-around.

- Finally, it is adaptive and co-creative, more characteristic of learning organizations,[29] as it is inherently a learning activity, constantly conscious of situation and environment.

In essence, civil-military coordination at its best is a form of applied grand strategy. In other words, it is thinking globally and acting locally — or, in military terms, thinking strategically at the operational and tactical levels. It is a compass, not a cookbook; a mindset, rather than a skill set.[30]

The paradox of strategically applied civil-military coordination is that, while it can generate transformative outcomes, the operational purpose of civil-military coordination is not to transform the host country — only the host country can do that, with the assistance of external actors, among them a foreign military. The purpose of civil-military coordination is more pragmatic — to channel the military's engagement efforts in such a way as to maximize their impacts while minimizing the commitment of military resources, preserving them for core security tasks.

ACTING LOCALLY: THE APPLIED CIVIL-MILITARY RELATIONSHIP AND DEMOCRATIC VALUES

In order to realize the above potentialities of civil-military coordination, policymakers and practitioners need to do more than think globally (or strategically).

Civil-military coordination in local action must, in turn, be reflective of and conducive to this strategic conscientiousness. The focus here is thus on the nature of the relationship between civil and military elements and players.

This is where one aspect of Huntington's analysis of the civil-military relationship is constructive:

> The military institutions of any society are shaped by two forces: a functional imperative stemming from the threats to society's security and a societal imperative rising from the social forces, ideologies, and institutions dominant within the society. Military institutions which reflect only social values may be incapable of performing effectively their military functions. On the other hand, it may be impossible to contain within the society military institutions shaped purely by functional imperatives. The interaction of these two forces is the nub of the problem of civil-military relations.[31]

What we could say about the current imbalance in terms of civil-military coordination is that there has been too much emphasis on the functional imperative in an era when the societal imperative is more appropriate. What we could also say is that, as in civil-military relations, strategically driven civil-military coordination is managing the tensions between those two imperatives. Thus, civil-military coordination in practice (in whatever form or institutional point of reference) is mainly about two things:

- First, managing the relationship and interaction between civilian and military actors that maximizes the comparative advantages of these actors as they apply to the situation; and,
- Second, enabling, shaping, and supporting the process of transition to peace, stability, and

self-sustained development along civil-military lines, with the aims of "civilianizing" external assistance and "localizing" essential internal public services and governance functions.

Civil-military coordination is thus first and foremost a management function — specifically, the risk-reward structure. As the private sector is teaching us:

> What accounted for fundamental shifts in longer term advantage was not operational-level innovation. It wasn't technology or product innovation, or new business models, or a new way of thinking about the whole industry. Again and again, it was management innovation — breakthroughs in how to organize and mobilize human capabilities.[32]

Given an understanding of the "nub" of civil-military relations, the basic management functions of civil-military coordination, and a more global and strategic understanding of civil-military coordination in an environment mostly in human security terms, it becomes clear that civil-military coordination is not just a matter of linking strategy and tactics, security with development, and hard and soft power. It is a matter of "how to organize and mobilize human capabilities."

Thus, the replication of the civil-military relationship in democratic societies in operational approaches in human security settings becomes all-important. It demands unprecedented moral and ethical commitments, in which the military is subservient to and supportive of "civilian power" (to use the term in the *Quadrennial Diplomacy and Development Review*) and that the military's role — as the major (but not leading) civil-military actor — is that of an enabler, especially with respect to the security sector. More appropriate civil-military approaches are thus an application of Liddell Hart's strategy of the indirect approach, demonstrably placing the military in a supporting and not supported role. They are less concerned with "winning hearts and minds," which is a tactic and not a strategy:

> The goal is not simply to be liked. *It is to be more influential and therefore more effective at lower cost.* In a world where foreign public opinion has ever greater impact on the success or failure of vital American national interests, it should be weighed in making policy decisions and should shape *how* the United States pursues its policies and how U.S. leaders talk about American policies. Listening, understanding and engaging makes for better policy, helps to avoid unnecessary conflicts, and should ideally allow policymakers to foresee and pre-empt objections to policies that sound worse in the field than they do in Washington.[33]

More democratic civil-military approaches have currency and effect on the narrative not because of their direct appeal to democracy *per se*, but because they resonate with more universal values, such as those encoded in the 1948 Universal Declaration of Human Rights, that lead to democracy. Even in hard power terms, it appears to be no coincidence that democracies are unusually successful in war. The reasons for this seem to be superior human capital, more harmonious civil-military relations, and Western cultural values and norms — once again, invoking Napoleon's dictum.[34]

Civilian control of the military is inclusive within and not exclusive from civil society — something very much taken for granted in the United States but yet far from a given in most developing countries. Yet, "civilian control means more than the absence of a military coup. As long as the military possesses autonomous decisionmaking power, the democratically elected authorities' power to govern and the quality of democracy remain limited."[35] Harmonized with the democratic civil-military relationship, civil-military coordination as explained in this chapter is an application of democratic values, a way to an end and not an end in itself. More importantly, it helps to close the "say-do" gap that has bedeviled especially American applied foreign and national security policy for decades. It also reduces the image of U.S. domination and strong-arming and facilitates internationalizing the overall effort, thus giving it greater cumulative power, persuasiveness, and influence and making it much more difficult to counter. Moreover, it helps promote a democratic culture in general in which the military itself becomes a civil society organization:

> Democratic military professionals do not pursue their responsibilities to the state in isolation. They are part of a broader national security community comprised of national security professionals from both the civilian and military spheres, other actors such as journalists and academics who contribute intellectual capital and foster debate, legislative bodies with constitutional responsibilities to oversee and provide resources for national security policy, and, finally, the public at large to whom all of the above are ultimately responsible.[36]

Whether for us or them, the full integration of the military in civil society, and reflexively its integration into the engagement of that society, including its government institutions and the private sector — with the all-important caveat of the primacy of civilian authority—will ensure that the civilianization of security occurs more than the militarization of aid and development. The idea of "third-generation" civil-military coordination is intriguing, and deserves further examination. The Focused District Development (FDD) program in Afghanistan, as an example of this approach, is certainly more collaborative, partnering, and "broadens the civil-military relationship contact face to local governance and political authorities." However, "the FDD is a military-driven police mentoring program."[37] Thus, precisely because the distinction between military and civilian work practically vanishes under this concept, the supreme qualifier of civil authority becomes even more vital:

> If militaries are to be mobilized to assist in addressing the challenges facing much of Africa, the clear expectations need to be established and safeguards need to be put in place. . . . Trust can only be built if the military communicates effectively and regularly with the population. . . . In pursuing this mobilization goal, the essential element that helps ensure success is maintaining civilian oversight of the military and its projects. Doing so begins with clearly defining the military's new role as temporary and supplemental to the public and private sectors. Projects should be designed in such a way that it is always clear that the military is not taking over or dominating but rather is assisting the other sectors and alleviating the pressure being placed upon them. . . . The circumstances in which the military can be mobilized to deal with nontraditional security concerns need to be clearly outlined in the state's national security policies and in law.[38]

Although a more democratic approach to civil-military coordination has yet to be socialized across the board, there are numerous examples of exceptional best practices, including the author's own experience as Chief of Civil-Military Coordination for the UN Mission in Liberia:

> ... the CIMIC [civil-military coordination] intent in Liberia has been to use the capabilities of the Force to '. . . enable and multiply civilian initiatives, and conducted in coordination with the UNMIL [United Nations Mission in Liberia] civil component (jointly) and UN agencies as well as NGOs and the GoL (collaboratively).' This entails a more indirect role for military assets — more clearly in support of civilian agencies and leading less from the front and more from behind the UNMIL civil component, UN agencies, and the GoL, aligned with them and their frameworks and benchmarks, in order to promote local ownership of civil administration and essential public services responsibilities, and to help build civil authority and public confidence. To de-emphasize 'winning hearts and minds,' the moniker for UNMIL CIMIC became: 'it's not about us; it's about them.'[39]

Like good aid workers, good practitioners of civil-military coordination engage in an enabling process of helping their civilian partners build local capacity as well as confidence — teaching locals how to fish rather than simply giving them a fish. As a former Commander of the NATO International Security Assistance Force in Afghanistan stated: "At the end of the day, it's not about their embrace of us, it's not about us winning hearts and minds; it's about the Afghan government winning hearts and minds."[40] Put another way:

> Military involvement in aid is driven in part by the 'winning hearts and minds' (WHAM) theory. This operates on the basis of a charity paradigm, which sees beneficiaries as the deserving poor, and provides

handouts and services while ignoring the complexity of the local context, and the unintended consequences of injecting resources into conflict-affected communities. NGOs have been working for many years to erase the handout mentality, emphasizing the importance of 'ownership,' involvement and empowerment of beneficiaries.[41]

The visualization of this more strategic, indirect, and democratic approach to civil-military coordination, as applied in Liberia, is depicted in Figure 8-1. The idea is to work the military out of a job by providing its stabilization efforts increasingly through civilian and local entities in an enabling process.

Figure 8-1. Civil-Military Echelons of Assistance.

Another important aspect of this approach is that, in order to facilitate the end state depicted in Figure 8-1, the military must adopt the rule sets, ways, measures, and means of the civilians it is supporting. Another CIMIC aphorism used at UNMIL: "Their game plan is our game plan."

While this model was designed originally with transitional civil-military coordination (the second major management function of civil-military coordination) in mind, the principles of "civilianizing" external assistance and "localizing" essential internal public services and governance functions by gradually placing the military to the rear of the assistance chain (behind civil society organizations and local government structures) and taking on an increasingly indirect and enabling role do not apply just to post-conflict transition management. Indeed, it could apply to conflict prevention and "building partner capacity" efforts such as in the Horn of Africa and the Trans-Sahel. U.S. involvement, for example, in low-level counterinsurgency operations in the Philippines after 9/11 eventually took the approach of following local lead in civil action programs. "Filipino doctors, dentists and veterinarians come in to provide free care. Of utmost importance . . . is putting a Filipino face on all these operations."[42]

Perhaps even more illustrative of the shifting paradigm is the U.S. civil-military response to the earthquake in Haiti, where the military clearly played a supporting role, and the U.S. Government sought to work within multilateral frameworks rather than expend the resources to create a parallel structure, exemplifying a prepositional term that has gained currency among U.S. civil affairs and other special operations personnel — "by, with, and through":

> Early on, the United States decided not to create a combined Joint task force. With the UN already on the ground, a robust multinational force was in place. In addition, MINUSTAH countries contributing additional resources and personnel already had links to their local UN representatives. Creating a *combined* Joint task force would have conflicted with those efforts. Instead, Joint Task Force-Haiti deployed to conduct humanitarian assistance and disaster response operations. The purpose of Joint Task Force-Haiti was

to support U.S. efforts in Haiti to mitigate near-term human suffering and accelerate relief efforts to facilitate transition to the Government of Haiti, the UN, and USAID. The military possesses significant capabilities that are useful in emergencies, but long-term plans for relief and reconstruction are best left to nonmilitary government agencies.[43]

As mentioned earlier, however, the paradigm has not yet shifted for everyone. From its inception, AFRICOM has been beset with problems of credibility on the continent, due largely to the "say-do gap" of an essentially military organization—a regional combatant command—that originally tried to look and act like a whole-of-government organization.

> The new U.S Africa Command was created with the intention of a more deliberate (rather than *ad hoc*) civil-military and interagency teaming approach—from the top down, and with a much heavier civilian content and lead, and thus with more soft than hard power at play, than in other combatant commands. . . . The real problem, however, at AFRICOM is that, despite its large civilian component, it still largely serves military missions (in particular, counterterrorism) rather than vice-versa—at least on the ground. This conflicts with AFRICOM's central message. By and large, the military staff there defines security requirements. This is one of the reasons why AFRICOM has had such great difficulty in gaining credibility and acceptance in Africa—the greatest evidence for which is that it is still headquartered in Stuttgart, Germany. This is a strategic and not an operational issue.[44]

Indeed, focusing more on the democratic civil-military relationship as an operational application, not only in terms of security and defense sector reform and partnership capacity development but also under the rubric of the country team, can only improve the strategic effectiveness of "comprehensive engagement" as defined in the 2010 *National Security Strategy*. This is because by walking the talk, closing the say-do gap, and leading through civilian power, U.S. civil-military practitioners would then be doing abroad what they do at home, clearly connecting strategy with operations and the whole-of-society with the whole of government.

It does more than this. With respect to building partnership capacity, demonstrating the democratic civil-military relationship helps address the concern expressed by former Secretary of Defense Robert Gate's admonition that, beyond the traditional national security centric tendency to focus almost exclusively on operational development of the armed forces:

> . . . there has not been enough attention paid to building the institutional capacity (such as defense ministries) or the human capital (including leadership skills and attitudes) needed to sustain security over the long term.[45]

In Liberia, for example, the Office of Security Cooperation is synchronizing AFRICOM's Operation ONWARD LIBERTY program designed to enhance military institutional leadership and DoD's Defense Institution Reform Initiative (DIRI, similar to the Ministry of Defense Advisory program in Afghanistan) to build capacity among the Ministry of Defense staff providing civilian oversight. This kind of applied foresight and synchronization of stovepipes, however, was more the result of personalities than policies or programs.

Systemically, U.S security assistance efforts in places like the Horn of Africa and particularly the

Trans-Sahel, are based on a counterterrorism model—the coup in Mali being only the latest example of a problematic approach to U.S. security sector reform focused almost entirely on operational rather than institutional capacity building and with almost total disregard of the civil-military relationship:

> ... something is very wrong about the U.S. approach to counterterrorism cooperation in the Sahel. . . . Indeed. The two-pronged military-civilian strategy has been to (a) build security capacity of the Malian and other regional militaries to control territory and fight terrorists and (b) take steps to prevent the spread of violent extremism. . . . Unfortunately, the early signs aren't good that the USG really recognizes the scale of the problem. . . . If we really believe that fighting terrorism in Africa is in our national interest, then the disaster still unfolding in Mali begs for an honest and aggressive rethinking of both the what and the how.[46]

Another outcome of a more democratic approach to civil-military coordination is that it tends to go far to mitigate the nettlesome strains from military force employment of humanitarian methods to "win hearts and minds" in the face of the NGO claim of exclusivity in humanitarianism. Such a civil-military approach is inherently more supportive of the efforts of these organizations, which are more appropriate for humanitarian and nation-building tasks formerly performed by military organizations, at least in U.S. experience.

On the other hand, civil society organizations must, in turn, recognize that military organizations, for better or worse, are themselves extensions of civil society and thus have a role in making peace, albeit more indirect than direct. More pragmatically, it facilitates an eventual relationship with indigenous military, paramilitary, and police forces and encourages them to maintain an appropriate balance between Huntington's imperatives in their own security sector, having seen that example in foreign forces. Beyond helping external militaries work their jobs, it helps achieve a more sustainable security sector reform process and a more secure and stable environment for both the civil society organizations and the emerging government institutions long after those forces leave.

Thus, both kinds of entities need to employ a qualitative blend of realism and idealism, respecting and accommodating, as best as possible, particular principles and equities. This can only come through establishing relationships, dialogue, and even rule-sets for operational civil-military interaction in order to learn about comparative advantages as well as limitations:

> CSOs generally take a long-term, relationship-based approach to development. Because of security, political and economic pressures, U.S. government and military officials often attempt shorter-term, quick-impact development. The challenge is to design short-term programming that contributes toward long-term goals and to design long-term programming that supports short-term objectives. Addressing the contradictions in timeframes requires more extensive discussion between CSOs and ISAF policymakers.[47]

Another insight thus comes into play—what you do in the steady state (strategically) cultivates the capital you draw upon for crisis response or in the field in general (operationally). It is mainly because, in the 21st century security and development engagement environment, relationships, and influence matter more than throwing weight. This critical strategic and operational capital—beneficial to both sides—is, at best, difficult to obtain once the operation begins. This is a common, yet still underappreciated, lesson.

AMERICAN LEADERSHIP

All of this is actually good news for the United States. Despite the incongruities of its overwhelming national security, hard-power psychology, the United States, whose foundation of strength in its national ethos of *e pluribus unum* has been always morally based, is still the most ideally suited lead nation. Its dynamic, multicultural civil society and its democratic national values represent tremendous social capital. The democratic civil-military ethos of the United States is most clearly depicted in a symbol more than 2 centuries old — namely, the obverse of the Great Seal of the United States. The state, symbolized by the eagle, aspires for peace and civil society, looking in the direction of the olive branches in one talon while holding the arrows of war in reserve (or support) in the other. The Great Seal elegantly illustrates the alignment and application of these civil-military priorities. (See Figure 2.)

More concretely, for example, the United States possesses a unique comparative advantage, as it is already demonstrating in isolated cases, in assisting foreign governments and militaries in improving civil-military linkages and mechanisms, at all levels, due to its own program equities in areas like civil affairs. The problem is that these equities are not consistently arrayed in a comprehensive and coordinated way, in accordance with the realities of the 21st century and the need to find more democratic balance in Huntington's imperatives as applied overseas.

Figure 8-2. Great Seal of the United States.

Besides addressing the sheer imbalances in budgets and authorities, "civilianizing" security, "demilitarizing" foreign policy and "developmentalizing" foreign aid, there are other areas to address. There are no civilian counterparts, for example, to the geographic combatant commander at the Department of State or the U.S. Agency for International Development, let alone a counterpart regional coordination entity, that would go far to facilitating a more comprehensive, civilian-led U.S. strategy in the geographic regions of the world.[48]

Civil affairs—the only true civil-military coordination entity in the U.S. Government, going back over a century, has evolved from military government, which is a suspension—not an extension—of democracy. Civil affairs must also transform from recent "bad guy" centric counterinsurgency and counterterrorism and become more strategic than tactical, with greater steady state linkages to and operational partnering with, for example, the State Department's Bureau of Conflict and Stabilization Operations, from which civil affairs should take greater strategic direction. In yet another example, there should be a more strategically-driven synchronization of programs such as DoD's DIRI program and the State Department's Global Peace Operations Initiative and Africa Contingency Operations Training & Assistance program in order to build partnership civil-military teaming capacity and confidence in the civil-military relationship in democratic societies.

There are many more changes to mention. Moreover, their scope and extensiveness spell implications for U.S. foreign policy and national security are profound and far-reaching. This runs not just from Washington to the field, but from the field to Washington. Locher remarks that:

> We have always been able to win ugly by throwing money at a problem, but that is no longer the case. We have lost our margin for error and we are headed for a decade of austerity, when even great programs are being killed. The times call for a national security system that is effective, efficient, participatory and agile. Unfortunately, we don't have it—we have the opposite of that, a system that is archaic, designed 63 years ago, that still clings to Cold War concepts. At PNSR, we have a saying, 'How can we secure our children's future with our grandparents' government?' We are not going to win the future with that government.[49]

There is greater impetus for this kind of transformation not only from the strategic imperatives observed abroad, but from the American people themselves. In a remarkable study conducted by the Fund for Peace, involving scores of town hall type meetings around the United States held over a 2-year period, a major conclusion was that, while Americans still expected the United States to maintain its global leadership role, "It leads best when it's true to its values and when it works with others." Additionally:

> . . . there was remarkable consistency that America must lead in the world—but it leads most effectively when it 'walks the talk,' i.e., adheres to its own stated principles. . . . America's ideals impel it to lead in the world, and the world looks to America to play that role. But how America leads is as important as whether it leads. . . . Reorienting American policy priorities not only would enhance U.S. global leadership, but was seen as yielding lasting influence. . . . America was a stronger nation when it listened to people, and indeed, could learn from different countries, cultures, and experiences. . . . Finally, there was significant discussion in most forums about the differences between 'American power' and 'national strengths.' Many participants associated the former with an emphasis on coercive behavior in the world, while they viewed the latter as concerning principles and values, such as democracy, liberty, and tolerance. While coercive means might be necessary in some cases, an over-reliance on them was seen as counterproductive and even disastrous; whereas pursuing policies on the basis of the nation's strengths was seen as the most effective way to produce lasting influence in the world. In addition, people viewed a predominantly coercive approach as out of touch with new global realities.[50]

While the perils of the 21st century are coming more or less on their own, the promises emerging from the same paradigm are not as such. This calls for greater, not less, American international leadership, for no other nation is better suited to exploit and lead this transformation.

> There was nothing inevitable about the world that was created after World War II. No divine providence or unfolding Hegelian dialectic required the triumph of

democracy and capitalism, and there is no guarantee that their success will outlast the powerful nations that have fought for them. Democratic progress and liberal economics have been and can be reversed and undone. The ancient democracies of Greece and the republics of Rome and Venice all fell to more powerful forces or through their own failings. The evolving liberal economic order of Europe collapsed in the 1920s and 1930s. The better idea doesn't have to win just because it is a better idea. It requires great powers to champion it.[51]

The qualitative difference between then and now, however, is that "real leadership is not dominance."[52] Every military officer learns that the most effective, persuasive, and durable form of leadership is by example—whether from the front or behind. This is as true for nations as it is for individuals. Practicing at home what you preach abroad is a demonstration that what matters over there also matters over here, as Harry S. Truman observed in his message to Congress that launched the civil rights movement, in which he concluded:

> If we wish to inspire the peoples of the world whose freedom is in jeopardy, if we wish to restore hope to those who have already lost their civil liberties, if we wish to fulfill the promise that is ours, we must correct the remaining imperfections in our practice of democracy. We know the way. We need only the will.[53]

When Americans think globally and act locally, making their actions consonant with their core values and embracing a new ethos of collaborative engagement, in view of adversaries and partners alike, they transform both their environment and themselves. A more enlightened approach to civil-military coordination is not a tradeoff between idealism and realism, it is a fusion of both. It is a fusion of art and science that combines practical critical thinking with an imaginative synthesis of the most appropriate methods. It is at the heart of American grand strategy for the 21st century. Failure to recognize this risks further deterioration of American global leadership and the security and prosperity that comes with it.

ENDNOTES - CHAPTER 8

1. For a more detailed discussion, see Christopher Holshek, "Lessons of Iraq and Afghanistan—Looking from Outside the Box," Volker C. Franke and Robert H. "Robin" Dorff. eds., *Conflict Management and "Whole of Government": Useful Tools for U.S. National Security Strategy?* Carlisle, PA: Strategic Studies Institute, U.S. Army War College, 2012, pp. 275-305; also see Christopher Holshek, "From Afghanistan to Africa: Civil-Military Teaming in a Whole New World," Jon Gunderson and Melanne Civic, eds., *Unity of Mission: Civilian-Military Teams in Complex Operations,* Maxwell Air Force Base, AL: Air University Press, forthcoming.

2. The author uses the term "civil-military coordination" not as an operational or doctrinal term, but rather in a much larger, grand strategic sense that includes the coordination of civilian-based and military power and influence at the strategic, operational, and tactical levels.

3. The United Nations Development Programme's 1994 *Human Development Report* is considered a cornerstone publication for defining "human security" as including economic security, food security, health security, environmental security, personal security, community security, and political security as its main components—precisely how most underdeveloped nations, particularly in Africa, define "security" for them writ large. See Mahbub ul Haq *et al., Human Development Report 1994,* United Nations Development Programme, Oxford University Press, Oxford, 1994.

4. Mahbub ul Haq.

5. For a detailed explanation, see Lisa Schirch, "Where Does Whole of Government Meet Whole of Society?" Franke and Dorff, eds., *Conflict Management*, pp. 127-152.

6. Fareed Zakaria, "Fareed's Take: U.S. has made war on terror a war without end," *CNN GPS*, May 6, 2012, available from *globalpublicsquare.blogs.cnn.com/2012/05/06/national-security-state/*.

7. David Rothkopf, "The Enemy Within," *Foreign Policy*, May-June 2012, available from www.foreignpolicy.com/articles/2012/04/23/the_enemy_within_0; accessed 1 May 2012. See also Christopher Holshek, "The Enemies We Love," *The Huffington Post*, 4 May 2012, available from *www.huffingtonpost.com/christopher-holshek/defense-spending_b_1472725.html*.

8. Richard H. Kohn, "The Constitution and National Security: The Intent of the Framers," Richard H. Kohn, ed., *The United States Military Under the Constitution of the United States*, New York, New York University Press, 1991, p. 87.

9. Marybeth Peterson-Ulrich, "Infusing Normative Civil-Military Relations Principles in the Officer Corps," Don M. Snider and Lloyd J. Matthews, eds., *The Future of the Army Profession*, 2nd Ed., New York: McGraw Hill, 2005, p. 655.

10. Robert D. Kaplan, "Looking the World in the Eye," *Atlantic Monthly*, December 2001, pp. 70-72 (interview with Huntington). Huntington published *The Soldier and the State* while an assistant professor of government at Harvard. The book was initially dismissed as propagandist by skeptical academics, and so infuriated his colleagues that they voted to deny him tenure 2 years later. Forced to leave, he joined the faculty at the University of Chicago. In 1962, Harvard realized its mistake and lured him back as a full professor. Students on campus staged protests during his classes, so his graduate students organized details to patrol the halls so lectures could proceed. Huntington continued teaching at Harvard for the next 4 decades, twice chairing the same department that once rejected him.

11. Suzanne C. Nielson and Don M. Snider, eds., *American Civil-Military Relations: The Soldier and the State in a New Era*, Baltimore, MD: Johns Hopkins University Press, 2009, p. 387.

12. Suzanne C. Nielson, "American Civil–Military Relations Today: The Continuing Relevance of Samuel P. Huntington's *The Soldier and the State*," *International Affairs*, Vol. 88, No. 2, 2012, pp. 372-373.

13. Barack Obama, "The 2012 State of the Union," January 25, 2012, available from *www.whitehouse.gov/state-of-theunion-2012*.

14. Christopher Holshek, "National Service Day," *The Huffington Post*, November 11, 2011, available from *www.huffingtonpost.com/christopher-holshek/national-service-day_b_1086206.html*. For a discussion of the democratization of both sacrifice and service, see also Christopher Holshek, "Standing Up for All the Fallen," *The Huffington Post*, May 25, 2012, available from *www.huffingtonpost.com/christopher-holshek/memorial-day_b_1538896.html*.

15. Colin S. Gray, *Irregular Enemies and the Essence of Strategy: Can the American Way of War Adapt?* Carlisle, PA: Strategic Studies Institute, U.S. Army War College, March 2006, p. 5.

16. The German term, *Gleichschaltung*, or "co-ordination," refers specifically to the Nazis systematic co-opting of the major institutions of German society, among them the military, into the expanded German state in the 1930s. The case of the military, the politicization of its leadership, and the swearing of allegiance to Adolf Hitler rather than the nation characterize the logical conclusion of a process, begun in the 1920s, of the metamorphosis of a highly professionalized military into what was more famously known as a "state within a state."

17. See Richard Weitz's blog on Locher's April 11, 2012, keynote presentation at the U.S. Army War College annual strategy conference, in "The U.S. Strategy 'Deficit': The Dominance of Political Messaging," *Second Line of Defense*, available from *www.sldinfo.com/the-u-s-strategy-%E2%80%9Cdeficit%E2%80%9D-the-dominance-of-political-messaging/*. Quote obtained from Mr. Locher's personal notes for his April 11, 2012, presentation provided to the author.

18. Frederik Rosen, "Third-generation Civil-Military Relations: Moving Beyond the Security-Development Nexus," *Prism*, Vol. 2, No. 1, December 2010, p. 28.

19. Stephen M. Walt, "Top 10 Lessons of the Iraq War," *Foreign Policy*, March 12, 2012, available from *www.foreignpolicy.com/articles/2012/03/20/top_ten_lessons_of_the_iraq_war?page=full*.

20. George Friedman, "The State of the World: A Framework," *STRATFOR*, February 21, 2012, available from *www.stratfor.com/weekly/state-world-framework*.

21. Robert D. Kaplan, "How We Would Fight China," *The Atlantic Monthly*, June 2005, available from *www.theatlantic.com/magazine/archive/2005/06/how-we-would-fight-china/*.

22. *Human Security Report 2009/2010: The Causes of Peace and The Shrinking Costs of War*, Human Security Report Project, available from *www.hsrgroup.org/human-security-reports/20092010/overview.aspx*.

23. Jeffrey Gettlemen, "Africa's Forever Wars," *Foreign Policy*, March-April 2010, available from *www.foreignpolicy.com/articles/2010/02/22/africas_forever_wars*.

24. Anthony H. Cordesman, "The US Cost of the Afghan War: FY2002-FY2013," Washington, DC: Center for Strategic and International Studies, May 15, 2012, available from *csis.org/publication/us-cost-afghan-war-fy2002-fy2013?utm_source=The+US+Cost+of+the+Afghan+War%3A+FY2002-FY2013&utm_campaign=The+US+Cost+of+the+Afghan+War%3A+FY2002-FY2013&utm_medium=email*.

25. Rosen, p. 31.

26. Samuel A. Worthington, "Exporting Security: International Engagement, Security Cooperation, and the Changing Face of the U.S. Military," Book Review, *Prism*, Vol. 2 No. 1, January 2010, p. 167.

27. See Holshek, "Lessons of Iraq and Afghanistan—Looking from Outside the Box" and "From Afghanistan to Africa." See also Paul Fishbein and Andrew Wilder, *Winning Hearts and Minds? Examining the Relationship between Aid and Security in Afghanistan*, Medford, MA: Feinstein International Center, Tufts University, January 2012; as well as Mark Bradbury and Michael

Kleinman, *Winning Hearts and Minds? Examining the Relationship between Aid and Security in Kenya*, Medford, MA: Feinstein International Center, April 2010.

28. For a detailed discussion of the idea of a "postmodern military" whose soldiers are more internationalized and civil-military minded, see C. C. Moskos, J. A. Williams, and D. R. Segal, *The Postmodern Military*, New York, Oxford University Press, 2000.

29. For a greater understanding of the term "learning organization" in application, for a military perspective with respect to counterinsurgency operations, see John A. Nagl, *Learning to Eat Soup with a Knife*, Chicago, IL: University of Chicago Press, 2005; for a civilian bureaucratic perspective, see Thorsten Benner, Stephan Mergenthaler, and Philipp Rotmann, *The Evolution of Organization Learning in UN Peace Operations Bureaucracy*, Berlin, Germany: Global Public Policy Institute, 2011, available from *www.bundesstiftung-friedensforschung.de/pdf-docs/berichtbenner2.pdf*.

30. For a more detailed discussion of the strategic nature of civil affairs and civil-military operations, see Christopher Holshek, "Civil-Military Power and the Future of Civil Affairs," Reserve Officer Association National Security Report, *The Officer*, May 2007, pp. 45-48. The full version, based on a U.S. Army War College Strategic Research Project, appeared as "The Scroll and the Sword: Synergizing Civil-Military Power," *Cornwallis Group XI: Analysis for Civil-Military Transitions*, Nova Scotia, Canada: George Mason University–Pearson Peacekeeping Center, 2007.

31. Samuel P. Huntington, *The Soldier and the State*, Cambridge, MA: Harvard Press, 1985, p. 2.

32. Gary Hamel, "Management Must Be Reinvented," World Innovation Forum 2008, available from *www.youtube.com/watch?v=TVX8XhiR1UY*.

33. Kristin M. Lord and Marc Lynch, *America's Extended Hand – Assessing the Obama Administration's Global Engagement Strategy*, Washington, DC: Center for a New American Security, June 2010, pp. 10-12, 16.

34. Stephen Biddle and Stephen Long, "Democracy and Military Effectiveness: A Deeper Look," *The Journal of Conflict Resolution*, August 2004, Vol. 48, No. 4, pp. 525-546.

35. Aurel Croissant, David Kuehn, and Philip Lorenz, "Breaking with the Past? Civil-Military Relations in the Emerging Democracies of East Asia," *Policy Studies* Vol. 63, Honolulu, HI: East-West Center, 2012, p. ix.

36. Peterson-Ulrich, p. 656.

37. Rosen, p. 33.

38. Birame Diop, "Sub-Saharan African Military and Development Activities," *Prism*, Vol. 3, No. 1, December 2011, p. 94.

39. Christopher Holshek, "Civil-Military Coordination and Transition Management: The UNMIL Experience, *Conflict Trends*, Issue 3/2011, September 2011, p. 47. The quotes are from the UNMIL Force HQ CIMIC Force Directive for the Conduct of CIMIC by the UNMIL Force for the Drawdown Phase, Version 2, June 15, 2009, p. 6, which the author wrote while serving as UNMIL Chief of CIMIC in 2008-09.

40. General David Petraeus, transcript of interview with David Gregory on NBC's "Meet the Press," August 15, 2010, available from *www.msnbc.msn.com/id/38686033/ns/meet_the_press-transcripts/*.

41. Sippi Azarbaijani-Moghaddam, Mirwais Wardak, Idrees Zaman, and Annabel Taylor, *Afghan Hearts, Afghan Minds: Exploring Afghan Perceptions of Civil-Military Relations*, London, UK: British and Irish Afghanistan Agencies Group (BAAG) and European Network of NGOs in Afghanistan (ENNA), 2008, p. 7.

42. Stew Magnuson, "U.S. Special Forces Target Hearts and Minds," *National Defense*, February 2008, available from *www.nationaldefensemagazine.org/archive/2008/February/Pages/U2357.S2357.Special2357.aspx*.

43. Lieutenant General P. K. Keen, Major General Floriano Peixoto Vieira Neto, Lieutenant Colonel Charles W. Nolan, Lieu-

tenant Colonel Jennifer L. Kimmey, and Commander Joseph Alt-house, "Relationships Matter—Humanitarian Assistance and Di-saster Relief in Haiti," *Military Review*, May-June 2010, p. 8.

44. Holshek, "From Afghanistan to Africa."

45. Robert M. Gates, "Helping Others Defend Themselves: The Future of U.S. Security Assistance, *Foreign Affairs*, Vol. 89, No. 3, May-June 2010.

46. Todd Moss, "Lessons from Mali's Debacle: Time to Re-think Counterterrorism Cooperation," *Rethinking U.S. Foreign Assistance Blog*, Washington, DC: Center for Global Development, May 10, 2012, available from *blogs.cgdev.org/mca-monitor/2012/05/lesson-from-malis-debacle-time-to-rethink-counterterrorism-cooperation.php*.

47. Lisa Schirch, "The Civil Society-Military Relationship in Afghanistan," *Peacebrief*, Vol. 58, Washington, DC: United States Institute of Peace, September 24, 2010, p. 4.

48. See Retired Ambassador Edward Marks, "A 'Next Gener-ation' Department of State—A Proposal for the Consolidation of the Management of Foreign Affairs," *American Diplomacy*, March 2010, available from *www.unc.edu/depts/diplomat/item/2010/0103/oped/op_marks.html*.

49. James R. Locher III, quoted in Kathryn Boughton, "Na-tional Security Expert Who Spoke in Kent Says bin Laden Out-come the Exception; National Security System Flawed," *Litchfield Country Times*, May 2, 2011, available from *www.countytimes.com/articles/2011/05/02/news/doc4dbf1e831ef1e702049372*.

50. Will Ferroggiaro, *The Use & Purpose of American Power in the 21st Century—Perspectives of Americans from the 2008-2009 National Dialogue Forums*, Washington, DC: The Fund for Peace, June 2010, pp, 15-16, 32.

51. Robert Kagan, "Why the World Needs America," *The Wall Street Journal*, February 11, 2012, available from *online.wsj.com/article/SB10001424052970203646004577213262856669448.html?mod=WSJ_hp_LEFTTopStories*.

52. Christopher Holshek, "Over There Matters Over Here," *The Huffington Post*, March 22, 2012, available from *www.huffingtonpost.com/christopher-holshek/us-super-power_b_1362816.html*.

53. Harry. S. Truman, "Special Message to the Congress on Civil Rights," February 2, 1948, Independence, MO: Harry S. Truman Library and Museum, available from *www.trumanlibrary.org/publicpapers/index.php?pid=1380&st=&st1*.

CHAPTER 9

PEACEBUILDING AND DEVELOPMENT: CHALLENGES FOR STRATEGIC THINKING

Fouzieh Melanie Alamir

PROBLEM STATEMENT

It has become commonplace in the international strategic discourse to underline the importance of development aspects in international conflict and crisis management. This has been promoted by concepts such as Human Security,[1] the Whole-of-Government Approach (WoG),[2] or the Comprehensive Approach (CA),[3] and most recently reflected in the U.S. *National Security Strategy* of 2010.[4] Going back to the main-stream of U.S. national security thinking during the Cold War in terms of instruments of power (diplomacy, information, military, and economy [DIME]),[5] the latter two concepts implicitly presume that military strategic thinking can be utilized as a generic method to achieving broader policy goals. They imply that the comprehensive set of civilian and military instruments at the disposal of a nation-state can be employed in the same manner as military instruments. Development policy instruments in this context tend to be regarded as a lever, which can simply be added to the list of the other instruments of national power. All too smoothly, development policy domains such as the fight against poverty, promotion of human rights, good governance, democratization, or capacity building, have been lined up with security policy fields of action such as anti-terrorism, nonproliferation, or cyber security without reflecting whether the character and principles of development policy can be simply subsumed under this header.

It goes without saying today that peacebuilding efforts and development policy should be key elements of an up to date grand strategy. The question remains however, whether the approaches and cognitive premises of strategic thinking[6] are capable of capturing and embracing the characteristics of peacebuilding and development as policy domains *sui generis*.

This chapter argues that peacebuilding and development policy elude traditional presumptions and patterns of strategic thinking in numerous ways and analyzes why. Following a brief sketch of the cognitive premises of modern strategic thought, I will discuss how strategic thinking is challenged by several distinctive features of peacebuilding and development processes. The concluding section summarizes the findings with regard to adjustments required by strategic thinking.

COGNITIVE PREMISES OF MODERN STRATEGIC THOUGHT[7]

Although the logical structure of strategic thinking does not differ from other logical social science constructs, it is largely shaped by the professional self-conception, premises, and operational requirements of military actors. The point of departure of strategic thinking is the nation-state and its national security interests defined in predominantly realist terms of balance of power, territorial integrity, sovereignty, protection of the political and economic order, and availability of human and natural resources as prerequisites of sustained existence. Seen from this status-quo oriented and state-centric perspective, the strategic environment tends to be captured in elementary categories of risks, threats, power structure, allies, or adversaries. This neglects the complexity, dynamics, inconsistency, and ambivalence of social and political challenges relevant in peacebuilding and development contexts. However, scholars of strategic studies often stress that military power is but one means to achieve political ends and howsoever sophisticated and differentiated the categorical grid of assessing strategic environments, the major interpretation pattern in strategic thinking for locating phenomena in the strategic environment remains the power balance and risk-threat scheme.[8]

Moreover, derived from military professional self-conceptions, the major point of reference of strategic thinking is the question of whether and what action is required. This action orientation implies another key characteristic of strategic thinking, namely the premise of unlimited feasibility as long as — given political determination — it is technically and physically feasible. This, in turn, compounds a focus on those phenomena, which can be influenced by the given means and instruments, at the expense of those that cannot be immediately influenced or are not fully understood. In addition, it abets a widespread but false conclusion that those with high operational skills must also be good strategists, or, in other words, that strategy development can be handled in the same manner as operational management.

Another feature of strategic thinking that has been assigned by military thinking is the general confidence in instrumental rationality. It disregards the relevance of irrational elements in politics, is inclined to take political decisions for granted, and focuses on how to implement them rather than to question their wisdom. In the same vein, strategic thinking depends on clear goal formulation in order to derive strategy-driven action, even if the exact goals are not known. In consequence, blurred ends tend to be substituted by a focus on ways and means. A good example to demonstrate this is the prominence of the WoG/CA debate. While WoG/CA are useful concepts to improve how we implement policies, they do not reflect whether we are pursuing the right goals. However, both concepts have gained the status of almost strategic paradigms, indicating, in fact, a roll back of strategic thinking.[9] Furthermore, it is the military's need for hierarchy, predictability, order, simplicity, precision, and sequence — all derived from military operational requirements — that can be traced in strategic thinking, too. The military approach to compartmentalize processes and to break the processes down to hierarchical command and control patterns can also be found in the "engineering" mindset of strategic thinking. Last, but not least, strategic thinking is prone to focusing on hard facts and figures rather than on soft factors like will, perceptions, and emotions, thereby underrating the tremendous power the latter might engender.

Eventually, although it does not describe a cognitive premise but rather a condition, strategic thinking suffers from the same circumstance as military reasoning about ends, ways, and means, which is that it does not enjoy great popularity among policymakers. Having said this, it should be emphasized that strategic thinking is regarded from a cognitive-structural perspective without claiming to do justice to specific products of strategists. Moreover, there is no criticism in stating that strategic thinking has been coined by military thinking. On the contrary, it is acknowledged that strategic thinking has historically evolved in a military context, and that it naturally had to take account of military operational planning and execution requirements. The question is, however, whether peacebuilding and development objectives can be adequately pursued on the basis of these cognitive premises.

WHY PEACEBUILDING AND DEVELOPMENT ELUDE CONVENTIONAL STRATEGIC THINKING

Before going into the details of the argument, our understanding of peacebuilding and development policy needs to be clarified. As with most generic concepts, there is no commonly accepted definition of peacebuilding. The mandate of the United Nations (UN) Peacebuilding Commission highlights four aspects of post-conflict peacebuilding and recovery: integrated strategies, reconstruction and institution building, sustainable development, and coordination of all relevant actors.[10] The former President of the Alliance for Peacebuilding, a nongovernmental advocacy organization, described peacebuilding as "the set of initiatives by diverse actors in government and civil society to address the root causes of violence and protect civilians before, during, and after violent conflict. . . ."[11] Both definitions put emphasis on the long-term, comprehensive interagency and structural approach, as well as on tackling the root causes of violent conflicts. It is the focus on these aspects that marks our understanding of peacebuilding as a development-oriented concept different from peacemaking, stabilization, or peacekeeping. Although not explicitly stated, the reference to sustainable development or the root causes of conflict indicates the close link between peacebuilding and good governance; human rights; and political, economic, and social development as ingredients of sustainable development.[12] In other words, peacebuilding and development are inextricably linked. *The Journal for Peacebuilding and Development*[13] mirrors this understanding in its very title. Peacebuilding in poor and conflict prone societies is not feasible without a broader development framework, although peacebuilding and development are distinct policy domains. Whereas peacebuilding focuses on establishing mechanisms of peaceful conflict resolution, development creates the social, political, and economic conditions that enable and sustain them. While peacebuilding is a thoroughly civil-military endeavor with prominent contributions to be made by the military, the role of military actors in development is marginal and limited to military roles in security system reform. Peacebuilding can be seen as the element linking peacemaking, stabilization, and peacekeeping efforts as primarily military tasks to the broader development efforts. Regarding our question, however, peacebuilding and development pose a common set of challenges to strategic thinking and will therefore be dealt with in tandem.

How Do Ownership and Legitimacy Fit into a State-Centric Scheme?

As mentioned above, strategic thinking has a state-centric and status quo oriented bias that clashes with several tenets of peacebuilding and development policy. First, there is a clash of perspectives. Due to its inherent point of departure, strategic thinking tends to treat actors and societies in countries of concern as objects in relation to their own national interests. In contrast, peacebuilding and development rely on in-digenous actors and societies as their principal acting subjects. The notion of local ownership and legitimacy (not in the eyes of the international community, but in the eyes of local constituencies) as core development principles and precondition claims the right of self-determination of concerned polities on the one hand, while reminding them of their responsibility on the other. Moreover, it implies that external actors need to accept taking a backseat. In scenarios where exter-nal actors have not only spent human and technical resources to intervene in a crisis militarily, but have also sacrificed lives and are under political pressure to make the engagement a success, the temptation to impose policies is high. Combined with the often dis-played unwillingness or incapacity of local actors to agree on peaceful conflict resolution and to manage basic stabilization requirements, it is not hard to imag-ine why principles of local ownership and legitimacy are easily abandoned and cause international donors to either impose conditions and/or rely on bridge-heads. Yet, ownership and legitimacy are necessary to ensure sustainability and to avoid the peril of getting trapped in long-term engagements abroad.

Second, due to the state-centric bias of strategic thinking, the dynamics of awakening civil societies, the peace potential of opposition groups, the influence of individuals beyond the official political system, or socio-cultural sensitivities, tend to be overlooked. As external actors often lack knowledge and understand-ing of societies alien to their own cultural context, they tend to interpret phenomena within the parameters of their own system of meanings. For example, our re-liance on documents in political and administrative processes in the form of policy papers, memoranda of understanding, contracts, reports, etc., is not necessarily shared in other parts of the world. People there have learned that signing a document is necessary to receive material benefits, but a signature may have a less binding character to them than a gift, a handshake, or a word of honor. In addition, the state-centric perspective abets a focus on actors who are in power, or at least in command of armed forces, without asking too many questions on how they came to power or how they use their power. This is in conflict with the general people-centered orientation of development policy and its human security approach where the conventional instruments of power encounter their limits. This applies even more so when it comes to the particular concern of development policy for vulnerable groups such as the poor, women, children, disabled, or other minorities.

Strategic thinking will not be able to overcome the limits of its state-centric and status quo oriented bias unless it opens up for civil societies and organized groups beyond the official political system as potential partners in creating stability and peace. This also requires more careful and more critical examination of the roots, background, power base, goals, methods, ideological reference, and possible future profile of those who receive backing or support.

Facing Dynamic Complexity and Cultural Outland — Are Conventional Methods of Acquiring Knowledge Up to the Task?

Strategy development begins with an analysis of the strategic environment. Based on the premise that "facts are value neutral,"[14] categories for analyzing the strategic environment in conventional strategic thinking are the physical environment, the national character, the interplay between states, balance of power considerations, and the nature of conflict.[15] Although Colin S. Gray highlights the necessity of a skeptical mindset and creative thinking for strategists,[16] in practice it tends to be neutralized by the requirements of operational command, which hardly leave space for lengthy reflections or thinking out of the box. Hence, although clear-sighted scholars suggest otherwise, the process of strategy-related knowledge development in actual practice is at best stuck in limited conceptual frameworks or, more often than not, overshadowed by short-term constellations and interests which rather blur than enlighten the view.

Moreover, as data collection, collation, and interpretation in general cannot be "neutral," products of analysis always mirror underlying premises, hypothesis, interests, and cultural parameters of the analyst. Apart from general epistemological problems that are not going to be reflected here and that are not specific to strategic analyses, the methods and approaches to gaining awareness and understanding of the strategic environment face particular challenges, namely the problems of complexity, dynamics, and bias.

As strategic thinking is preoccupied with risks, threats, and power structures, it tends to neglect the complexity, dynamics, inconsistency, and ambivalence of social and political processes and phenomena, which characterize peacebuilding and development processes. Since they are all but consistent, linear, simple, and definite, the methods of analyzing and understanding peacebuilding and development issues through the lens of strategic thinking require modifications.

In order to better grasp complexity and understand the interdependencies, linkages, and cumulative effects, systemic analysis will yield better results than conventional approaches. To capture dynamics, knowledge development should be a concomitant process throughout the different stages of strategy development and implementation. Effects achieved should be under recurrent review and reappraisal as to whether the overall objectives are still valid and whether the general approach is still appropriate. The integration of periodic assessment and evaluation loops has long been established in developmental project management methods. If we want to minimize bias, misinterpretations, or false conclusions, we need to include experts and actors with genuine insider perspectives into the very process of analysis and understanding. This is where the inclusive, cooperative approach of development policy comes in. This approach may not be immediately transferrable due to security regulations, but it calls for the development of new formats and procedures that enable more direct involvement of subject matter and first-hand expertise into strategy development processes.

Goal Formulation—Can We Know
Where We Are Heading To?

"To travel the correct road, you need to know where you are going."[17] All literature on strategic thought concurs with this formula. There is also consensus that political goals are to be set by politicians and hence are sometimes not sufficiently clear to derive strategic guidance. Therefore, the task of the strategist is to translate political goals into strategic guidance, which may sometimes require entering into a dialogue with policymakers and demanding a clarification of political goals. As strategy makers are familiar with a certain tension between policy and strategy, this tension increases when it comes to formulating peacebuilding or development goals.

In most recent international crisis management scenarios, peace arrangements were highly volatile and foresaw specified goals only for the relatively short immediate stabilization period. The reasons were manifold. In Kosovo, for example, the major bone of contention, namely the question of status, had been deliberately excluded because the Dayton Accord could otherwise not have been signed. The Pretoria Accord, signed by warring Congolese parties to end the fighting and establish a government of national unity, was flawed from the outset as none of the conflict parties had been sincerely interested in the establishment of a stable central state, and as fighting was ongoing in the East. Major conflict parties had been excluded from the process that led to the Petersberg Agreement for Afghanistan and international post-conflict reconstruction efforts.

These examples should suffice to point out that strategic goal formulation in the immediate aftermath of war is almost impossible. In most cases, peace agreements are nothing but a respite, a door opener under more or less conducive conditions for potential future comprehensive conflict solution and reconciliation. Realistic political visions, and the road thereto can hardly be anticipated in the face of destroyed economies, humanitarian catastrophes, socio-psychological legacies of war, and a fragile truce with armed factions about to regroup, just waiting for the spark that reignites the fire. As conflict parties are not able and often also not willing to formulate political visions, external actors are in an even weaker position to do so as long as they do not intend to fully take over responsibility.

With regard to goal formulation as a precondition for strategy development, peacebuilding and development leave us in a very uncomfortable position. The subject, and our role as external actors, deny the development of clear and realistic strategic political goals. But how can external actors who claim to be strategy-driven engage under these circumstances? What happens, in fact, is that the long-term strategic horizon is often curtailed and, lacking political visions, is replaced with short-term objectives. The supposedly top-down approach of strategy-driven policy is turned upside down and replaced by a bottom-up approach with open ends. This is understandable and, given the structural conditions of international politics, to a certain extent inescapable. However, for external actors this bears high risks of long-term engagement without a clear exit, mission creep, or political entanglement, which make pro-active moves ever more difficult.

Strategic thinking cannot really overcome this dilemma. But it should not surrender the claim for political vision all too easily. The very existence of a vision, even if it does not find the necessary political support and may seem rather academic than politically realistic, might positively shape the debate. Moreover, strategic thinking can install systematic and perpetual risk assessment as an integral element of the strategy development and implementation process. Since we seem to be doomed to bottom-up approaches to a certain extent, we should at least conduct recurrent review loops to early identify those effects that may undermine what has already been achieved or that may increase risks and vulnerabilities of the peace process. In this context, the systematic use of simulation methods to anticipate possible effects and outcomes might provide added value.

How Should Guidance be Given to Actors That Cannot Be Guided?

The previously cited formula from Robert Kennedy "to travel the correct road, you need to know where you are going" also implies a claim to provide comprehensive strategic guidance. As strategic thought to date has predominantly given strategic guidance to the military instrument of power — true also for grand strategy — the potential tension between policy and strategy making has been relatively easy to overcome. The military as an instrument can be deployed and commanded top down along clear principles.

However, if strategic guidance is sought for the complex set of civilian instruments that come to bear in peacebuilding and development processes, the vagueness of political goals compounds the inherent blur of roles and responsibilities. Compared to the military as a quasi unitary actor, civilian actors comprise national and international governmental organizations (IGOs) and nongovernmental organizations (NGO), civil society groups and organizations (CSOs), as well as private enterprises. These actors work in vastly different areas such as humanitarian relief, economic recovery, institution building, education, reconciliation, gender balance, child protection, and many other areas. Apart from the diversity of actors, there are no guidelines or binding arrangements regulating who gets engaged where, how, and for how long. Moreover, there is the problem of ensuring that actors at least do not work in opposite directions, if not share common political goals. Only governmental agencies can be politically controlled to make sure they follow the same objectives. NGOs, as long as they work with governmental donor funds, can be controlled to a limited extent via budgetary instruments. The bulk of the remaining actors, however, can at best be controlled via indirect levers (bilateral voluntary agreements, public pressure, voluntary adherence to norms, etc.), or not at all since they do not operate within common structures or rules of political hierarchy and accountability.

Against this background, the very idea of any kind of comprehensive strategy for civilian programs and activities in peacebuilding and development processes seems to be forlorn. This, in consequence, makes it very difficult for implementing any broader strategy. We lack institutional or procedural levers to translate political goals into strategic guidance beyond the traditional diplomatic, informational, military, and economic instruments of power. Being aware that the better part of activities able to support and/or induce sustained peace and development do not fall into this category of instruments, means to accept that we lack direct steering mechanisms for many relevant peacebuilding and development activities.

This does not mean, however, that there are no possibilities of improving political coherence among the multiple actors and agencies. But it should be clear that we might at best get closer to assembling NGOs, CSOs, or private business actors under the banner of a unified effort, whereas we may never achieve any organizational setting similar to a unified command. As this cannot be imposed upon independent actors, the only way to gain better political coherence is to build long-term institutional relationships and mutual trust. We can do so by improving mutual knowledge and common situational understanding, by including actors and building consensus early on, and by developing institutionalized formats of consultation and cooperation in all phases.

For strategic thinking, again this requires learning from approaches and procedures that are common in development policy. Nevertheless, we face clear limits to what can be achieved in this respect from a strategist's point of view. Apart from security considerations, conflicting policy and institutional interests between actors and agencies involved will most likely impede more than temporary coalitions of the willing. Hence, if more control is wanted, international donors would have to dedicate significantly more governmental resources, and by the same token take over extensively more political responsibilities in international conflict and crisis management: But this would very likely exceed existing capacities and political will. Otherwise, whether we like it or not, we will have to live with the fact that only a limited number of activities (and thereby outcomes) can really be subjected to (grand) strategy-driven action and steering mechanisms, i.e., we will have to learn to live with a considerable extent of anarchy.

Which Instruments Does Strategic Thinking Have to Create Political Will and Influence Perceptions?

Strategic thinking is characterized by an instrumental logic[18] that is applied not only with regard to the mode of utilization of instruments at one's disposal, but also with regard to the way of achieving effects. It aims at diminishing the scope of maneuver of adversaries, influencing their behavior, and preventing them to achieve their goals mainly by denial of opportunities. Another feature of this instrumental rationality is its inclination to disregard the so-called soft factors in politics such as perceptions, emotions, identities, and beliefs.

Peacebuilding and development, on the contrary, are primarily about setting up opportunities, about creating ownership and encouraging political will to reform, whereas influencing the activities of local actors is of secondary importance. Peace and development cannot be simply engineered by combining a blueprint with resources, instruments, and manpower. They rely to a large extent on hopes and fears, on the capacity and credibility of local stakeholders to mobilize, lead and convince people, on the strength of identities, the willingness to tolerate frustrations, on the belief that the future holds better prospects.

But can ownership and political will to reform be created by external actors at all? The instrumental logic of strategic thinking clearly reaches its limits when it comes to creating opportunities and incentives for local ownership and reform-oriented political intentions. Development policy has been dealing with the challenge of creating local ownership and engaging local stakeholders for many years, but has not come to satisfactory conclusions yet. Practical levers are limited to participatory methods of program planning and implementation.[19] Empirical analyses have shown that despite efforts to improve inclusive methods, the relationships between donors and local stakeholders often remain asymmetrical and, moreover, participatory approaches often exclude civil society.[20]

Can the soft factors in politics be influenced by the traditional instruments of power? Public information, intelligence, cyber operations, psychological and information operations — all of which can be subsumed under the information instruments of power[21] — would be considered the most suitable levers to tackle perceptions, beliefs, and emotions of people. Indeed, their potential impact should not be underestimated as long as the following conditions are met: messages are understood in the local context, messages are credible in the local context, and messages are consistent with the behavior of the sender. However, perceptions, beliefs, and emotions are inextricably linked to expectations, and if expectations are not met, they easily reverse to the opposite. That means, in a peacebuilding and development context, traditional information instruments of power can and should be utilized, but need to be handled with particular care. If they are not, they are likely to produce rather short-term effects, whereas influencing soft factors of politics also require instruments with more long-term effects such as basic and political education, societal discourses, reconciliation processes, or the like.

In consequence, it seems strategic thinking has to cope with the dilemma of investing resources and sacrificing lives in international crisis management, while not being able to fully control processes. We are often forced to take a backseat, particularly when taking account of the frequently witnessed unwillingness or incapacity of local actors to make peace or manage peace processes. This dilemma cannot be overcome. This means that strategic thinking requires more systematic risk analysis, and either more courage to nonaction if we cannot estimate the risks, or more courage to name and face the possible negative effects.

How Can Strategic Planning Cope with the Unforeseeable?

Closely linked to the instrumental logic described above is the "engineering" mind set of strategic thinking, characterized by hierarchy, predictability, order, simplicity, precision, and sequence—all derived from military operational requirements. Consequently, the process from strategic planning to actual implementation breaks the complexity of reality down to operationally manageable levels, units, and activities. Although the operational and tactical level may considerably shape the situational picture generated at the strategic level through the data they provide, strategic planning essentially remains a top-down process.

In stark contrast, peacebuilding and development processes can by no means be compartmentalized and broken down to hierarchical command and control relationships of a military operation. Because more often than not, it is uncertain who the stakeholders are and what goals they pursue, i.e., the level of contingencies is very high and can be compared only to counterinsurgency operations in urban terrain in military terms of complexity of the operational environment. Most peacebuilding and many development scenarios lack an established common set of norms and rules, a precondition for reliable command and control mechanisms. The simultaneous challenges of maintaining peace, diminishing humanitarian crises, creating viable institutions, alleviating poverty, encouraging economic recovery, fostering reconciliation, and allowing for better overall living conditions evade any attempt to fit peacebuilding and development processes into any setting of sequential steps. Orderly top-down planning and implementation procedures, particularly if we take into account the diversity and huge number of actors involved, are not applicable under the given circumstances.

Peacebuilding and development processes take place in multilevel, multiactor, and multinational contexts that lack all preconditions to apply top-down, hierarchical, orderly, sequential, or precise unified command and control. This forces strategic planning ambitions to confine themselves to giving guidance to those actors who are willing and able to act in a concordant effort. Realistically, in most cases this will be governmental actors representing one donor state only.

How Can Strategic Thinking Cope with Conflicting Time Rhythms?

Presuming a defined strategic end-state, strategic thinking, and even more so strategic planning, needs clear timelines to allocate budgets, ensure political acceptance, and set up activities. While operational and tactical goals remain to be specified by subsequent planning stages, a guiding vision of the political end-state is supposed to inform strategic planning and the overall time frame of implementation. Programs, campaigns, and operations are implicitly assumed to be terminable within the legislative period of the initiating government.

Peacebuilding and development policy, on the other hand, follow a somewhat converse logic. Due to their high level of contingency, the anticipatory focus lies on short- to mid-term objectives at best, while the political end-state remains diffuse with the responsibility to carve it out in the hands of local actors in a remote and uncertain future. Consequently, while strategic planning often tends to fall behind the actual dynamics and requirements on the ground, peacebuilding and development processes with their bottom-up logic tend to undermine the pace and time frames of budgetary planners, administrative procedures, and legislative periods.

In particular, progression of political attention in donor countries does not conform to the needs of recipient peacebuilding or developing countries. In the immediate aftermath of conflict, political attention and acceptance levels of home constituencies are high, but rapidly wane, be it due to a "normalization" of conditions, due to fatigue, or simply due to the emergence of new crises on the international agenda that overlap the images of the former. But peacebuilding and development processes require political attention at a constantly high level by international donors for much longer periods than those shaped by mass media and election cycles. When it comes to early recognizing and reacting to negative dynamics that may imperil what has already been achieved, political mechanisms to readjust strategic guidance are slow. In addition, expectation management, pertaining to home constituencies as well as the populace of recipient countries, is often neglected in strategic thinking.

For strategic thinking, political and procedural time frames of the political system in general and the particular administration in charge have to be taken as a given, i.e., there is little room for realistic changes with regard to domestic political and procedural conditions for strategy formulation and strategic planning. Therefore, the scope of adjustments to strategic thinking so as to better cope with conflicting time frames is limited. Certainly, systematic expectation management can and should be improved. The dynamics of political attention and levels of acceptance of domestic audiences can be anticipated to a large extent and should therefore be more systematically included as a potential constraining factor that requires systematic coping strategies. The expectations of audiences in recipient countries can be better managed by unanimous and honest communication. Unanimous communication can best be assured by making strategic communication an integral part of not only the military, but all strands of international crisis management activities.[22] Particularly, messages to recipient country audiences have to be unanimous among national and international donor nations and organizations.[23] Honesty in strategic communication is about caution with regard to what we promise to audiences in recipient countries and how we explain our own motives of engagement, but even more so it is about congruence between what we say and what we do.

CONCLUSION

We have shown that peacebuilding and development processes evade the cognitive premises and conventional approaches of strategic thinking in many respects. Strategic thinking, therefore, will have to adjust in order to better cope with the challenges posed by peacebuilding and development.

With regard to one of its fundamental tenets, namely its state-centric reference point, strategic thinking will have to adapt to a more open reference framework, accepting civil societies and organized groups beyond the official political system as potential partners in creating peace and development. This implies more attention and more thorough scrutiny of the roots, background, power bases, goals, methods, ideologies, and possible future roles of those who are chosen as partners and who receive political backing and development aid. Though practical constraints often do not allow us to be too select in the choice of local partners, more attention should be lent to their

261

adherence to the norms and principles we intend to foster, and it should be more carefully examined to show whether they are part of the solution rather than part of the problem. After all, backing elites, who are not interested in peace and pursue only self-seeking interests, not only imperils the peace process, but also calls into question the credibility and legitimacy of international engagement as a whole.

Procedures for gaining awareness and understanding of the strategic environment can be improved by systematically applying systemic analysis approaches. Knowledge development should be a concomitant process throughout the different stages of strategy development and implementation. Moreover, the volatility and dynamics of peacebuilding and development processes require recurrent review processes of the effects achieved and open-ended political reappraisals on whether the overall objectives are still valid and whether the general approach is still appropriate. Last, but not least, knowledge development, as well as monitoring and evaluation, require more and systematic inclusion of subject matter experts from many disciplines and actors with genuine insider perspectives in order to minimize bias and avoid misinterpretations or false conclusions. Promising approaches of improving knowledge development as a distinct method and perpetual process, accompanying strategic and operational planning, have been developed and tested within the military domain,[24] but have to date never gained attention in the interagency arena.

The challenges of formulating strategic goals pertaining to a highly contingent and volatile subject like peacebuilding and development processes can, if not fully tackled, at least be addressed by strategic thinking via systematic and perpetual risk assessments.

The latter should be integral elements of strategy development and implementation. Combined with recurrent review loops to early identify effects that may undermine the intended direction of the peacebuilding or development process, this will help avoid the wrong path, dwelling on the wrong path for too long, or quickly adjusting strategy. In this context, the systematic use of simulation methods to anticipate possible effects and outcomes—not only at the military strategic and operational planning levels, where it has been established for decades, but also at the political strategic level—might provide added value.

When it comes to the political and structural constraints of unifying diverse actors behind a common strategic guidance, one of the very premises of strategic thinking has to be questioned. More control of a peacebuilding or development scenario for international actors requires more donor resources, and by the same token, the political will to take more political responsibilities. Otherwise, we will have to live with the fact that external actors can be subject only to a limited number of activities (and thereby outcomes) and to some form of political steering mechanisms. In consequence, we will have to say good-bye to the strategic premise of "anything goes" and learn to live with a considerable extent of anarchy and uncontrollability.

Another cognitive premise of strategic thinking that requires adjustments is the instrumental logic. We cannot overcome the dilemma that one of the main challenges of peacebuilding and development processes, i.e., the creation of political will on the side of local elites, is not feasible with the conventional instruments of power. One conclusion is to reconsider the DIME concept of instruments of power and related concepts.[25] Another conclusion is that we will have to live with a backseat role in many cases, even if local actors display unwillingness or incapacity to act. The only lever for strategic thinking, therefore, is — again — to include more thorough and more systematic risk analysis prior to a political decision to engage. Political decisionmakers need more courage to decide either not to engage if risks cannot be estimated or are too high, or more courage to face and prepare for the possible negative effects.

By the same token, the engineering logic of strategic thinking and planning needs a review when it comes to peacebuilding and development processes. If we acknowledge that multilevel, multiactor, and multinational contexts lack all preconditions to apply top-down, hierarchical, orderly, sequential, or precise unified command and control, strategic planning ambitions will have to be confined to giving guidance to those actors who are willing and able to act in a concordant effort. This limits the scope of actors that can be subjected to any form of coordinated planning and implementation to governmental actors representing one donor state. The recent debate on WoG approaches in international conflict and crisis management shows, however, that the concept does not meet the high expectations connected to it when it comes to practice.[26] Hence, the limits of achieving greater coherence even among the governmental actors of one donor country remind us to be realistic and humble.

Finally, the range of options for adjustment in strategic thinking is also limited with regard to conflicting time rhythms between domestic political decisionmaking processes and dynamics of peacebuilding and development processes. As political and procedural time frames of the domestic political system in general and the particular administration in charge are a given, there is little room for realistic changes. However, much can be improved with regard to systematic expectation management. The dynamics of political attention and levels of acceptance of domestic audiences should be anticipated and more systematically taken into consideration as a potential constraining factor requiring coping strategies. Audiences in recipient countries can be better addressed if coordinated strategic communication is an integral part of all strands of international crisis management activities. In addition, strategic communication should be carefully designed with regard to what we promise to audiences in recipient countries and how we explain our own motives of engagement. Most importantly, the gap between what we say and what we do must not widen under all circumstances, as this undermines our credibility.

In a broader perspective, we may need to accept that there are things we will never understand, and that many people may not want to share our norms and values. Having said this, strategic thinking in general needs increased flexibility regarding basic assumptions and cognitive patterns, making the possibility of delay, setbacks, detours, or even failure, integral elements of our thought. The main challenge is to reconcile top-down approaches and the instrumental/engineering logic of strategic thinking with the ambiguity, unpredictability, and uncontrollability of peacebuilding and development processes. We may also have to reconsider our understanding of feasibility in international politics in general and learn to better live with contingency and risks. All in all, strategic thinking would be well advised to adopt more humility in its outlook on the world.

ENDNOTES - CHAPTER 9

1. As the most prominent example, the European Security Strategy puts high emphasis of aspects of human security though it does not explicitly refer to the concept. See *A Secure Europe in a Better World*, Brussels, Belgium: European Security Strategy, December 2003, available from *www.consilium.europa.eu/uedocs/cmsUpload/78367.pdf*. In its guidelines on preventing violent conflict, the Organization for Economic Cooperation and Development (OECD) Development Assistance Committee (DAC) explicitly refers to the Human Security concept. See "Helping Prevent Violent Conflict," OECD DAC *Guidelines*, Paris, France: OECD DAC, 2001, available from *www.oecd.org/dataoecd/15/54/1886146.pdf*.

2. The WoG concept has been utilized in different contexts. See, for example, *Whole of Government Approaches to Fragile States*, OECD DAC Reference Series, Paris, France: OECD DAC, 2006, available from *www.oecd.org/dataoecd/15/24/37826256.pdf*; Joseph R. Cerami and Jeffrey A. Engel, eds., *Rethinking Leadership and "Whole of Government" National Security Reform: Problems, Progress, and Prospects*, Carlisle, PA: Strategic Studies Institute, U.S. Army War College, May 2010, available from *www.dtic.mil/cgi-bin/GetTRDoc?AD=ada522339.pdf&Location=U2&doc=GetTRDoc.pdf*; Volker C. Franke and Robert H. Dorff, eds, *Conflict Management and "Whole of Government": Useful Tools for U.S. National Security Strategy?* Carlisle, PA: Strategic Studies Institute, U.S. Army War College, April 2012, available from *www.strategicstudiesinstitute.army.mil/pubs/display.cfm?pubID=1102*; or the most prominent example: *U.S. National Security Strategy*, Washington, DC: The White House, May 2010, available from *www.whitehouse.gov/sites/default/files/rss_viewer/national_security_strategy.pdf*.

3. The Comprehensive Approach is a concept that has evolved and is being used mainly in the NATO context. See *Political Guidance on ways to improve NATO's involvement in Stabilisation and Reconstruction*, available from *www.nato.int/nato_static/assets/pdf/pdf_2011_09/20111004_110922-political-guidance.pdf*.

4. *U.S. National Security Strategy*, Washington, DC: The White House, May 2010, available from *www.whitehouse.gov/sites/default/files/rss_viewer/national_security_strategy.pdf.*

5. Hans Binnendijk and Patrick Claswon, "Tuning the Instruments of National Power," *Joint Forces Quarterly*, Winter 1995-96, pp. 82-88.

6. When we speak of strategic thinking, we refer to the discourse on grand strategy or national security strategy in the context of strategic studies as a subject in Armed Forces colleges and the like.

7. For the purposes of this chapter, literature on teaching strategy was the main source of reference. Among many others, the following works were particularly useful: *Grand Strategy: Theory and Practice*, No. 8802, Quantico, VA: U.S. Marine Corps, Command and Staff College, unknown date, available from *www.au.af.mil/au/awc/awcgate/usmc/csc_8802_lesn1_grand_strat.pdf; U.S. Marine Corps Doctrinal Publication (MSDP) 1-1, Strategy,* Washington, DC: November 1997, available from *www.dtic.mil/doctrine/jel/service_pubs/mcdp1_1.pdf;* John Lewis Gaddis, "What is Grand Strategy?" Paper prepared as the Karl Von Der Heyden Distinguished Lecture, Duke University, February 26, 2009, the keynote address for a conference on "American Grand Strategy after War," sponsored by the Triangle Institute for Security Studies and the Duke University Program in American Grand Strategy, available from *www.duke.edu/web/agsp/grandstrategypaper.pdf;* Colin S. Gray, *Schools for Strategy: Teaching Strategy for 21st Century Conflict*, Carlisle, PA: Strategic Studies Institute, U.S. Army War College, November 2009; Gabriel Marcella, ed., *Teaching Strategy: Challenge and Response*, Carlisle, PA: Strategic Studies Institute, U.S. Army War College, March 2010.

8. The author of the U.S. Marine Corps Command and Staff College manuscript of a seminar on grand strategy admits that "[A]lthough strategy is as much about peace as it is about war, it is generally recognized that, if we fail to properly manage the former, we must be prepared to execute the latter." See "Lesson Introduction," Lesson 1: Grand Strategy: Theory and Practice, first paragraph.

9. Fouzieh Melanie Alamir, "Security System Reform in Weak or Fragile States Implemented Through a Whole of Government Approach: A Threefold Challenge," Franke and Dorff, eds., pp. 153-184.

10. General Assembly Resolution 60/180 on the UN Peacebuilding Commission, December 30, 2005, available from *www. un.org/ga/search/view_doc.asp?symbol=A/RES/60/180.*

11. Chic Dambach, former President and CEO, quote available from *www.allianceforpeacebuilding.org/?page=aboutmission.*

12. For this understanding of development, see the European Consensus on Development, *Official Journal of the European Union*, C 46/01, February 24, 2006, available from *ec.europa.eu/ development/icenter/repository/european_consensus_2005_en.pdf.*

13. A publication hosted by the American Unversity`s Center for Global Peace and the Peacebuilding and Development Institute, in partnership with the University of Peace, available from *www.journalpeacedev.org/.*

14. Robert Kennedy, "The Elements of Strategic Thinking: A Practical Guide," Gabriel Marcella, ed., p. 27.

15. The MCDP 1-1 understands the national character as being derived from the location, the language, the culture, the religion, the historical circumstances, and other factors specific to a state or political entity (p. 23). By assessing the nature of conflict, it considers questions like these: What value do both sides attach to the political objectives of the war? What costs are both sides willing to pay? What is the result of the "value compared to cost" equation? What material, economic, and human sacrifices will the participants endure? For how long? Under what circumstances? Will the societies expect regular, measurable progress? Will they patiently endure setbacks and frustration? (p. 81). See MSDP 1-1.

16. Gray, p. 47.

17. Kennedy, p. 30.

18. See also Gray, p 8.

19. See, for example, Handbook on Stakeholder Consultation and Participation in ADB Operations, Tunis-Belvedere, Tunisia: African Development Bank, 2001, available from *www.afdb.org/ fileadmin/uploads/afdb/Documents/Policy-Documents/Handbook%20 on%20Stakeholder%20Consultaion.pdf.*

20. Tobias Pietz and Leopold von Carlowitz, *Ownership in Practice: Lessons from Liberia and Kosovo*, Berlin, Germany: Deutsche Stiftung Friedensforschung, Georgsmarienhütte, 2001, available from *www.zif-berlin.org/fileadmin/uploads/analyse/dokumente/veroef-fentlichungen/Pietz_von_Carlowitz_2011_Ownership_in_Practice. pdf*; Hannah Reich, "Local Ownership in Conflict Transformation Projects: Partnership, Participation or Patronage?" Berghof Occasional Paper No 27, Berlin, Germany, Berghof Research Center for Constructive Conflict Management, September 2006, available from *www.berghof-conflictresearch.org/documents/publications/ boc27e.pdf.*

21. Jeffrey L. Caton, Cori E. Dauber, Jeffrey L. Groh, and David J. Smith, "Information as Power. An Anthology of Selected United States Army War College Student Papers," Vol. 4, Carlisle, PA: U.S. Army War College, January 2012, available from *www. carlisle.army.mil/DIME/documents/Information%20as%20Power%20 Vol%204%20(web-final).pdf.*

22. Report of the Defense Science Board Task Force on Strategic Communication, Washington, DC: Office of the Under Secretary of Defense for Acquisition, Technology and Logistics, September 2004, available from *www.fas.org/irp/agency/dod/dsb/ commun.pdf*; "Principles of Strategic Communication," Washington, DC: Department of Defense, August 2008, available from *www.au.af.mil/info-ops/documents/principles_of_sc.pdf.*

23. See *U.S. Public Diplomacy. Interagency Coordination Efforts Hampered by the Lack of a Communication Strategy*, Washington, DC: U.S. Government Accountability Office, April 2005, available from *www.gao.gov/new.items/d05323.pdf.*

24. In the context of military concept development and experimentation, the Multinational Experimentation Series (MNE) served as a framework where the method was developed and tested over several years. Concepts and findings of this process

have influenced NATO and NATO member-state approaches to gaining situational awareness and understanding, but have not been taken up by civilian agencies.

25. Related concepts are the so-called 3D (Diplomacy, Development, and Defense) concept that is being used at the political-strategic level, or the Political, Military, Social, Economic, Information, and Infrastructure (PMSEII) concept developed in the context of operational planning for courses of action.

26. Franke and Dorff, eds., see especially chaps. 4, 5, 6, and 10.

CHAPTER 10

FORCES OF ORDER AND DISORDER: SECURITY PROVIDERS AND CONFLICT MANAGEMENT

Michael Ashkenazi

The author would like to thank Volker Franke for the opportunity to write this chapter, and S. M. Stirling for *In the Court of the Crimson Kings*, which stimulated the concept of "security provider." The participants of the 2012 KSU-SSI Symposium, "Conflict Management and Peacebuilding: Pillars of a New American Grand Strategy," at Kennesaw State University, are thanked for their comments. Particular thanks go to Dr. Andreas Heinemann-Grueder for incisive and supportive criticism of an earlier draft. All errors and misrepresentations are my own.

INTRODUCTION

The term "security" is a notably contentious one (e.g., Huysmans, 1998). In the traditional realm, security implied first the security of the state and its institutions, and then, in some but not all conceptualizations, the security of the individual from violence or harm *not directly mandated by the state*. In the past decade, the interpretation of the term "security" has expanded to encompass virtually all aspects of human life — security from hunger, want, and lack of education.

Crucially, *most* security (in the state sense) has been in the hands of security specialists: individuals and organizations specializing in providing security. As noted, this is, of course, challengeable: What is it that these specialists actually provide and to whom, has been an enduring issue (Krahmann, 2008; Shearing & Wood, 2007). No less crucially, it is these same security specialists — *security providers* in the terminology used here — that have been at the core of *insecurity* in two related ways. On the one hand, toward "nonmembers" however defined, historically, the military (a type of security provider) have at all times been the major threat to individuals' lives, bodies, and property. On the other, internal security providers — police, the military, and guerillas — have been major forces threatening the integrity of individual bodies, rights, and property within many polities.

The recent concept of conflict management implies, sometimes is even predicated, on the presence of individuals and groups who will, following some principle, effectively provide this security (Bercovitch & Jackson, 2009; Elde *et al.*, 2005; Miall *et al.*, 1999). This chapter will demonstrate that this perception — that security providers will automatically be positive vectors in conflict management — needs some serious rethinking. The features of security providers will be described and characterized, notably those in less-developed and fragile states (LDFS). Varied and sometimes unexpected interests of these security providers help "manage" conflict, albeit in ways that the theoretical genitors of the concept might not like. Both the terms "security" and the nature of the security providers need to be approached from a different perspective.

Much of the data is derived from studies by myself and others in less-developed and post-conflict countries. From 2009 to 2011, I conducted field studies on security providers in several countries in Asia and Africa. Some of the issues arising from those studies

272

are raised here. For the rest, I rely on the vast mass of publications on the militaries, traditional defense organizations, and commercial security formations in LDFS.

MANAGING CONFLICT

The idea that conflict is "manageable" in some form encompasses a wide range of possible activities and potential outcomes. Conflict management is an activity that is poly-specific: most primates engage in processes of conflict management, both to avoid conflict and to mitigate its effects (Aureli & de Waal 2000). That human primates do so as well should be no surprise. Peacekeeping by United Nations (UN)-mandated and other forces constitute part of the repertoire of international conflict management. Positive reinforcement comes in the form of economic aid, trade, and other rewards. The establishment of legal agreements (albeit, often buttressed by either the threat of force or economic reward) constitute a third part of conflict management. Whatever the peace management paradigm involved, the actual application relies on individual and collective security, which, in turn, is a function of police agencies (local or international) internally, and military or quasi-military agencies against external threats. Both of these types of organizations—police and military—are engaged within the conflict management process as security providers. Security providers are individuals and institutions that are able to bring force to bear to ensure that conflict parties actually abide by "the rules," whatever they may be, or by the decisions of whomever is attempting to manage conflict in the society concerned. Given that conflict is endemic in human societies, it is unsurprising to find

273

that most violent conflict management requires some form of executive force *in potentio.*

While all the elements of conflict management are worthy of study, this chapter addresses the issue of individuals and groups that are able to bring force to bear to ensure that conflict parties actually abide by the rules, whatever they may be, for conflict management in the society concerned. At the lower levels of organization — inter-individual and community levels — these enforcers may be neighbors, kin, bystanders, village elders, or groups assigned to this role by custom and local law (e.g., Evans-Pritchard, 1949; Barth, 1959). At higher levels of organization — tribe, ethnic organization, and nation-state — the role is assigned to organized formations: police, military, and international peacekeepers. In other words, *all* conflict management depends, to some degree or another, on security providers. Reorienting the discussion of conflict management in this way forces us to consider the point that security providers are a multi-faceted and compound category that dispense both security and insecurity. Understanding how such organizations and individuals shift their "output" between some degree of security and some degree of insecurity is necessary if we are to ensure that conflict management goes beyond theory and planning into the realms of practice.

It is useful to recognize and accept some basic behavioral statements as framing conditions to help in understanding security providers:

- People make conflict. Conflicts are not created, sustained, or carried out by abstractions such as states, but by real people.
- People manage conflict. Managing conflict is something that all primates, including humans,

engage in. If they do not, they stand likely to suffer as a community (or troop, in the case of primates, Aureli & De Waal, 2000).

- Conflict management depends on culturally defined roles. We can identify several generic roles that are expressed culturally in all conflicts among humans: the conflict parties, mediators and enforcers, and onlookers.

Certainly, the analysis above points to a major assumption: that security providers should contribute to managing and abating conflict. However, in practice, this is not necessarily the case. Several case studies of security providers will be examined to understand why this is not the case and to show the limits of their contribution to conflict management.

CHARACTERIZING SECURITY PROVIDERS

A security provider is an individual or formation that purports to be engaged in activities that affect the degree to which groups and individuals can ensure (or at least predict to some degree) their physical, social, and material integrity. By defining both security providers and security in this fashion, I am able to avoid the lengthy arguments about the nature of security, to encompass broader strategic understanding of security such as "human security," and to use the definition to encompass a range of security providers beyond the commonly accepted one.

Following this approach, at least four different types of security providers, distinguished by their formal *and* their substantive characteristics, can be identified. *State* security providers are individuals and formations mandated by the state and, in theory, controlled by its governing bodies, to provide security. *Commercial* security providers are formations who are involved in security activities in return for monetary payment. *Traditional* security providers are mandated by the social and cultural systems of pre-modern and local social organization. Finally, *Out-law*[1] security providers encompass a wide range of formations that either engage in negative security (they actually threaten physical, social, and material integrity), or conditional security ("us or no one").

State Security Providers.

State security providers encompass all types of legally mandated forces that we are familiar with: police, military, gendarmerie, prison guards, and, in at least one case, the fire brigade. These formations are characterized by functioning on the basis of legal frameworks, mandated and paid for by the state. Often (e.g., the military), there is a psycho-social dimension to their activities that is motivated by, and makes strong reference to, positive ideological and moral support, downplaying financial rewards (Franke, 1997). State security is *supposed* to provide *universal* service: a public good. In practice, this is, of course, not always the case. State security providers are also expected to provide *homogenous* services; that is, all beneficiaries are supposed to be protected to the same degree. Certainly, since early in the 20th century, public, state-provided security has been viewed as a public good to which all are entitled (Mandel, 2001).

Commercial Security Providers.

While strictly speaking, security organizations motivated overtly and strictly by financial rewards are
not a new phenomenon (*landsknecht* and *condottieri*
in Renaissance Europe), commercial security formations providing internal policing services have been
relatively uncommon until the middle of the 20th century (Mandel, 2001). Commercial security formations
in the modern state are typically organized as profit-
making corporations operating to supplement internal
security forces. They are also, in theory and often in
practice, regulated by a state authority, and the scope
of their action is typically restricted by a state authority. Commercial security formations provide *restricted*
service. That is, they *choose* to provide security to particular individuals or groups, depending on their fee.
Thus their services are *specific* and *particularistic*.

Traditional Security Providers.

The twin and related problems of internal and
external security provision did not spring into being
in the 20th century, and nonmodern states and other
political and social structures have needed to provide
security for themselves. This has usually been solved
by diffusing security provision among a number of
different systems, appealing to self-help being the
first. To avoid confusion, traditional security providers in this chapter refers to *formations*, rather than individuals (or kin groups) acting on their own to ensure
self-help (see Fry 2002 for a concise classification).
Many such formations of security providers are based
on the recruitment of young men as they make their
life's journey. Age-grade groups (*lo-mua* in China,

wakamono-kai in Japan, *elmorani* in East Africa) where young men of given age cohorts are expected to perform public service, performance-based groups (dog soldiers among the Cheyenne), or voluntary societies (so-called "Secret Societies" in many West African societies) are common bases for recruitment and organization of traditional security providers. Typically, such formations' authority is based on community consensus bolstered by ritual (that is "appeal to traditions and practices encoded by remote, often moot beings") (Guthrie, 1980). Traditional security providers provide a *community* service: those outside the community, physically or socially, may not benefit, and may even suffer, from their activities.

Out-law Security Providers

Predation on others is a universal fact of life. Both externally and internally, where groups and individuals prey on their neighbors, they are actors within what we can call the security network—those actors concerned with security activities. Out-law security providers affect the provision of security in many ways. The category includes out-and-out predators who provide no services to their victims (Vikings and Somali pirates). Many, however, provided restricted security, whether in the form of banditry (Hobsbawm, 2010) where they support and enjoy class or ethnic solidarity, or in the form of protection services ("you pay me, and nothing will happen to you, and I will keep other predators away") such as a traditional Mafia source of income (Gambetta, 1996). At the far side of the predatory scale are OAGs, the "wannabes" who would like to be able to have a monopoly of force (and sometimes have it locally), and who prey on their neighbors, albeit with excuses (the Maoist insurgents in Nepal gave out formal receipts for extortion money "valid against extractions by other units of the PLA"[2]). Out-law service is *opportunistic* and *situational*.

To the degree the state actually owns a monopoly on violence, out-law security providers largely provide *negative* security. However, where the state does not have an effective, substantive monopoly, out-law providers become one of a mass of commercial and even traditional security providers.[3]

SECURITY PROVIDERS IN ACTION: SOME EXAMPLES

To draw together the strands raised to this point, it is useful to provide some empirical examples. In each case, I have tried to demonstrate the *mutability* of the role any particular security provider formation assumes. As we can see, we always need to account for *multiple* rather than single action types. Moreover, we need to try and understand, globally, *how* and *why* security providers change what they are doing, since they constitute, in some situations, a positive vector for conflict management, and in almost but not quite identical situations, a negative influence on conflict management. Several examples, all from recent studies, bolster the argument that we need to look very carefully at the implications of different types of security provider.

State Providers: Post-Soviet Policing in Albania, Georgia, and Afghanistan.

I rely here heavily on a study by Stephan Hensell (2011), as well as some first-hand observations from

Afghanistan and elsewhere. With the emergence of post-Soviet states, the position of the police as security providers changed radically. Their secure position as guardians of the state's interests was replaced by a variety of arrangements in which the police were either heavily politicized (in Albania, for instance) or were forced to become entrepreneurs, using their privileged position as security providers to engage in economic activities (as in Georgia). In the latter form, internal security services typically "rent" areas of activity — traffic control, border control, and issuance of licenses — by paying a tribute to a superior (leading all the way to the presidency). They finance this, and themselves, by extracting fees for activity in their "assigned" areas. Lucrative positions are competitively sought after.

Kabul airport is an example in miniature. Formal security practices are set in place: security check of luggage and of persons, border control (exit permit and exit stamp), and customs. This is part of local and international security provisions with which we are all familiar. At Kabul airport, however, one can hire an armed individual policeman as a security provider: that individual will whisk the client through all the security checks in 10 minutes flat, rather than the 2 hours that are not uncommon.

In both cases, the issue *here* is not corruption, however defined. What is important is how a particular type of security provider — a state provider — assumes, for whatever environmental or structural reasons, a posture that would be located more closely to commercial and out-law security provision than the universalistic state mode.

Traditional Security Providers: Mafias and Chiefs.

In common with many other East and Southeast Asian societies, in village society in Timor Leste, young men between puberty and marriage are ex-officio members of village and neighborhood youth groups. These groups serve partly as a socialization medium and partly as a village defense force against fires, floods, and external attack. Members often train in the local martial art (*Timor Silat* in this case, though *taekwondo* is increasingly popular). The Timorese protest that they always settle disputes peacefully. Yet, the youth groups engage in both culturally permissible violence and petty harassment to establish their claim to being "security providers" for the community.

Youth unemployment is very high in Dili, the Timorese capital. Commercial security is the major cash employment sector (that is, aside from subsistence farming. See Ashkenazi and Boemcken, 2011). Every *suco* (neighborhood) in Dili has groups of unemployed young men sitting around, playing football, and generally idle. In Timor Leste, as in many other places in South East Asia, neighborhood/village security is entrusted to young men. This perception still exists. We collected numerous reports of incidents where newcomers (mainly foreigners) to neighborhoods were subject to minor harassments—stones thrown at the roof at night and small items misplaced—until they hired a local guard through the mediation of the *xefe da suco* (neighborhood head).[4]

Traditional security provision is focused on protecting *the community*, not individuals within it. Provided the community's interests are not at stake, a certain amount of violence can be shrugged off. The youth groups may defend themselves and their turf or attack others, so long as the community-first principle is maintained. The groups do so through providing the threat and actuality of force, as well as through ensuring social and even economic support to groups, households, and individuals within the community.

Commerce Is About Profits; Commercial Security Is About. . . .

In 2011, we surveyed commercial security in Timor Leste and Liberia (Boemcken and Ashkenazi, 2011). Crucially, while commercial security seemed to offer a halo effect[5] — commercial guards *did* report on the commission of crimes even in properties they were not protecting — the actual process of protection against deadly force was restricted to their clients, by definition, the richer segment of society. It needs to be mentioned that both societies are extremely poor least developed countries (LDCs).

In Dili, where the institution of neighborhood guards has a lengthy cultural history as noted previously we found a full spectrum of commercial security that blended on the one end with traditional security provision by neighborhood and village youth and on the other with state security provision. Over 9,000 guards employed by three commercial security companies vastly outnumber the 6,000 or so state security organs (military, police, and gendarmerie). To add to that, *some* households hired members of youth groups from the community to protect their property. Most households relied on the presence of the young men in the streets — reinforced by occasional public events and support activities by the neighborhood headmen — for security. At the other end, the commercial security formations were considered, and believed themselves to be a supplementary part of the state security forces. In a third direction, there is evidence that some of the neighborhood youth groups in Dili are adopting a security posture that brings them closer to the fourth corner of potential security formation postures.

Out-laws Want To Be . . .

While a great deal of criminal activity is just that — criminal — some of it must be looked at with more nuance. Out-laws, such as some of the Timorese youth groups and so-called Martial Arts Groups (MAGS), survive by skirting close, or allying themselves with criminal activity (Scambary, 2006). They have been linked to smuggling, prostitution, and street intimidation. Most of these groups *still* claim adherence to traditional norms, and cite the need for *kampong* protection as a cause for their activities.

Other examples can also be found, the most extreme of which is the Lord's Resistance Army (LRA) in Uganda. Led by a charismatic prophet-general, Joseph Kony, the LRA is an offshoot of traditional Acholi conflict management (Allen, 2005). Crucially, because many out-law groups are "wannabe" state authorities, they mix structures and practices of order and disorder. Even out-and-out bandits, as Hobsbawm points out, can be strongly embedded within their societies as providers of security. (2010)

An interview in Dili with the *xefe da suco* of a centrally located neighborhood is instructive:

> I am responsible for order in the <u>suco</u>. The young men want jobs. They see the private security guards make good money, but the demand for such jobs is great, the

supply limited. Some of the young men have started pressuring local merchants to give them jobs as guards. There have been cases of minor irritation—throwing stones and so on—but also cases of major intimidation. If the government wants to ensure peace and law, it should channel some of the money through the <u>suco</u> structure. I know who these young men are, I know the merchants, and I can ensure that the young men do not behave like criminals, and the merchants get the good protection they need for their goods and shops.[6]

This example highlights what would otherwise be called a "hybrid" system, between criminality and traditional security. In practice, I argue, what we are looking at is the fourth of four possible "postures" that any security provider must adopt.

CONFLICT MANAGEMENT AND SECURITY PROVIDERS

The field of conflict management is a growing body of knowledge that is speculative, proven, and, sometimes frankly hopeful. In this section, I want to address the role of security providers in conflict management, as reflected in the literature. As can be seen from the examples above, the role that any particular security provider can play varies extensively. The problem, from a strategic perspective, is that there are many motivations that drive even the purest example of a particular type: a state army or police force, a group of traditional warriors.

The strategic problem of managing conflict thus becomes an exercise in *identifying* what these influences are, what their relative weight is, and how they can be strengthened or weakened (by no means a puerile task), and trying to provide necessary reinforcements to ensure the particular formation is assisting in transforming the conflict in a particular direction. Given that there are often many players in a particular conflict (not all of them security providers, of course), this is a daunting task. To add to the problem, a particular organization can easily morph from one type to another: from state to commercial, for example, or vice versa.

Security Provider Structure Dynamics.

To explain these somewhat different phenomena, and to relate the empirical evidence to the issue of conflict management, it is important to look at the dynamics of security provision as a series of potential points, or "postures" on a plane defined by four ideal types: state, commercial, traditional, and out-law security providers (see Figure 10-1). Under an appropriate external stimulus, any group may drift from a position near one of the ideal poles into a position closer to any of the others. State security providers can become involved in the provision of services-for-cash (commercial security), or into outright predation (out-law security). Traditional security providers can morph into state militias or out-law security providers. Commercial and out-law security providers can approach other roles, including becoming state security apparatuses themselves.

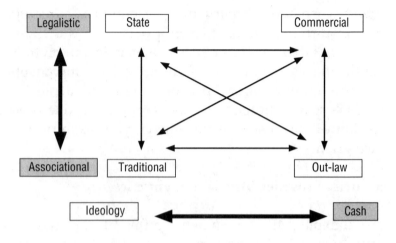

Figure 10-1. Dynamics of Security Formation Type.

Posture.

To clarify what I mean by morphing into another form, I want to introduce a concept I call posture. Posture is a composite of tendencies that position any particular security formation on the two-dimensional surface. Two critical variables (and they may not be the only ones) are financial/ideological motivation and legal/associational motivation. Any randomly selected security formation is influenced by both, albeit to different degrees.

Out-law formations can be influenced largely by cash (in the case of criminal gangs). State security providers by ideology (national police) but there will *always* be some mixture: an ideological or cash component. Similarly, the associational understructure may be based purely on social needs or on legal formulations, but in practice, there is some degree of mix even at the poles.

The dynamics—how an organization changes its posture toward one or another of the poles, depends on what influences the particular organization. "Influenced" in this case means that the organization (or individual) receives rewards in one of those two dimensions. The rewards—which are the equivalent of behaviorist positive reinforcement (Skinner, 1978) may be in cash or in social esteem, authority, services, goods, etc. As the formation accrues more positive reinforcements of one or another of those two variables, its posture (its location on the notional plane) will tend toward one or another of those four types.

Timorese neighborhood defense group A can serve as an example. 'A' essentially has four models to follow. One is that of a pure neighborhood defense group (rewarded by social esteem, some handouts, and wide social network support). The other is as a commercial company (rewarded by cash, and by social and presentation benefits). The third is out-law, in which cash rewards and individual machismo constitute the major rewards. As a state mandated group, the rewards are access to power, public ideological support ("defenders of the nation"), job security, and potential promotion. We can examine the group's options in terms of the kinds of reinforcement they receive and can foresee receiving. In practice, a neighborhood youth group receives a certain amount of social recognition and support. However, this is diffuse, highly conditional (on their being trouble-free), and does not solve the major problem of most members: making a living. The possibility of becoming a state group is nonexistent: the state is poor, and state security formations have been filled by former guerillas (in the army, police, and gendarmerie). This particular neighborhood in the center of Dili, does have, however, a resource: a commercial sector of small and larger retail shops. Cash reinforcement can be manufactured by offering security services to local merchants, and when these do not agree to pay the (nominal) fee, incidents can be arranged to demonstrate that security by the local youth group is really necessary. Now, this would be simply a tale of extortion (that is, the traditional group is changing its posture to out-law) except for the intervention of the *xefe da suco* and his council. These have argued *against both the merchants and the youth group* that the youth group has a traditional role to play in neighborhood security, and that the merchants must pay for this service, via the traditional neighborhood administration. Community members, on the whole, agree with this formulation (and indeed, so do the merchants). The youth group is on the verge of becoming an extortionate network. However, by reasserting the authority of the *suco*, the *xefe* offers them a lower income but additional social reinforcement. Had he not done so, the youth group would have become an extortionate gang, (as have others in Dili).

Conflict management depends highly on being able to offer combatants or opposed sides reinforcement for appropriate behavior. Reinforce aggression and violence, and groups will become more aggressive and violent, *and* other groups, too, will become aggressive and violent. Moreover, contemporary conflict management is highly reliant on an assumption that the four types of security providers *will act as they do in Western societies, including the United States*; that is, that they are close to their Weberian ideal type. This is not necessarily the case. Professional commercial security organizations in Timor and in Liberia see themselves as an informal, but nevertheless essential, part of the state security apparatus. The Lou Nuer White Army see themselves as protecting traditional privilege and activity, not as out-laws. Indeed, both of these types of security provider (as well as others such as the police in Georgia and Albania) have multiple reinforcements and consequently multiple roles.

POLICY IMPLICATIONS

What policy implications can we draw about conflict management from the above? There are three general implications we need to keep in mind.

1. Security providers (whether the individuals who make them up or the groups that structure individual activity) operate on the basis of a variety of reinforcements. Economic reinforcements are important, even crucial, but other factors such as social approval have great consequences as well.

2. The more reinforcements of a particular sort are received, the more the form of the security provider morphs toward a particular pole: offering cash to traditional security providers will very quickly bring them to adopt a commercial posture. Reduce their prestige and social approval, and they easily become out-law.

3. As with all forms of reinforcement, there is a need to refresh reinforcement from time to time. In the real world, this means one cannot say, "the job is done," and turn away.

We also need to recognize some more specific issues having to do with the connection between security providers and conflict management. Crucially, since the posture adopted by a security provider is plastic, the time and resource dimensions need to be assessed. To ensure that security providers have a posture that supports the goal of conflict management, one needs to ensure that *resources can be allocated for the long time*; that is, not years, but decades. This implies, in the interests of continuity, that these resources are generated from inside the system (the state or community) and not gifted from the outside, since the latter will, inevitably, end. Second, working on that basis, we can look at how security providers can be induced to participate in conflict management. Conflict management is a practice that emerges from and reflects internal dynamics, while also affecting them. The situation will remain dynamic and unstable, unless underlying issues, which push potential security providers into other profiles, are dealt with society-wide. While external reinforcements may be necessary, what is desirable are internally generated reinforcements that will ensure a more-or-less homeostatic situation of low or no conflict.

REFERENCES

Allen, Tim. 2005. *War And Justice In Northern Uganda: An Assessment Of The International Criminal Court's Intervention*. London, UK: London School of Economics.

Ashkenazi, Michael and Marc von Boemcken. 2011. "Timor Leste." Pp. 21-34 in Marc von Boemcken, ed., *Commercial Security and Development Findings from Timor-Leste, Liberia and Peru*. Brief 45. Bonn, Germany: Bonn International Center for Conversion (BICC).

Aureli, Filippo, and Frans de Waal. 2000. *Natural Conflict Resolution*. Berkeley, CA: University of California Press.

Barth, Fredrik. 1959. *Political Leadership among Swat Pathans*. London, UK: School of Economics Monographs on Social Anthropology. The Athlone Press.

Bercovitch, Jacob, and Richard Jackson. 2009. *Conflict Resolution in the Twenty-First Century: Principles, Methods, and Approaches*. Ann Arbor, MI: University of Michigan Press.

Evans-Pritchard, E. E. 1949. "Two Nuer Ritual Concepts." *Man*, Vol. 49. pp. 74-76.

Eide, Espen Barth, Anja Therese Kaspersen, Randolph Kent, and Karin von Hippel. 2005. *Report on Integrated Missions: Practical Perspectives and Recommendation*. ESS Reports. New York: United Nations.

Franke, Volker C. 1997. "Warriors for Peace: The Next Generation of U.S. Military Leaders." *Armed Forces & Society*, Vol. 24, No. 1, pp. 33–57.

Guthrie, Stewart Joseph Agassi, Karin R. Andriolo, David Buchdahl, H. Byron Earhart, Moshe Greenberg, Ian Jarvie, Benson Saler, John Saliba, Kevin J. Sharpe and Gambetta, Diego. 1996. *The Sicilian Mafia: The Business of Private Protection*. Cambridge, MA: Harvard University Press.

Hensell, Stephan. 2011. "Privatizing the Police: The Political Economy of Law Enforcement in Eastern Europe." *Security and Peace*, Vol. 4, pp. 237-243.

Hobsbawm, Eric J. 1992. "Inventing Tradition," pp. 1-14, in Hobsbawm, Eric J., and Terence O. Ranger, eds., *The Invention of Tradition*. Cambridge, MA: Cambridge University Press.

Hobsbawm, Eric J. 2010. *Bandits*. London, UK: Weidenfeld & Nicolson.

Huysmans, Jef. 1998. "Security! What Do You Mean? From Concept to Thick Signifier." *European Journal of International Relations*, Vol. 4, No. 2, June 1, 1998, pp. 226–255.

Kondoch, Boris. 2001. December 1. "The United Nations Administration of East Timor." *Journal of Conflict and Security Law*, Vol. 6, No. 2 December 1, 2001, pp. 245-265. doi:10.1093/jcsl/6.2.245.

Krahmann, Elke. 2008. "Security: Collective Good or Commodity?" *European Journal of International Relations*, Vol. 14, No. 3, pp. 379–404.

Mandel, Robert. 2001. "The Privatization of Security." *Armed Forces & Society*, Vol. 28, No. 1, pp. 129 –151.

Miall, Hugh, Oliver Ramsbotham, and Tom Woodhouse. 1999. *Contemporary Conflict Resolution: The Prevention, Management and Transformation of Deadly Conflicts*. Hoboken, NJ: Wiley-Blackwell.

Scambary, James. 2006. *A Survey of Gangs and Youth Groups in Dili, Timor-Leste*. Canberra, Australia: AusAID.

Shearing, Clifford and Jennifer Wood. 2007. *Imagining Security*. Portland, OR: Willan.

Skinner, B. F. 1978. *Reflections on Behaviorism and Society*. Englewood Cliffs, NJ: Prentice-Hall.

Smith, Daniel Jordan. 2004. August. "The Bakassi Boys: Vigilantism, Violence, and Political Imagination in Nigeria." *Cultural Anthropology*, Vol. 19, No. 3, pp. 429–455.

Tissot, Georges. 1980. "A Cognitive Theory of Religion [and Comments and Reply]." *Current Anthropology*, Vol. 21, No. 2, pp. 181-203.

ENDNOTES - CHAPTER 10

1. The hyphen is intentional, since a major characteristic of these formations is that they operate outside government or local legal sanction.

2. Question to the American readers: could you itemize this as a valid expense for the IRS?

3. The Bakassi Boys in Nigeria (Smith 2004), who provide security, but also engage in extortion are one example. A nascent system evolving in Dili, Timor Leste, is described below.

4. It should be noted that these guards take their job seriously, and that given their ability to rapidly mobilize their peers, *and* the social supervision of the neighborhood elders, the service rendered is quite good.

5. That is, security is enhanced even in properties not formally protected by the hired guards, since the mere presence of a uniformed observer tends to deter crime.

6. "Author's diaries. Interview with xefe da suco "C', August 6, 2010."

CHAPTER 11

MASS ATROCITY PREVENTION AND RESPONSE OPTIONS: ADDRESSING THE POLICY CHALLENGES

Dwight Raymond

BACKGROUND

Strategy entails choices to integrate ends, ways, and means in order to pursue national interests that are often conflicting. The *National Security Strategy* states:

> The United States is committed to working with our allies, and to strengthening our own internal capabilities, in order to ensure that the United States and the international community are proactively engaged in a strategic effort to prevent mass atrocities and genocide.[1]

Also referenced in documents such as the *Quadrennial Defense Review* (QDR) and the *Quadrennial Diplomacy and Development Review* (QDDR), mass atrocity prevention has been more recently emphasized in a Presidential Study Directive on Mass Atrocities (PSD-10) and subsequent governmental efforts to respond to the PSD. PSD-10 states that "Preventing mass atrocities and genocide is a core national security interest and a core moral responsibility of the United States" and "requires a level of governmental organization that matches the methodical organization characteristic of mass killings."[2]

This chapter describes a policy formulation methodology and relevant considerations contained in *Mass Atrocity Prevention and Response Options (MAPRO): A*

Policy Planning Handbook, which is intended to help policymakers address these issues comprehensively. After providing an overview of mass atrocities, it identifies guidelines, a proposed framework for policy formulation, interests, how elements of national influence can be employed, and the risks and challenges associated with efforts to prevent or respond to mass atrocities.

One of the prominent themes of mass atrocity literature is that national governments and the rest of the international community are disposed toward inaction.[3] This is due to several factors, such as competing national interests that dissuade action, risk-averse decisionmaking and bureaucracies that support *status quo* approaches, and the often-complex context of potential problems that may not be reducible to a clearcut case of stopping identifiable evil perpetrators and protecting innocent victims. As described in one masterpiece of political satire, governments often appear to follow a four-stage approach to crisis management:

- Stage 1: We say that nothing is going to happen.
- Stage 2: We say that something may be going to happen, but we should do nothing about it.
- Stage 3: We say that maybe we should do something about it, but there is nothing we can do.
- Stage 4: We say that maybe there was something we could have done but it is too late now.[4]

The list of mass atrocities since the end of the Cold War is disturbing, including Rwanda, Srebrenica, Sierra Leone, East Timor, Darfur, other parts of the Sudan, South Sudan, the Congo, Sri Lanka, the Lord's

Resistance Army (LRA) activities in Uganda and elsewhere, and others. In part because of these crises, and the checkered results of the international community in addressing them, an expanding community of interest has developed on the Protection of Civilians (PoC) in general and mass atrocity prevention in particular. This community of interest includes past and present representatives of national governments, human rights advocates, scholars, international organizations, nongovernmental organizations (NGOs), and the media. The United Nations (UN) and some national governments have created focal points to coordinate collective efforts regarding mass atrocity prevention and response. Other developments have also contributed to improving the international community's will and capacity to address mass atrocities.

Despite continuing harsh criticism of the UN, to include from some of its staunchest advocates, that institution has been steadily pursuing peacekeeping reform initiatives since the 2000 *Brahimi Report on UN Peace Operations*, which essentially concluded that without marked transformation, the UN would recede into irrelevance. Subsequent related efforts include the "New Horizons" report, the *Considerations for Mission Leadership in United Nations Peacekeeping Operations*, and emphasis on PoC and robust peacekeeping.

In 2001, the International Commission on Intervention and State Sovereignty (ICISS) released *The Responsibility to Protect*,[5] a study that changed the terms of the debate about when outside actors have the right to intervene in a sovereign country's internal affairs. The ICISS report concluded that sovereignty implies responsibility and, in the case of serious harm when the state is unwilling or unable to protect its population from extreme harm, the principle of nonintervention yields to the international responsibility to protect. The report developed a three-stage approach for the responsibility to protect, including prevention, reaction, and rebuilding.

The Responsibility to Protect concept (also known as R2P or RTP) was subsequently endorsed at the 2005 UN General Assembly Summit and, within the UN, later evolved into a framework of three "pillars:"[6]

- Pillar 1: Protection Responsibilities of the State.
- Pillar 2: International Assistance and Capacity-Building.
- Pillar 3: Timely and Decisive Response.

In 2008, the first UN Special Adviser on the Responsibility to Protect who collaborates closely with the Special Adviser on the Prevention of Genocide (first appointed in 2004), was designated. Despite tangible steps toward institutionalizing R2P, however, many have strong reservations about its implications for state sovereignty, its potential license for intervention, and the extent to which "responsibility" translates into a legal international obligation to act.

In the United States as well, incremental steps have been taken to improve the government's coherence regarding mass atrocity prevention and response. The most noteworthy catalyst was the 2008 Genocide Prevention Task Force (GPTF) report, *Preventing Genocide*, which included 34 recommendations.[7] Since the publication of the GPTF report, government documents, including the *National Security Strategy*, the QDR, and the QDDR, have referenced mass atrocities. On December 22, 2010, Senate Concurrent Resolution 71 on Genocide Prevention provided additional emphasis, and PSD-10 specified the creation of an Atrocity Prevention Board, in accordance with a GPTF recommendation.

Mass atrocity mitigation is also included in military references including the Guidance for the Employment of the Force (GEF) and the Army Operating Concept. The 2010 publication of the unofficial Mass Atrocity Response Operations (MARO) military planning handbook was followed by a MARO appendix in the new *Joint Publication (JP) 3-07.3 Peace Operations*.[8] These documents are intended to assist military commanders and staffs in the planning and conduct of operations to prevent and respond to mass atrocities.

The MAPRO Handbook[9] was published in March 2012 as a reference for members of the policy community. It is intended to support recommendations from the GPTF report and to assist with the implementation of PSD-10's intent by supporting informed and structured policy formulation. The Handbook addresses considerations for mass atrocity situations, describes a policy formulation process, and provides templates that can be adjusted as necessary. While it primarily addresses mass atrocity situations (arguably the worst-case threats to peace and development), much of the Handbook is also applicable to other complex situations involving conflict because many of the national interests, actors, policy processes, potential lines of effort, and potential elements of national influence are similar. Indeed, mass atrocity situations will often have to be addressed as a part of the wider context within which they occur, such as insurgencies, civil war, or interstate conflict.

MASS ATROCITY PREVENTION AND RESPONSE OPTIONS

Genocide was defined at the 1948 Convention on the Prevention and Punishment of the Crime of Genocide as:

> any of the following acts committed with intent to destroy, in whole or in part, a national, ethnical, racial or religious group, as such: Killing members of the group; causing serious bodily or mental harm to members of the group; deliberately inflicting on the group conditions of life calculated to bring about its physical destruction in whole or in part; Imposing measures intended to prevent births within the group; Forcibly transferring children of the group to another group.[10]

It notably includes intent to eliminate some groups. Strictly speaking, genocide does not apply when an eliminationist intent is not present, or if the groups targeted for elimination fall outside of the categories included in the definition (e.g., political groups, economic classes, sexual orientation, or others).

A mass atrocity may be defined as:

> Widespread and systematic acts of violence against noncombatants including killing; causing serious bodily or mental harm; or deliberately inflicting conditions of life that cause serious bodily or mental harm.[11]

Mass atrocities include genocides as well as cases that are excluded by the 1948 definition of genocide. There can be a blurry line between mass atrocities and other problematic situations such as atrocities, massacres, political violence, and large scale human rights violations. Additionally, atrocities can include acts such as rape and torture, and are not necessarily limited to killing.

MAPRO may be defined as:

U.S. Government efforts to anticipate and prevent when possible and — if prevention fails — to respond by mitigating or stopping genocide or mass atrocities.[12]

MAPRO includes relevant policies and programs regarding general government capacity and its efforts regarding particular mass atrocity situations. Mass Atrocity Response Operations (MARO) is a related subset of MAPRO and refers to "Military activities conducted across the operational spectrum to prevent or halt mass atrocities."[13]

MAPRO Guidelines.

Effective policymaking for mass atrocity mitigation should adhere to the following six guidelines:
- Prevention is preferable to response.
- The United States has a wide range of diplomatic, informational, military, and economic tools that should be considered and integrated.
- Policymakers must understand the complete context of the situation.
- Quick action is important to address concerns and take advantage of opportunities.
- Multilateral efforts are preferable to unilateral action.
- Planning for transitions and endstates should begin as early as possible.

Prevention Is Preferable to Response.

Prevention is superior to response for three main reasons, the first of which is that effective prevention implies that large-scale human suffering has been avoided. The second reason is that the resources required for prevention are likely to be modest in comparison to those required for a major intervention and post-crisis reconstruction. Finally, prevention precludes the requirement to obtain political and international support that could prove elusive when a controversial response is contemplated. Prevention, however, poses its own challenges; it requires a pre-crisis investment of attention and resources that must compete with other issues that may be more immediate.

The United States Has a Wide Range of Diplomatic, Informational, Military, and Economic Tools that Should Be Considered and Integrated.

The GPTF report famously stated that the United States has "a wide range of options between the extremes of doing nothing and sending in the Marines."[14] Various diplomatic, informational, military, and economic (DIME) measures can mitigate mass atrocity situations by addressing underlying conditions; exposing, dissuading, stopping, isolating, or punishing perpetrators and their enablers; establishing the resolve, credibility, and capability of the U.S. Government or the international community; protecting or empowering potential victims; diminishing perpetrator motivation or capability to conduct mass atrocities; or convincing bystanders and other actors to take constructive action or refrain from supporting perpetrators. It should be noted that military tools are not limited to coercive interventions; lesser operations can be quite useful in supporting diplomacy.

Policymakers Must Understand the Complete
Context of the Situation.

A mass atrocity situation will frequently occur within the context of a broader conflict such as civil war, insurgency, or interstate conflict. Regional and international dynamics will be relevant, and a particular situation will both be influenced by recent experiences and will influence future situations (e.g., the 1994 international response to Rwanda was in part shaped by experiences in Somalia, and Libya 2011 subsequently affected Syria in 2012). Policymakers must understand the different actors (perpetrators, victims, interveners, bystanders, positive actors, and negative actors), although actual categorization to include perpetrators who may have some legitimate or understandable objectives and that their cooperation may be required to achieve a peaceful settlement. They must also comprehend the geographic, political, military, economic, social, infrastructure, and informational considerations (especially those that affect conflict dynamics). Local and community contexts will often be significant.

Quick Action Is Important to Address Concerns
and Take Advantage of Opportunities.

Country teams are often in the best position to monitor developments and act expeditiously, while anticipating unintended second-order effects. Delayed action may encourage perpetrators, allowing them time to build strength and mobilize, while allowing potential victims to become even more vulnerable. Appropriate quick action is facilitated by a responsive policy formulation process that efficiently provides information and options to senior decision makers and secures their rapid guidance and decisions.

Multilateral Efforts Are Preferable to Unilateral Action.

Multilateral prevention and response efforts tend to have greater legitimacy, reduce the likelihood that U.S. DIME measures will be diluted by circumvention, spread the cost and burden of the actions (and any post-conflict stabilization efforts), and reduce the likelihood of negative consequences, such as regional anti-Americanism that might arise from a unilateral approach. Moreover, some nations may be more capable than the United States of taking effective action in some situations. A UN Security Council Resolution provides the preferred level of mandate legitimacy. In its absence (for example, if a resolution is vetoed by one of the permanent five members), majority votes in either the Security Council or General Assembly or backing from a regional or sub-regional organization may be an acceptable alternative.

Planning for Transitions and Endstates Should Begin As Early As Possible.

The main focus in a mass atrocity situation is to prevent or halt the atrocities. However, policymakers may also have to address the aftermath including: prevention of mass atrocity recurrence; the root causes of the crisis; or achieving a peaceful, stable, and just political settlement. The former government may or may not remain in power. The country's territory may or may not remain under unified governance. Perpetrators may or may not be brought to justice, and compensation to victims may or may not be arranged. Policymakers in the U.S. Government, other national governments, and international organizations should develop plans and make the necessary arrangements regarding post-crisis roles, responsibilities, and authorities. Situations and plans are likely to change, but policymakers ideally should shape these changes rather than merely watch them occur.

MAPRO Policy Planning.

The MAPRO Policy and Planning Framework generally conforms with various interagency planning processes that have been advanced in recent years. It is suitable both during deliberate contingency planning for hypothetical situations as well as when planning for short-term crisis situations. The MAPRO Handbook supplements the framework with formats and examples of planning products, such as briefings and memoranda, which can be tailored as necessary. While such guidance may seem mundane and pedantic, it is useful for structuring efforts and to minimize floundering.[15]

MAPRO Policy and Planning Framework.

Continuous situational understanding is critical, and it is particularly important to have an appreciation of relevant actors and the U.S. national interests. Actors may, however loosely, be categorized as perpetrators, victims, interveners, and others (including bystanders, positive actors, and negative actors).[16]

U.S. national interests in a specific situation will be among the most important determinants in formulating policy. These interests may often conflict with each other and policy should reflect how the interests are balanced and weighted. Mass atrocity situations are likely to involve any of the following national interests:[17]

- Escalation or resumption of violence is prevented.
- Conflict spillover into the wider region is avoided.
- Effects on transnational issues such as terrorism are minimized.
- Timely and effective humanitarian aid is provided to save lives and alleviate suffering.
- Rights of refugees, displaced persons, and vulnerable populations are protected.
- Political stability and good governance are supported.
- Economic interests are secured by promoting stability and rule of law, or by averting crisis.
- U.S. citizens and property are protected.
- U.S. actions do not have unacceptable adverse impact upon relations with allies, regional countries, or other nations.
- The international community, (particularly the UN or relevant regional organization) takes appropriate action in concert with the United States.
- The United States acts in accordance with its values and maintains its credibility and legitimacy.
- Refugee/Internally Displaced Persons/humanitarian crisis is avoided.
- U.S. willingness to protect civilians and support international laws and norms is demonstrated.
- Perpetrators are delegitimized.
- Human rights violators are brought to justice.
- Terrorist threats are reduced.
- The anticipated costs (including money, personnel, and other resources) of U.S. actions are acceptable.

A MAPRO plan may be structured in accordance with Figure 11-1. A key inference is that thoughtful advance planning may result in effective prevention measures that preclude any need to implement the later stages of the plan.[18]

Phase I: Prevention
- Stage IA: Steady-State Engagement
- Stage IB: Targeted Prevention
- Stage IC: Crisis Management

Phase II: Response
- Stage IIA: Stop Mass Atrocities
- Stage IIB: Stabilization

Phase III: Transition
- Stage IIIA: Build Host Nation Capacity
- Stage III B: Transition to Steady-State Posture

Figure 11-1. Suggested MAPRO Plan Phases.

A MAPRO plan should address the critical Lines of Effort (LOEs) that comprise the necessary and sufficient elements (or functions) required for success. The LOEs should include a concept for implementation, relevant activities and objectives, and lead and supporting agencies. A representative set of LOEs may include the following:
- Situation Understanding;
- Diplomacy & Strategic Communication;
- Unity of Effort;
- Military Efforts;
- Economic Efforts;
- Safe and Secure Environment;
- Governance and Rule of Law;
- Social Well-Being.[19]

APPLYING THE ELEMENTS OF NATIONAL INFLUENCE

Approaches to mitigate a mass atrocity situation may be broadly categorized as *suasion,* which involves persuasion, dissuasion, and deterrence; *compellence,* which incorporates higher levels of pressure and sanctions; and *intervention,* in which a solution is imposed to include through the use of coercive military force. In practice, these approaches may not have clear distinctions between them. During a response, the role of discrete actors such as the United States could, in turn, be generally viewed as that of a *bystander, enabler* of other actors, *leader of a multinational effort,* or *unilateral actor.* The approach and role of U.S. efforts will be determined by U.S. interests; the urgency of the situation; other issues that must be addressed; the potential leverage possessed by the United States and other actors; the likelihood that the United States can achieve constructive results without undesired second-order consequences, domestic political considerations, and the opinion and actions of the international community including the UN and regional organizations.

A wide array of DIME tools can be employed to prevent, respond to, and aid in the recovery from mass atrocity situations. Many of these are included in Figure 11-2, and are roughly grouped in accordance with the general approach that the tools support. In general, "suasion tools" are less resource-intensive, incur less risk, and are not as intrusive on host nation sovereignty as are the "compellence" and "intervention" tools. They can be integrated into a "carrot-and-stick" approach and, of course, there is no requirement to exhaust all less extreme measures before firmer tools are attempted.

308

	DIPLOMATIC	INFORMATIONAL	MILITARY	ECONOMIC
SUASION	•Pressure/Inducements/Contacts •Informal Negotiations •Fact Finding Missions •Coalition/Consensus Building •IGO/NGO Coordination •USG Planning/Augment Embassy •Meet with Victims •Formal Negotiations •Speeches/Leader Engagements •Mediation •Use Intermediaries •Summits •Coalition Building •UNSC Resolutions	•Policy Statements •Strategic Comm Program •Media Relations •Conflict Assessment •Information Sharing •Enhanced Media Activities •Influence Local Civil Society •Arts Promotion •Congressional Testimony •"MAPRO Orchestra"	•Theater Security Cooperation •Security Assistance •Exercises •Port Visits •Other Military Support to: • Deter Perpetrators • Support Diplomacy with Credible Threats	•Foreign Aid •Debt Relief •Other Economic Support to incentivize perpetrators and their enablers
SANCTION	•Travel Bans •Travel Advisories •State Sponsor Terrorism List •Reduce Embassy/Consulates •Criminal Investigations •International Law Enforcement •Extradition/Legal Actions •Amnesty/Immunity •Restrict Diplomatic Activity •Culture/Sporting Events •Isolation •Recognize Opposition Groups •Recall Ambassador •Break Diplomatic Relations •Noncombatant Evac Ops •Enabler Sanctions •Ultimatums	•Human Rights Monitoring •Atrocity Reporting System •Increased Intelligence Gathering •HUMINT Networks •Gain Control of Media	•Force Activation •Increased Alert Status •Deployment Preparations •Expanded Military Presence •Basing Arrangements •Expanded ISR •Blockade or Quarantine •Shows of Force •Headquarters Deployment	•Technology Controls •Exchange Rate Adjustment •IMF/World Bank Advocacy •Trade Policy Alteration •Freeze/Seize Assets •Foreign Direct Investment •Embargoes •International Sanctions
INTERVENTION	•Treaty Compliance •Stationing/Overflight Rights •Other Diplomatic Support: • Mandates • Legitimacy • Int'l Support • End Conflict • Post-Conflict Preparations	•Electronic Countermeasures • Jamming/disrupting • Cyber •Military Info Spt Ops (MISO) •Release Intelligence •Truth and Reconciliation Commissions •Other Information Support to: • Build/Maintain Int'l Support • Divide Perpetrators • Encourage Positive Actors • Support Operations • Capitalize on Success • Mitigate Setbacks • Manage Expectations • Set Post-Conflict Conditions	•MISO •Combat Camera •No Fly Zones •Mine Clearance •NEO •Limited Temporary Intervention •Humanitarian Assistance •Electronic Warfare •SOF Operations •Strikes/Raids •Coercive Military Intervention	•Humanitarian Assistance •Other Economic Support to: • Support Victim Groups • Support Partners • Support Regional Countries • Post-conflict R&S Efforts

Figure 11-2. Diplomatic, Informational, Military, and Economic (DIME) Tools.[20]

The *MAPRO Handbook* discusses several "cross-cutting considerations" when policy is formulated and DIME tools are applied. These are:

- Host Nation Ownership and Capacity;
- Political Primacy;
- Legitimacy;
- Unity of Effort;
- Security;
- Conflict Transformation;
- Regional/International Engagement;
- Strategic Communication.[21]

Policymakers will be confronted with hard choices and tough decisions during a mass atrocity situation, and the decisions are apt to become more challenging as circumstances change and the situation develops. It will be difficult to predict the outcome with any real certainty, requiring continual reassessment of the problems, the desired endstate, and the solution set. Some of the potential anticipated policy decisions are as follows:

- Whether to treat the host nation government as a partner or adversary.
- How to handle setbacks (e.g., mass atrocities that occur).
- Whether to commit additional resources.
- Whether to transition from one phase to another.
- When to transfer responsibility to another actor (e.g., the UN or host nation).
- Whether to modify the plan radically (e.g., change objectives).
- Whether to intervene (in fact or appearance) on one side of the conflict.
- Whether to await a UN Security Council Resolution.

- Whether to intervene without a clear exit strategy.
- Whether to develop or implement a branch plan.
- Whether and to what extent to accommodate concerns expressed by other actors.
- How to gain/sustain domestic and international support.
- Whether to sacrifice political goals, such as bringing perpetrators to justice, to stop conflict or maximize humanitarian benefit.

MAPRO-related decisions will incur risks regardless of whether action is taken or not taken. Policymakers should attempt to anticipate the major risks (that is, what can go wrong?) and identify measures to lessen the probability of the risks or their impact if they, in fact, materialize. Negative second-order effects are particularly difficult to predict.[22] In some cases, policymakers will have to accept risk, but they should do so with an understanding both of the risks and the potential consequences. Some of the general potential risks in a mass atrocity situation include the following:

- Ineffectiveness (especially if actions are too little or too late).
- Unintended Escalation.
- Collateral Damage.
- Anti-Americanism or Anti-American Sentiment.
- Quagmire and Mission Creep.
- Losses.
- Increased Resistance because of Pride or Nationalism.
- Politicization of Humanitarian Assistance.

- Negative Second-Order Effects.
- Risks of Inaction.

RECOGNIZING THE MAPRO CHALLENGES

There are three inherent difficulties associated with a mass atrocity situation: (1) recognizing that a genocide or mass atrocity situation potentially exists; (2) deciding what to do about it, and (3) mobilizing, deploying, employing, and orchestrating the complex set of resources necessary to address the situation.

The first difficulty can be partially remedied by institutional measures such as identifying, monitoring, and interpreting early warnings and indicators. Part of the solution includes responsive information sharing with other governments, international organizations such as the UN, NGOs, and civil society within the country of interest. However, policymakers and their constituencies will demand a high level of certainty regarding mass atrocity situations, and perfect information will never be possible (particularly for events that have not yet occurred or which may be masked by an existing background of political violence or human rights violations). Perpetrators will also conceal, obfuscate, deny, minimize, or rationalize their actions (e.g., claiming that any casualties are insurgents or violent protestors, not helpless victims).

The MAPRO Handbook is intended to assist policymakers as they wrestle with MAPRO decisions and the associated risks by providing a rational yet feasible process for contingency planning as well as crisis response. The framework discussed in the Handbook is generally suitable for other interagency planning efforts that require a structured approach to complex strategic issues. By itself, however, it is not a panacea for effective government action to prevent and respond to mass atrocities. It can support the necessary fusion of three governmental groups: those in government who are experts about a particular country or region, those who focus on transnational functional matters (such as international law, financial sanctions, war crimes, military operations, or peacekeeping), and those who make policy decisions within an extremely diverse portfolio.

Effective policy planning requires a modest commitment of resources, perhaps not quite "a level of governmental organization that matches the methodical organization characteristic of mass killings,"[23] but the resources are needed nonetheless. The rudimentary requirements include dedicated planning space, a handful of dedicated planners with senior leader access and clearly delineated authorities (particularly necessary when mass atrocities are but one dimension of a complex situation and multiple department and intergovernmental agencies are stakeholders), and the active participation of other "part-time" planners who contribute their expertise when needed.

More importantly, planning's effectiveness hinges on senior leader involvement. Senior leaders must devote the time to understand the planning process and plans (shaping both as they so desire), provide guidance, approve planning products, make decisions, and ensure that their organizations are providing adequate support and participation. If senior leaders are not involved in policy planning and do not seriously expect a high quality process, they in effect are saying that they do think that planning is really that important. If they do not think it is important, it will not be.

ENDNOTES - CHAPTER 11

1. *National Security Strategy*, Washington, DC: The White House, May 2010, p. 48.

2. Barack Obama, *Presidential Study Directive on Mass Atrocities*, Washington, DC: The White House, available from *www.whitehouse.gov/the-press-office/2011/08/04/presidential-study-directive-mass-atrocities*.

3. See, for example, Samantha Power, *A Problem from Hell*, New York: Basic Books, 2002.

4. Antony Jay and Jonathan Lynn, *Yes Prime Minister*, Topsfield, MA: Salem House Publishers, 1986, p. 160.

5. International Commission on Intervention and State Sovereignty, *The Responsibility to Protect*, Ottawa, Canada: International Development Research Center, 2001.

6. United Nations General Assembly, Report of the Secretary General A/63/677, *Implementing the Responsibility to Protect*, New York: The United Nations, January 12, 2009.

7. Genocide Prevention Task Force, Madeleine K. Albright and William S. Cohen, Co-Chairs, *Preventing Genocide: A Blueprint for U.S. Policymakers*, Washington, DC: The United States Holocaust Memorial Museum, The American Academy of Diplomacy, and the Endowment of the United States Institute of Peace, 2008.

8. Sarah Sewell, Dwight Raymond, and Sally Chin, *Mass Atrocity Response Operations (MARO): A Military Planning Handbook*, Cambridge, MA: The President and Fellows of Harvard College, 2010.

9. Dwight Raymond, Cliff Bernath, Don Braum, and Ken Zurcher, *Mass Atrocity Prevention and Response Options (MAPRO): A Policy Planning Handbook*, Carlisle, PA: Peacekeeping and Stability Operations Institute, U.S. Army War College 2012, available from *pksoi.army.mil/PKM/publications/collaborative/collaborativereview.cfm?collaborativeID=11*.

10. The text of the Genocide Convention is available from *www.hrweb.org/legal/genocide.html.*

11. *MAPRO Handbook,* p. 10.

12. *Ibid.*

13. *Joint Publication (JP) 3-07.3, Peace Operations,* Draft, p. GL-5.

14. GPTF, p. xvii.

15. See *MAPRO Handbook,* Part II and Annex D.

16. *Ibid.,* pp. 27-29.

17. *Ibid.,* pp. 32-32.

18. *Ibid.,* pp. 61-64.

19. *Ibid.,* pp. 53-54.

20. *Ibid.,* p. 84. See pp. 84-120 for a brief description of each of the tools.

21. See *MAPRO Handbook,* pp. 73-77, for discussion of the cross-cutting considerations.

22. For example, a second-order effect of the 2011 Libyan intervention was the 2012 coup in Mali; mercenaries employed by the Gaddafi regime left Libya with large quantities of heavy weapons and joined the Tuareg insurgency. Mali military officers, contending that their government was not providing adequate resources to counter the insurgents, overthrew the democratically-elected President.

23. Obama, *Presidential Study Directive on Mass Atrocities (PSD)-10,* August 4, 2011.

CHAPTER 12

THE UNITED STATES, CHINA, AND INDIA IN THE NEW WORLD ORDER: CONSEQUENCES FOR EUROPE

Liselotte Odgaard

INTRODUCTION

In the debate on a new world order, policymakers and analysts appear to focus on three developments. First, the U.S. reorientation away from the Atlantic to the Pacific is at the center of the debate. This reorientation has come about because the geographical center of gravity in the new world order has moved away from Europe with the implosion of the Soviet Union, and over to Asia with the rising power of countries such as China and India. This development raises the question of the extent to which Washington will pursue Asian integration into the existing world order or, alternatively, treat Asia's rising powers as opponents. The growing economic challenges faced by the United States make it clear that in the coming decades, Washington will increasingly direct its resources toward Asia. Second, China's growing economic and military capabilities are major topics in the debate on the future world order. The economic reform process that was set in motion under the leadership of Deng Xiaoping in 1978 has led to consistently high economic growth rates and a military modernization process that has caused the rest of the world to consider the extent to which China will embrace or reject the liberal international order of integration. Third, subsequently India has joined the club of rising economic powers, with annual economic growth rates of 8-9 percent.[1] This development has raised the issue of whether India might gradually overtake China as the main rising power.

This chapter makes the argument that the U.S. pursuit of an integrationist world order and China's pursuit of a coexistence world order will dominate the future world order. India and Europe will be takers rather than makers of order, facing the challenge of carving out a position in-between these two competing world orders. The remainder of the chapter first outlines the characteristics of the integrationist value-based order pursued by the United States. Second, I describe the characteristics of the coexistence interest-based order pursued by China.[2] Third, I argue that India's rise is limited and does not translate into growing strategic influence on the future world order. Fourth, I discuss the implications for Europe of an order dominated by two incoherent alternatives.

THE US INTEGRATIONIST WORLD ORDER

The United States pursues a strategy of influence suitable for a great power that aims to consolidate the existing world order beyond its position of superior power. The United States remains the only full-blown global great power, with a gross domestic product (GDP) of $14.256 trillion in 2010, which is approximately three times as large as China's GDP of $5.068 trillion in 2010.[3] Militarily, superior capabilities, combined with a global alignment system, means that U.S. power projection remains second to none, and this system forms the principal basis for Washington's world-wide politico-strategic influence. At the same time, the United States is a great power in decline, with estimates of U.S. GDP at only two-thirds of China's

GDP in 2050, if current economic growth rates continue to apply.[4] Although this time frame is too long to predict that Washington will lose its status as a global great power, these prospects influence Washington's concern to consolidate the existing world order. In particular, the United States is concerned to preserve its influence on right and wrong international conduct beyond its position of dominant power.[5]

The United States took the lead in formulating Western political aspirations as a program aiming at enhancing international integration.[6] The world order pursued by the United States is based on liberal values, and its central principles are well-known. These are, first, that market economic structures form the basis of international integration because they engender transnational links, which allegedly promote greater wealth for all. The liberal idea of the market entails that economic growth is the road to prosperity. This economic philosophy implies that the state plays a minor role in the economy, which allows the decisions of market agents to engender the most effective use of resources. A second principle is that democracy engenders peace and stability by virtue of its reliance on popular opinion and checks and balances on political authorities. The liberal idea of democracy declares that the people are sovereign and that the will of the people is respected by means of the right to elect representatives for the management of political authority. In essence, the liberal democratic model implies that political structures are established that allow adult members of society to pursue their interpretation of the good life and how it is realized. A third principle is that the interpretation of the United Nations (UN) Charter should be revised so as to allow for compromises with absolute sovereignty in the event of serious breaches of individual civil and political rights. In other words, states may intervene in the internal affairs of each other if incumbents managing sovereignty fail to provide basic security for their citizens, even if the regime in the target state has not endorsed intervention from external parties. Liberal state-society relations take the individual rather than the state as the fundamental unit whose rights are to be protected. This requires the protection of civil rights by means of law to ensure the right to life and property as well as the obligation to respect agreements. No entity, not even the state, ranks above the law, and, as such, the state apparatus itself is also obliged to respect the law. A fourth principle is that the U.S. alignment system based on liberal democracy and civil and political rights defines the states that form the core of world order. In other words, U.S. allies subscribing to the liberal economic and political integrationist values are entrusted with primary responsibility for promoting and securing world order.

The United States considers itself to have a mission to build and preserve a community of free and independent nations with governments that answer to their citizens and reflect their own cultures. Thus, the 2012 *Strategic Guidance* for the U.S. Department of Defense (DoD) states that the United States seeks:

> a just and sustainable international order where the rights and responsibilities of nations and peoples are upheld, especially the fundamental rights of every human being.[7]

Because democracies respect their own people and their neighbors, the advance of freedom will lead to peace. The United States believes in the concept of democratic peace, meaning that international peace is best engendered by democracies governed by law. Such states are less likely to go to war against each other because they consider each other legitimate entities behaving in accordance with common rules of state conduct.[8] Democracies committed to the rule of law are less likely to go to war against each other since democracies are seen as entities that play by the rules. They are considered less legitimate targets of enforcement strategies by default because it is not merely the government, but the people represented by the government, whose decisions and activities are consequently called into question, since, in democracies, governments are answerable to their citizens.[9] The U.S. goal of spreading democracy may be traded in for stability in the short term, but it remains the long-term goal of the U.S. Government. This is the case even for the Barack Obama administration, which inherited the problems of peacebuilding emerging in the Afghanistan operations and has tended to prioritize stability rather than democratization. On the basis of the logic that peace and international stability are most reliably built on a foundation of freedom defined as democracy, the United States has been heavily engaged in fighting terrorism and rogue regimes such as Gaddafi's rule in Libya. Military means are applied with the intention of creating the preconditions for the spread of liberal democracy in the long run.

One core element in Washington's program for international order is the U.S. alliance system. It originates from the Cold War threat of Sino-Soviet expansion and does not merely encompass the customary understanding of alliances as pacts of mutual military assistance. Rather, the United States developed an extensive system of alignments of which the actual military alliances formed the iron core. Initially, the Soviet Union was surrounded by a virtual power vacuum along its entire periphery, from Scandinavia and the British Isles, along the rim lands of Eurasia, to Japan and Korea. The United States therefore established and maintained a substantial military presence in and close to the chief Eurasian danger areas, projecting U.S. power across the water barriers.[10] After the Cold War, the U.S. alliance, or perhaps more precisely, alignment system, has remained in place. One of the core strategic objectives of U.S. national defense is to strengthen the country's security relationships with traditional allies and to develop new international partnerships, working to increase the capabilities of its partners to contend with common challenges. The U.S. overseas military presence operated in and from four forward regions: Europe, Northeast Asia, the East Asian Littoral, and the Middle East-Southwest Asia. The United States has embarked on a comprehensive realignment of the U.S. global defense posture to enable U.S. forces to undertake military operations worldwide, reflecting the global nature of U.S. interests.

The means used by Washington to pursue the consolidation of this liberal world order are to expand the role of the liberal world order as the basis of interaction in Asia. This strategy encompasses entering into free-trade agreements such as the Trans-Pacific Partnership with Asian countries strengthening economic and military cooperation with Asian democracies, restructuring the U.S. alignment system so as to place the U.S. Pacific Command at the center, and involving Asian countries in peacemaking operations where grave breaches of civil and political rights are seen to engender threats to international peace and stability. Liberal economic globalization is, by and large, accepted around the world, including in China, as a role model for other states and nations to imitate. The United States considers China's intentions, with its integration into global economic market structures, to be potentially disturbing; however, Washington's liberal understanding of international relations encourages it to entertain the hope that China's economic integration will socialize the population into adopting a positive view on the political ideas of liberalism. Therefore, the United States adopts a positive attitude toward the fact that contemporary China is fully integrated into the international economic system. Thus, the element of market economic structures is not at the top of the U.S. security agenda, although issues of contention remain, such as Beijing's reluctance to include the Chinese currency, the renminbi, in a system of floating exchange rates. By contrast, liberal democracy and legal globalization have yet to take root and hence remain a long-term goals of U.S. Governments. The U.S. aim to spread democracy across the world is, however, not necessarily pursued by peaceful means. The war on terror was principally conducted by military means, but they are considered an element in creating the preconditions for the spread of liberal democracy and the rule of law in the long run. In the U.S. *Defense Strategic Guidance* dated 2012, it is formulated as the belief that:

> [r]egime changes, as well as tensions within and among states under pressure to reform, introduce uncertainty for the future. But they also may result in governments that, over the long term, are more responsive to the legitimate aspirations of their people, and are more stable and reliable partners of the United States.[11]

So the United States supports democratic reform. Elections are vital. However, democracy also requires the rule of law, the protection of minorities, and strong, accountable institutions that last longer than a single vote. In general, the eradication of terrorism is one of several ways by which stability at the domestic and international level is promoted. Stability is seen as a precondition for democratization since it is difficult to bring about lasting changes in governmental and legal practices without some measure of predictability in the basic political and military structures. Stability may entail working with authoritarian political establishments in the short run to pave the way for long-term liberal political and legal reforms. The enhanced prioritization of the Asia-Pacific in the U.S. military force posture testifies to the fact that this region is of primary significance to U.S. interests. As such, it is pivotal for the United States to assure partners, dissuade military competition, deter aggression and coercion, and be able to take prompt military action in this region. The continued U.S. ability to perform in these capacities constitutes the structure that aids Washington's attempt to implement the other aspects of its program for international order.

The U.S. world order is called integrationist because it is based on values. The drawback to this type of order is that it is fairly rigid in its definition of legitimate and illegitimate conduct, and it excludes numerous states from becoming core members due to the economic, military, and political structures that form the basis of state-society relations. The strength of this order is that the limits of acceptable behavior are clearly defined. Only democracies subscribing to market economic principles can form part of the core of the liberal world order. It is also clear that the agenda of this world order is extensive in the sense that integration toward a community of states operating on the basis of the same values is the long-term objective. The liberal basis of world order also clarifies the purposes of the U.S. use of its great power since the objectives and values are clearly defined and have already been pursued for decades, especially after the implosion of the Soviet Union in the post-Cold War era. Consequently, the standard by which U.S. performance is measured is well-defined. Washington may often fail to live up to its standard of free economic competition, democracy, and civil and political rights, but the standard itself is clearly defined and well-known.

CHINA'S COEXISTENCE WORLD ORDER

China pursues a strategy of influence suitable for a power that does not yet have the material capabilities to claim great power status. In economic terms, China only has a GDP that is one-third the size of the United States. At the same time, China has all the problems of developing countries on a large scale, including corruption, pollution, malfunctioning health care, socioeconomic inequality, and insufficient social security. These issues lead to fast growing problems of social unrest that threaten the political authority of China's Communist Party. In military terms, ongoing military modernization is reflected in an estimated defense budget growth of 7.5 percent in 2012. Nevertheless, China's defense budget, which is estimated to be $98.36 billion in 2009, remains more than six times below the levels of U.S. defense spending.[12] In addition, China does not have an alliance system and hence its power projection capabilities remain strictly limited.

In terms of economic and military capabilities, China has risen in the group of secondary powers. Beijing has not yet reached global great power status. However, in terms of political power, China already exercises influence at global great power level. After the implosion of the Soviet Union, China seemed like the best bet for a great power successor, and China has been skillful at filling this role without having the capabilities basis to play the role of a global great power. Beijing has done this by gradually developing a coexistence type of world order that has emerged as an alternative to the U.S.-led world order. It is a coexistence type of proposal in the sense that it aims at limited cooperation to avoid great power conflicts that jeopardize international order. This type of order is designed to avoid China losing its current global political great power status and descending into secondary power status rather than continuing its rise to full-blown great power status. In view of China's numerous domestic social and economic challenges, Beijing sees it as imperative to spend the bulk of its resources to this end.

The world order pursued by China is based on the common interest of numerous developing states in peaceful coexistence. Peaceful coexistence encompasses noninterference in the internal affairs of others, mutual nonaggression, equality and mutual benefit, and mutual respect for sovereignty and territorial integrity. These principles correspond to the rules of the game of the UN system. China's concern to limit the use of force in the international system and to demonstrate its commitment to international law means that the UN system has become an important factor in China's attempt to revise the existing international order to suit Chinese interests and world views. China's numerous domestic socio-economic problems prompt Beijing to promote peace and stability and try to avoid the use of force in external relations. Instead, China focuses on the common responsibilities between contending states to produce peaceful conflict management that respects the Cold War principles of absolute sovereignty and noninterference in the internal affairs of other states. For example, after the Cold War, Beijing has been reasonably successful in its attempts to avoid zero-sum contests and the use of force over relative territorial and maritime gains in negotiations on border disputes.[13]

Peaceful coexistence at a more practical level of implementation involves four types of practices. One practice is to aim for compromises between conflicting positions when there is a risk of use of force that involves the United States and China. Due to China's modest economic and military capabilities, Beijing cannot afford to end up in a great power conflict that involves the use of force. For example, in the case of Taiwan, China reserves the right to use force against what it considers to be a province under the jurisdiction of mainland China. However, Beijing stops short of exercising this alleged right in practice. Instead, in the post-Cold War era Beijing has gradually adopted a pragmatic approach of policy coordination and negotiation to avoid using force against an entity that is likely to be defended by the United States. Second, China requires consent from host governments to accept peacemaking operations unless the UN system and its affiliated institutions present evidence of threats toward international peace and security. For example, China has accepted Chapter VII operations in the case of Sudan when irrefutable evidence has been presented by the UN or by UN-affiliated institutions that regime behavior engenders threats to international peace and security. At the same time, China has succeeded in limiting the number and scope of UN-approved punitive actions by insisting on consent from the government in Khartoum. Third, China pursues equality and mutual benefit as a top-down principle that involves treating states rather than individuals as legal equals and promoting social and economic development. For example, China's involvement in activities in Sudan such as building schools and a new presidential palace and in reducing import tariffs contrasts with the U.S. calls for punitive actions directed against excluding the Khartoum regime from international relations. Also, China supports the efforts of regional and functional organizations of the UN system to help with conflict management and to determine when threats to international peace and stability require intervention. For example, in the run-up to the UN Security Council vote on establishing a joint UN-African Union (AU) hybrid force in Darfur in July 2007, China's special envoy to Darfur, Liu Guijin, commented that "It is not China's Darfur. It is first Sudan's Darfur and then Africa's Darfur." According to Guijin, peace negotiations need to be prioritized over peacekeeping efforts to ensure that real and long-lasting peace could be restored to the region.[14] Fourth, China defends the fundamental status of absolute sovereignty in international law. For example, in the case of Myanmar China has accommodated the concern of developing countries about the regime's violations of civil and political rights by endorsing nonbinding presidential statements on the unsolicited domestic use of force. Such actions strengthen China's image both as a principled power whose political practice corresponds to the principles of international conduct that it promotes, and also as a pragmatic and equality-oriented power that listens to the demands of secondary and small powers. This set of coexistence principles is a mixture of a conservative defensive form of diplomacy based on old UN principles and an offensive form of diplomacy, which involves revisions of the old UN system. China's version of international order receives widespread support in non-Western regions of the world and justifies China's status as a maker rather than merely a taker of international order. China's influence is based on its relations with secondary powers such as Indonesia and Russia and its engagement in regional security institutions all over the world such as the AU, the Association of Southeast Asian Nations (ASEAN), and the Shanghai Cooperation Organization (SCO). These are used as a basis for exercising politico-strategic influence on a par with the United States. This network of engagement in regional security institutions constitute Beijing's alternative to the global U.S. alignment system. As a consequence, Beijing is able to participate in defining the rules of the game of international politics and thereby determine the foreign policy choices that are open to other international actors.

The advantages of China's coexistence version of world order is that it is inherently flexible because it refrains from defining values requiring implementation of specific economic, military, and political state structures to form part of the order. China's world order allows for a plurality of political systems and swift adjustments to changes in the international context. The drawback to this type of order is that it does not involve clarifying Beijing's long-term objectives. Insofar as China achieves full-blown global great power status, we do not have substantial objectives comparable to those derived from U.S. liberal standards that can give an idea of what kind of global great power China will be. China is undergoing a transition from communism as the basis of legitimacy to a new ideological basis that has yet to be clearly defined. The Confucian concept of harmonious society remains a rhetorical device without much practical applicability. The idea has not been translated into essential political structures, such as feedback mechanisms from society to government agencies, or into processes, such as the use of elections in facilitating political succession. The absence of a strategy at this level means that in the interim, the Chinese Communist Party relies on continued economic growth and improved standards of living to secure its domestic legitimacy.

During this process, which is likely to take decades, China's identity as a great power is unknown, and we have no standard by which to measure China's performance beyond pure Sino-centric national interests in restoring what China defines as its motherland. Socio-political transition, combined with Sino-centric interests, means that the majority of secondary and small powers will not become loyal to China to an extent that will allow Beijing to replace Washington as the dominant power in the international system. The secondary and small powers are more comfortable with the United States as the dominant power since it is the devil they know compared to the enigmatic quality of China's great power ambitions.

INDIA'S SECONDARY ROLE IN THE GLOBAL WORLD ORDER

The debate about India's rise is based on high economic growth rates of 8-9 percent per year. However, even if India sustains these growth rates for the next 40 years, it will remain below the U.S. GDP in 2050 at current economic growth estimates. It is also worth remembering that if we take the GDP of the five BRICS countries (Brazil, Russia, India, China, and South Africa), India's share of GDP as a percentage of the BRICS total in 2009 constituted 13.6 percent against China's 51.9 percent in 2010.[15] Militarily, India proceeds with military modernization. In 2009, the defense budget for personnel, operations, and maintenance was $23.1 billion, and for procurement and construction, $8.5 billion. In 2010, the budget for personnel, operations, and maintenance had risen to $25.3 billion, and for procurement and construction $13.1 billion.[16] This modernization process is predominantly intended to enable India to match the Chinese and Pakistani military build-up, which is partly directed against India. India's long-standing border dispute with Pakistan is more serious than ever following Pakistan's engagement in Afghanistan with the emergence of the Taliban as a political movement. China has deployed medium-range ballistic missiles in the Qinghai-Tibet plateau. In turn, this has caused India to consider acquisition of an anti-missile defense system. China spends over four times as much on defense as India. In addition, China has established strategic partnerships with states such as Pakistan, Myanmar, Nepal, and Bangladesh along the rim of the Indian subcontinent, which will allow China to move down alongside India westwards in the Arabian Sea and eastwards in the Indian Ocean. This has caused India to draw closer to the United States, Southeast Asia, and Japan for purposes of getting access to arms and counter the political-strategic influence of China in India's backyard. Despite these efforts, China's influence is growing, whereas India's influence is waning. New Delhi's rapprochement to states such as the United States and Japan indicate that India becomes less and less able to manage peace and stability on the subcontinent on its own and has to look for partners that can help India counter the growing Chinese influence.[17]

Despite New Delhi's recent rapprochement with the United States and its continuous disagreements with China over their mutual border and resentment on both sides over issues such as Tibet and Pakistan, India has an independent identity that will ensure that the country maintains a distance to both great powers, much in the same way as Russia does although by different means and for different reasons. India is often seen as the exemplar of democracy in the developing world, being a secular democratic republic with a parliamentary form of government.[18] India has had aspirations to cash in on this status not by moving closer to the West, but by playing a leading role as a representative of developing countries in forums such as the Non-Aligned Movement (NAM) and the UN. However, NAM never took off as a political force in international relations, and India's bid for a permanent seat in the UN Security Council remains an aspiration rather than a reality. India is a secondary power that maintains relations with China as well as the United States without choosing sides. Consequently, India will remain a secondary power in the current world order, predominantly playing the role of a taker rather than a maker of order.

CONSEQUENCES FOR EUROPE

The different U.S. and Chinese versions of international order give rise to an international system without clear rules of the game because of the lack of one coherent set of principles of international conduct. In this in-between system, security threats are addressed by means of ad hoc frameworks of conflict management. The membership and rules of these frameworks are defined on a trial-and-error basis. Also, in this system secondary and small powers are quite influential because the United States and China compete for their backing and loyalty. This enables secondary and small powers to maximize their influence by gravitating toward both the U.S. and the Chinese order without choosing sides.

The North Atlantic Treaty Organization's (NATO) 2011 intervention in Libya may provide clues as to the consequences for Europe of the existence of two competing international orders. Despite the difficulties with contributing to civil and political rights regimes in Iraq and Afghanistan, the Western U.S.-led grouping continues to pursue a greater role for humanitarian intervention. This implies that the United States and Europe will continue to pursue liberal value-based objectives as alliance partners. On the other hand, European leadership in the military intervention in Libya implies that the Western countries support the calls for regionalization of UN Security Council security management that has formed part of China's program for international order for some time. Consequently, the United States is not likely to take the lead in this type of operation outside of the core of the U.S. sphere of interest in the Asia-Pacific. Moreover, Germany's agreement with China's abstention regarding UN Security Council Resolution 1973 on the grounds of unwillingness to authorize the use of force in Libya indicates that the dividing lines between those supporting an integrationist order and those supporting a coexistence-style order are becoming more and more blurred. This development does not indicate a merger between the U.S. and Chinese-led programs for international order. Instead, it indicates that increasing regionalization is necessary in the absence of one coherent set of principles that universally define right and wrong international conduct.[19]

Germanys' UN Security Council abstention also implies that Europe is not a unitary actor. Europe appears to be in disagreement over the future direction of cooperation at a time when two competing international orders are on offer. The United Kingdom's (UK) refusal in December 2011 to consider European Union (EU) plans to tighten budget controls to fix the Euro is an example of this problem. Moreover, as indicated by Germany's abstention on the UN Security Council 1973 Resolution, individual countries in Europe appear to align themselves in different ways with respect to the U.S. and the Chinese version of global order. Another example is the Greek decision to assist China in its operation to lift Chinese nationals out of Libya. The May 2012 election in Greece, putting the country's future in the Euro zone at risk, threatening to revive Europe's debt crisis and forcing a new election to be held in June 2012, testifies to the severe problems facing European cooperation and the future of the regional integration aspirations. The economic, financial, and political challenges facing the region point to the possibility of a disintegrating Europe of individual countries that reorient themselves toward Washington and Beijing on the basis of different interests and values. In this environment, European states may continue to engage in conflict management in their near abroad in the Balkans, the Middle East, and Africa to promote stability in the region's periphery. However, the days of major peacebuilding efforts such as those undertaken in Iraq and Afghanistan appear to be over because a fragmented Europe is becoming unable to muster the unity and long-term commitments that such efforts involve.

The fundamental issue that is raised by developments in the post-Cold War global order is whether the Western order can survive a disintegrated Europe with different policies toward China. Will the United States have faith in European countries that side with China and oppose the United States on some issues? Will Europe be able to remain sufficiently coherent that Washington and Beijing will continue to see the EU as a unit to be reckoned with in international politics? It remains to be seen to what extent Europe will remain a unitary actor. However, by now it is already clear that the principal challenge for Europe is to find a place in the new international order on the basis of a reconsideration of what Europe has to offer in the economic, military, social, and political sectors that addresses the interests of China without compromising Europe's position as core member of the Western liberal order. Despite China's rising power, U.S. ideas and ideals remain prominent in the global landscape due to the innovative and problem solving qualities of the U.S. economy and society.[20] As a consequence, it is pertinent for Europe to continue to remain an attractive partner to the United States at the same time as it addresses the rise of China in a constructive manner. Only in this way is Europe likely to position itself as an independent voice in international politics that is seen as important by the United States and China.

ENDNOTES - CHAPTER 12

1. GDP growth estimates from the Royal Danish Embassy in Beijing listed on the basis of data from the International Monetary Fund.

2. The arguments on the U.S. integrationist and the Chinese coexistence world order are pursued in detail in Liselotte Odgaard, *China and Coexistence: Beijing's National Security Strategy for the 21st Century*, Washington, DC: Woodrow Wilson Center Press/Johns Hopkins University Press, 2012.

3. GDP at MER (2009 USD bn), PWC World in 2050 & Goldman Sachs, and the Royal Danish Embassy in Beijing.

4. *Ibid.*

5. A similar argument has been made in Ian Clark, "China and the United States: A Succession of Hegemonies?" *International Affairs*, Vol. 87, No. 1, 2011, pp. 13-28.

6. The approach to liberal integration used in this article is based on G. John Ikenberry, *After Victory: Institutions, Strategic Restraint, and the Rebuilding of Order after Major Wars*, Princeton, NJ: Princeton University Press, 2001, pp. 3-79.

7. U.S. Department of Defense, *Sustaining U.S. Global Leadership: Priorities for the 21st Century Defense*, Washington, DC: U.S. Department of Defense, January 2012, available from *www.defense.gov/news/Defense_Strategic_Guidance.pdf*.

8. Francis Fukuyama, "Democratization and International Security," *Adelphi Paper* No. 266, London, UK: The International Institute for Strategic Studies, 1991/92, p. 18. The democratic peace argument has been defined and tested by Zeev Maoz and Bruce Russett, "Normative and Structural Causes of Democratic Peace, 1946-1986," *American Political Science Review*, Vol. 87, No. 3, September 1993, pp. 624-638. The origins of the democratic peace argument can be found in Immanuel Kant, *Den evige fred* [Zum ewigen Frieden] (*The Eternal Peace*), Copenhagen, Denmark: Det sikkerheds- og nedrustningspolitiske Udvalg, 1990 [1795/1796], p. 29, who argued that a republican constitution would promote peace.

9. See, for example, Bruce M. Russett, *Grasping the Democratic Peace: Principles for a Post-Cold War World*, Princeton, NJ: Princeton University Press, 1993.

10. Arnold Wolfers, *Discord and Collaboration: Essays on International Politics*, Baltimore, MD: The Johns Hopkins Press, 1962, pp. 206-209.

11. *Sustaining U.S. Global Leadership*.

12. For purchasing power parity estimate, see *The Military Balance 2011*, London, UK: International Institute for Strategic Studies, 2011.

13. Liselotte Odgaard, *China and Coexistence: Beijing's National Security Strategy for the Twenty-First Century*, Washington, DC: Woodrow Wilson Center Press/Johns Hopkins University Press, 2012, pp. 87-127.

14. Su Qiang, "Confrontation over Darfur 'Will Lead Us Nowhere'," *China Daily*, July 27, 2007, available from *www.chinadaily.com.cn/2008/2007-07/27/content_5445062.htm*.

15. The data comes from the Royal Danish Embassy in Beijing, which has based the calculations on data from the International Monetary Fund.

16. *The Military Balance 2011*.

17. Liselotte Odgaard, *The Balance of Power in Asia-Pacific Security: US-China Policies on Regional Order*, London, UK: Routledge, 2007, pp. 157-160.

18. Sumit Sarkar, "Indian Democracy: the Historical Inheritance," Atul Kohli, ed., *The Success of India's Democracy*, Cambridge, UK: Cambridge University Press, 2001, pp. 23-46.

19. Liselotte Odgaard, "China's National Security Strategy and Its UNSC Policy on Libya," *AMS-ISDP Joint Conference Proceedings 2011, The Situation in West Asia and North Africa and Its Impact on the International Strategic Configuration*, Conference

held in Beijing, People's Republic of China, September 15-17, 2011, pp. 36-39.

20. Fareed Zakaria, "The Future of American Power: How America Can Survive the Rise of the Rest," *Foreign Affairs*, Vol. 87, No. 3, May/June 2008, pp. 18-43.

CHAPTER 13

NEGOTIATING THE PITFALLS OF PEACE AND SECURITY IN AFRICA AND A NEW AMERICAN GRAND STRATEGY: AFRICAN UNION PEACE AND SECURITY ARCHITECTURE AND THE U.S. AFRICA COMMAND

Kwesi Aning
Festus Aubyn

INTRODUCTION

With the failure of the Organization of African Unity (OAU) to fulfill the ambitions, expectations, and optimisms stimulated by its establishment in the 1960s, it was finally transformed into the African Union (AU) in 2002, which sought to respond to Africa's multi-faceted security challenges through expansive and deepening multiple institutional processes. Establishing a security architecture through which the AU and its Regional Economic Communities (RECs) are building blocks would respond to these challenges. These robust initiatives have been introduced concurrently with partner states and institutions, both offering support while at the same time implementing their own national strategic interests. One such critical partner has been the United States, which through multiple engagements and its own grand strategies has become one of the key partners of the AU's institutionalization processes. But over the past decade, following such pathways has not always been mutually beneficial to either the AU or the United States. In this chapter, we explore and examine the history of U.S. engagements in Africa, especially in the peace and security arena, and juxtapose such grand strategic calculations with Africa's own perceptions of and responses to its security challenges. Furthermore, we explore how, in the face of common challenges, both the AU and United States can identify and respond to their security challenges in a manner that makes this relationship a win-win one instead of the present one driven by suspicion, competition, and outright hostility.

This chapter is divided into five sections. The first section examines U.S. security policy toward Africa in the post Cold War era, with particular emphasis on the various training programs and initiatives. The second section explores the present state of American grand strategy and how the new U.S. Africa Command (AFRICOM) fits into it with respect to Africa.

To demonstrate how Africa is responding to its own security challenges, the third section focuses on the new AU Peace and Security Architecture (APSA). The fourth section assesses how AFRICOM is enhancing Africa's emerging peace and security architecture and the drawbacks. The chapter concludes that U.S. interests in Africa would be best assured not by using military means to check China or the terrorist activities of al-Qaeda or al-Shabaab on the continent, but rather by looking to meaningfully address and reconcile its interests with the continent's human security needs. Africa is also advancing democratically, economically, and developmentally and, as such, it is essential that the United States engage the continent not as conflict-ridden, but as a mutual partner in advancing global peace and stability by pursuing long-term strategic objectives that address both U.S. and African interests.

U.S. SECURITY POLICY TOWARD AFRICA AFTER THE COLD WAR

Africa has historically remained in the periphery of American foreign policy interests except where a specific American interest or objective was at stake (e.g., containment of Soviet expansion). After the Cold War, Africa was seen by many U.S. policymakers as insignificant to U.S. strategic interests. However, attention toward the continent was reinvigorated by a presidential directive known as the *National Security Review 30: American Policy towards Africa in the 1990s (NSR 30)* that assessed America's policy toward Africa.[1] This presidential directive concluded that post-Cold War developments in Africa provided both "significant opportunities for, and obstacles to, US interests" and that the United States should remain militarily engaged on the continent.[2] Consequently, in 1992, President George H. W. Bush responded to the humanitarian crisis in Somalia by launching Operation RESTORE HOPE, which was made up of 25,000 troops from 24 countries.[3] Also known as Unified Task Force (UNITAF), Operation RESTORE HOPE was later transformed in 1993 to the United Nations Operations in Somalia II (UNOSOM II). Sadly, with few of the mission mandate objectives achieved, UNOSOM II was terminated in 1994 after the death of 18 U.S. Rangers in Mogadishu, which led to the subsequent withdrawal of U.S. troops.[4] Thereafter, in 1994, President Bill Clinton's *Presidential Decision Directive 25 (PDD-25)* decreed that the United States would not intervene in any future crisis situation in Africa unless American interests were directly threatened.[5] The United States became very reluctant to intervene directly or support UN interventions elsewhere in Africa, notably in Rwanda, where its interests were not directly at stake. But although the horrors of the Rwanda genocide and the subsequent crises in Burundi led to a partial reversal of this policy, the United States did not revert to direct military intervention in Africa even in the post-September 11, 2001 (9/11) period.[6] Instead, U.S. policy shifted toward developing the capacities of African countries to undertake peace operations under the guise of "African solutions to African problems" — a notion that some viewed as a convenient alibi for U.S. inaction.[7] These capacity-building initiatives centered on bilateral-level engagements, with a limited focus on the regional and sub-regional groupings. They included several training programs meant to build the capacity of individual African countries to participate in multilateral peace operations.

The first of such training programs was the African Crisis Response Force (ACRF) proposed by former U.S. Secretary of State Warren Christopher. ACRF was to consist of an African force that could be rapidly deployed in a theater of conflict primarily to protect civilians in designated areas. However, this training program was not well received by most African states, as some African Leaders like Nelson Mandela saw it as a U.S. excuse to establish its foothold in Africa after the U.S. failure to intervene in Rwanda.[8] In deference to African sensitivities, the Clinton administration launched the African Crisis Response Initiative (ACRI), incorporating some elements of ACRF in 1996. Unlike ACRF, ACRI was embraced by several African countries and had the possibility of direct military assistance to sub-regional bodies such as the Economic Community of West African States (ECOWAS), although it also operated at the bilateral level. The main objective of ACRI was to train African contingents for

Chapter VI-style peacekeeping on the continent and also to enhance their humanitarian relief capacity. Although many African countries such as Mali, Senegal, Ghana, Uganda, and Tanzania benefited from this training program, others like Nigeria and South Africa remained opposed to what they described as a foreign initiative that did not address African conflicts.[9] Other important programs initiated by the U.S. Government include the International Military Education and Training (IMET), the Enhanced International Peacekeeping Capabilities (EIPC) program, and the Africa Regional Peacekeeping (ARP) program.[10] Collectively, these initiatives contributed immensely to building the military capacity of African states for peacekeeping operations in accordance with Chapter VI of the UN Charter.

In response to the growing trend toward robust peacekeeping in Africa, ACRI was later transformed in 2004 to African Contingency Operations Training and Assistance (ACOTA) by the George Bush administration. According to the U.S. Department of State, the mission of ACOTA is to:

> enhance the capacities and capabilities of African militaries, regional institutions and the continent's peacekeeping resources as a whole so that they can plan for, train, deploy and sustain sufficient quantities of professionally competent peacekeepers to meet conflict transformation requirements with minimal Non-African assistance.[11]

In contrast to ACRI, and perhaps one of the most significant innovations of ACOTA, was the training for multinational peace support operations and the provision of nonlethal military weaponry to undertake these peacekeeping operations.[12] Moreover, it was also tai-

343

lored to match the individual needs and capabilities of each recipient country, an innovation that was missing in the previous programs. Under ACOTA, the United States also provided financial and logistical support to the AU missions in Darfur, Burundi, and Somalia. The regional economic communities, such as ECOWAS, were also provided with training and other capacity-building assistance through its member states.[13] By 2008, a total of approximately 45,000 African soldiers and 3,200 African trainers were educated under the program and deployed to peacekeeping operations in the Democratic Republic of Congo, Liberia, Burundi, Cote d'Ivoire, Darfur, Somalia, and Lebanon.[14] However, like all previous training programs, ACOTA suffered from limited funding, which affected its depth and sustainability.[15] Another weakness was that private security firms instead of uniformed U.S. personnel were used to implement the training program, and most recipient states objected to this.[16]

In 2005, ACOTA became a constituent part of the multilateral 5-year Global Peace Operation Initiative (GPOI) program of the Bush administration, which aimed at improving the supply of personnel for peacekeeping operations.[17] Although it was designed as a program with worldwide reach, its emphasis was on Africa. The primary purpose of the GPOI program was to train and equip 75,000 military troops, a majority of them African, for peacekeeping operations. One major innovation of the GPOI was its recognition of the strategic significance of developing the capacities of regional and sub-regional institutions to ensure "sustainability and self-sustainment."[18] GPOI also supports efforts to operationalize the African Standby Force (ASF) and regional and sub-regional logistics depots. In the post-9/11 period, as a result of the U.S.-led war on terror and concern about the potential threats that can be posed by failed and fragile states, the United States focused on strengthening indigenous capacity to secure porous borders and help build law enforcement and intelligence infrastructure to deny havens for terrorists.[19] Various states such as Mali, Chad, Mauritania, and Niger were provided with equipment and training through the Trans-Saharan Counter-Terrorism Initiative (TSCTI) and the Pan-Sahelian Initiative (PSI). The United States provided weapons, vehicles, and military training to counter terrorism in these countries.

AMERICAN GRAND STRATEGY

There is widespread uncertainty about the present state of American grand strategy. Does it exist or not? Grand strategy is all about the necessity of choice. According to Niall Ferguson:

> Today, it means choosing between a daunting list of objectives: to resist the spread of radical Islam, to limit Iran's ambition to become dominant in the Middle East, to contain the rise of China as an economic rival, to guard against a Russian "reconquista" of Eastern Europe and so on.[20]

Colin Dueck, for example, argues that:

> great power counterbalancing against the United States is by no means inevitable. It can in fact be prevented through the use of careful strategy. If, however, the United States acts aggressively and unilaterally, it is likely to "undermine the sources of its own success.[21]

Grand strategy is a term of art from academia and refers to the collection of plans and policies that comprise the state's deliberate effort to harness political, military, diplomatic, and economic tools together to advance that state's national interest. Grand strategy is the art of reconciling ends and means. It involves purposive action—what leaders think and want. Such action is constrained by factors that leaders explicitly recognize (for instance, budget constraints and the limitations inherent in the tools of statecraft) and by those they might only implicitly feel (cultural or cognitive screens that shape worldviews).[22] But efforts to identify and assess the state of current U.S. grand strategy raise several questions. For example:

- Is there a new pragmatism that delineates U.S. action in Africa since Barack Obama has taken office?
- Is this reflected in a "new strategic isolation" within a broader receding West characterized by a United States beset by relative economic decline and dysfunctional politics?
- To what extent does the Obama administration's foreign policy vision of "leading from behind" become evident?
- Is there a distinctive Obama approach beginning to emerge? Can we speak of the "D" word, the emergence of an Obama doctrine—namely "a new form of high tech, low-budget, and politically astute intervention that maximizes U.S. influence while minimizing cost for a cash-strapped government"?[23] There seems to be an emerging new approach described by Zbigniew Brzezinski as "discriminating engagement,"[24] which in practical terms refers to a new approach in dealing with trouble spots around

the world, characterized by U.S. economic and political realism. If this new "discriminating engagement" is implemented, then where does the much-hyped new Africa Command fit into this grand strategy with respect to Africa?

- To what extent does this approach focus on using other tools of national power to determine and achieve outcomes that do not have a sole focus on the use of military might, but also use diplomatic tools to get others to pull their weight? From the above, there is an indication that recent discourse on such grand strategy raises more questions and does not provide clear-cut concrete answers. Previously, we have attempted to raise some of these questions and ideas.

U.S. AFRICA COMMAND (AFRICOM)

Created by a presidential order in 2007, AFRICOM is one of the nine Unified Combatant Commands of the U.S. Department of Defense (DoD). The establishment of the Command was the direct result of Africa's increasing strategic importance to the United States and also signified a new phase in U.S. foreign policy engagement with Africa. It became fully operational in October 2008, just a month before the election of President Obama. The command is currently headquartered in Stuttgart, Germany and is responsible to the Secretary of Defense for U.S. military relations with 54 African countries.[25] According to President George W. Bush, the idea behind the creation of AFRICOM was to strengthen America's security cooperation with Africa and create new opportunities to bolster the capabilities of African partners.[26] Additionally, the

Command will enhance U.S. efforts to bring peace and security to the people of Africa and promote common goals of development, health, education, democracy, and economic growth in Africa.[27]

Other countries such as Nigeria, Morocco, South Africa, Algeria, and Libya made policy statements that AFRICOM will not be welcomed on their soil. Nigeria in particular, rejected AFRICOM because it was believed to be counterproductive, unnecessary, and a derogation of the sovereignty of African states.[28] Many African governments also feared that AFRICOM will be used to destabilize and even overthrow regimes that the United States does not approve.

Before the creation of AFRICOM, the administration of U.S.-Africa military relations was divided among three different commands: European Command (EUCOM) located in Stuttgart, Germany; Hawaii-based Pacific Command (PACOM), and Central Command (CENTCOM) based in Tampa, Florida.[29] This division of responsibility of Africa among these three commands was reported to have posed some coordination challenges for the DoD. Therefore, as former Secretary of Defense Robert Gates argued, the establishment of AFRICOM was to enable the United States:

> to have a more effective and integrated approach than the current arrangement of dividing Africa between several commands.[30]

Its formation was to give Africa the attention that it deserves and also to demonstrate the importance of Africa for U.S. national security. According to DoD, the primary mission of the command is to:

> Protect and defend the national security interests of the United States by strengthening the defense capabilities of African states and regional organizations and, when directed, conduct military operations, in order to deter and defeat transnational threats and to provide a security environment conducive to good governance and development.[31]

The Command works jointly with other U.S. agencies such as the U.S. Department of State (DoS), the United States Agency for International Development (USAID), and U.S. embassies to support the implementation of U.S. foreign policy goals in Africa. In reality, AFRICOM is a diplomatic, developmental, and economic mission. The programs that AFRICOM monitors and assists include, among other things, the Pan-Sahelian Initiative (PSI), ACOTA, and GPOI. The activities of the command are meant to: build the capacity of partner conventional forces and security forces; conduct defense sector reform; counter transnational and extremist threats; foster regional cooperation, situational awareness, and interoperability; and contribute to the stability in current zones of conflicts.[32] These cooperation programs are all executed by AFRICOM's subordinate commands located in Italy, Germany, and Camp Lemonnier, Djibouti.[33] The focus of U.S. AFRICOM capacity-building programs and activities is to address three primary capacity-building functions that include operational capacity building, institutional capacity building, and developing human capital.

Some of the programs designed to address operational capacity constraints include the Africa Partnership Station (APS) and Operation ENDURING FREEDOM-Trans-Sahara (OEF-TS), Exercise Flintlock, and Exercise Natural Fire.[34] The APS program for instance is a multinational security cooperation initiative that aims to improve maritime safety and security in Africa and focuses on addressing four primary areas: maritime professionals, maritime infrastructure, maritime domain awareness, and maritime response capability. OEF-TS also supports the U.S. Government's Trans Sahara Counter Terrorism Partnership (TSCTP) program to help deter the flow of illicit arms, goods, and people and to preclude terrorists from establishing sanctuaries in their countries.[35] Ten African countries are currently part of this program: Algeria, Burkina Faso, Chad, Mali, Mauritania, Morocco, Niger, Nigeria, Senegal, and Tunisia.

The institutional capacity building programs include Operation ONWARD LIBERTY (OOL), the Africa Maritime Law Enforcement Partnership (AMLEP) Program, the Pandemic Response Program, and the PILOT-Partnership for Integrated Logistics Operations and Tactics.[36] While the OOL program supports the DoS broader Security Sector Reform (SSR) program in Liberia, the AMLEP program on the other hand addresses illicit transnational maritime activity, such as drug interdiction and fisheries enforcement, at the bilateral level. The programs designed to develop human capital comprise the International Military and Education Training (IMET) and Expanded IMET (E-IMET), The Combined Joint Task Force-Horn of Africa (CJTF-HOA), and the Partner Military HIV/ AIDS Program (PMHAP).[37] The IMET and E-IMET are the most widely used military assistance programs in U.S. AFRICOM's area of responsibility and aim at professionalizing militaries and reinforcing the democratic value of elected civilian authority.[38] The PMHAP aims at mitigating the impacts of the disease on African military readiness. The CJTF-HOA located at Camp Lemonnier also builds partner security capability, capacity, and infrastructure through regional cooperation, military-to-military programs, civil-military affairs projects, and professional military education programs.

In Fiscal Year 2010, AFRICOM received $274 million, and the Obama administration requested $298 million for the command for Fiscal Year 2011.[39] As of April 2011, AFRICOM had approximately 2,100 personnel, consisting of both military and civilian personnel from DoD and non-DoD agencies of the U.S. Government. In 2011, AFRICOM undertook its first major military operation named Operation ODYSSEY DAWN during the Libya crises, in which the AU became a mere observer, incapable of playing any major role. Operation ODYSSEY DAWN was the U.S. support to the multilateral military efforts to enforce a no-fly zone and protect civilians in Libya in support of UN Security Council Resolution 1973.[40] Before NATO's Operation UNIFIED PROTECTOR in Libya, AFRICOM also supported the U.S. humanitarian response in Libya through the delivery of relief supplies and the evacuation of foreign nationals fleeing the violence.

EVOLUTION OF THE NEW AFRICAN PEACE AND SECURITY ARCHITECTURE

The transformation of the OAU into the AU generated expectations that Africa's premier international institution would have the strength and capacity to deal with the peace and security challenges facing the continent.[41] While the OAU had achieved its stated objectives of decolonization, eradicating apartheid, and maintaining the colonially inherited boundaries at independence, the proxy wars in which Africa got entangled during the period of the Cold War resulted in the diversion of attention from the core economic and security challenges that the continent faced. By 1993, there was political recognition that the rhetoric of economic development could not be achieved if the conflicts that hounded the continent were not decisively dealt with. Consequently, the *Mechanism for Conflict Prevention, Management and Resolution* was established with the purpose to anticipate and prevent conflicts on the continent. Therefore, 1993 became the decisive year when the shift to the recognition of a need for a structured security architecture started to take shape. A decade later, with a Constitutive Act defining the parameters of a new AU, a *Protocol establishing a Peace and Security Council* (PSC) for the AU was promulgated in 2002 and eventually ratified by enough member states to make it operational. At its launch in May 2004, the PSC was characterized as "marking a historic watershed in Africa's progress toward resolving its conflicts and building a durable peace and security order."[42] The AU's new security regime is premised on several norms and principles that are both old (based on the Charter of the OAU) and new (emanating from the Constitutive Act).[43] They include:

- Sovereign equality of member states (Article 4a);
- Nonintervention by member states (Article 4g);
- African solutions to African problems;
- *Uti possidetis* (Article 4b);
- Nonuse of force/peaceful settlement of disputes (Articles 4e, 4f, 4i);
- Condemnation of unconstitutional changes of government (Article 4p); and,
- The AU's right to intervene in a member state in grave circumstances (Article 4h).

A combination of these values and norms plus the institutional mechanisms has given the AU an institutional vibrancy that creates opportunities for proactive responses to some of the continent's security challenges.[44] A case in point was the AU's deployment of peacekeepers to Burundi and the Sudan Darfur region to prevent a situation it terms as posing significant threats to legitimate order to restore peace and stability.

In addition to the Constitutive Act, which is the core document that defines the principle and objectives of the AU security policy and the PSC protocol, a Common African Defense and Security Policy (CADSP) was adopted in 2004. In particular, the PSC protocol and the CADSP together form the critical pillars underpinning the new AU peace and security architecture. The fundamental philosophical idea underlying CADSP was that of human security, based not only on political values but social and economic imperatives as well.[45] This notion of human security embraces such issues as: human rights; the right to participate fully in governance; the right to equal development, access to resources, and basic necessities of life; the right to protection against poverty; the right to education and health care; the right to protection against marginalization on the basis of gender; and protection against natural disasters and ecological and environmental degradation.[46] These issues represent Africa's primary security concerns that pose major threats to the stability of states and not the excessive focus of AFRICOM on terrorism and other transnational organized crimes on the continent.

The CADSP also aims to address some of the common security threats facing the continent such as the proliferation of small arms and light weapons, peace-building, and peacekeeping as well as post-conflict rehabilitation and reconstruction, terrorism, humanitarian issues, and diseases such as HIV/AIDS, tuberculosis, malaria, and other infectious diseases.[47] Its objectives and goals include: ensuring collective responses to both internal and external threats, advancing the cause of integration in Africa; enhancing AU's capacity for, and coordination of, early action for conflict prevention, containment, management, and resolution; and promoting initiatives that will preserve and strengthen peace and development in Africa.

KEY INSTITUTIONAL STRUCTURES AND MECHANISMS OF THE NEW APSA

The APSA is made up of a multifaceted set of interrelated institutions and mechanisms that function at the continental, regional, and national levels.[48] The AU member states form the national-level actors that house a majority of the capabilities relevant to conflict management on the continent. At the regional level are the regional economic communities (RECs), which constitute the building blocks of the continental security architecture. At the continental level, a variety of institutions and mechanisms coordinated by the AU PSC comprise the new APSA.[49] The Protocol Relating to the Establishment of the Peace and Security Council (PSC) establishes the PSC as a standing decision-making organ for the prevention, management, and resolution of conflicts. According to article 2 of the protocol, the PSC is meant to be a collective security and early warning instrument for timely and efficient response to both existing and emerging conflict as well as crisis situations in Africa.[50] The powers of the

PSC are extensive, dealing not only with "hard" peace and security issues, but also "soft" security or any aspects that influence human security. This enables the PSC to monitor elections and address issues of food security, natural disasters, and human rights violations.[51] It is supported by the AU Commission, a Panel of the Wise, a Continental Early Warning System, an African Standby Force (ASF), and a Special Fund. Among other things, the objectives of the PSC are to promote peace, security, and stability in Africa.[52] It is composed of 15 members, of whom 10 are elected for a 2-year term, while the remaining five are elected for a 3-year period on the principle of equitable representation of the five regions: North, West, Central, East, and Southern Africa.

The critical peace and security decisionmaking institutions include the Assembly of Heads of State and Governments (AHSG) of AU, the Executive Council, the PSC, and the Commission of the AU. Although the AHSG makes the final decisions on important peace and security issues such as the intervention in member states of the AU, the PSC is empowered to take most decisions on security issues on behalf of the AHSG.[53] The Chairperson of the AU Commission also plays an important conflict management role under the new APSA. The Chairperson assisted by the Commissioner in charge of Peace and Security is responsible for bringing issues to the attention of the PSC, the Panel of the Wise, and other relevant stakeholders and for ensuring implementation and follow-up actions.[54] The chair of the Commission performs this advisory role by relying on the information provided by the Continental Early Warning System (CEWS) which aims to facilitate the anticipation and prevention of conflicts (Article 12). The CEWS consists of a situation room located at the AU headquarters in Addis Ababa, Ethiopia, and is responsible for data gathering and analysis. It is linked to the early warning mechanisms of the RECs such as the ECOWAS, South African Development Community (SADC) and Intergovernmental Authority on Development (IGAD).

The Panel of the Wise, which is composed of five highly respected African personalities selected on the basis of regional representation, is tasked with advising the PSC and AU Commission Chair on any or all matters relating to the promotion and maintenance of peace and security in Africa. The Panel of the Wise could also be deployed to support the efforts of the Peace and Security Council (Article 11). Another important institutional mechanism of the APSA is the ASF (Article 13). It is established to enable the PSC to perform its responsibilities with respect to the deployment of peace support operations and interventions pursuant to Article 4 (h) and 4 (J) of the AU Constitutive Act.[55] The ASF provides for five sub-regional stand-by arrangements, each up to a brigade size of 3,000-4,000 troops, which will combine to give the AU a total of 15,000 to 20,000 troops who will be trained and ready to be deployed on 14 days notice.[56]

It was conceived to conduct, observe, and monitor peacekeeping missions in responding to emergency situations anywhere on the continent requiring rapid military response. The AU Peace Support Operations Division (PSOD) in Addis Ababa is the coordination mechanism and is expected to command an African-wide integrated communication system linking all the sub-regional brigades. Although the ASF was envisaged to be operational by 2010, challenges of coordination between the regional economic communities, finances, logistics, and equipment have prolonged its implementation.[57] But without doubt, the ASF represents a critical component of the APSA that will enhance the AU's capabilities to intervene to protect people in grave circumstances and to provide a prompt and robust response to manage and resolve conflicts on the continent. There is also the Military Staff Committee (MSC), which consists of senior military officers from PSC member states. When called upon, the MSC advises the PSC on questions relating to military and security issues that are on its agenda.[58]

AFRICOM AND APSA: WORKING TOWARD A COMMON END STATE

Traditionally, U.S. engagement with Africa has been on the bilateral level, supporting its allies with little focus on regional organizations, especially the AU. But the establishment of AFRICOM has led to a deepening interaction with the AU, an indication of its growing confidence in the organization as a crucial player in the maintenance of peace in Africa. According to Michael Battle, the U.S. Ambassador to the AU, this emerging partnership demonstrates how the U.S. Government sees the AU as being "critically important" to the development of its policy toward the African continent.[59] AFRICOM is currently offering enhanced support for many of the AU peace and security initiatives through both bilateral and multilateral initiatives. At the bilateral level, AFRICOM is focusing on improving the capabilities of individual member states of the AU to field well-trained and well-equipped troops for peace operations through programs such as EIPC, ARP, ACOTA, IMET, and E-IMET. These capacity-building programs and activities have significantly enhanced the operational and tactical dimensions of AU peacekeeping missions. For example, AFRICOM provides bilateral support to the troop-contributing countries (TCCs) of the AU mission in Somalia (AMISOM) such as Burundi and Uganda, through the provision of equipment, logistics support, advice, and training.[60] The AU/UN mission in Darfur is also being supported by AFRICOM. Between 2005 and 2010, the United States provided more than $940 million to support the AU missions in Darfur and Somalia, as well as capacity building through the ACOTA program.[61] The United States is also providing counterterrorism training to some selected military units in the Sahel and East Africa such as Mali, Chad, Niger, and Mauritania through the TSCTI and PSI programs.

AFRICOM is also supporting AU's effort to operationalize the African Standby Force through capacity building at the continental and sub-regional level, as well as AU member states.[62] These capacity building initiatives are targeted toward strengthening the capabilities and interoperability of the African Standby Force (ASF) and its sub-regional elements. Computers, software, and communication equipment have also been provided to bolster the CEWS and communication between the AU and regional ASF brigades. In order to build the capacity of the AU Secretariat to plan, manage, and sustain peacekeeping operations, the United States has provided a full-time Peace and Security Advisor to the AU Peace Support Operations division in Addis Ababa.

While all of these programs signify a significant milestone in U.S. support to the implementation process of the APSA, the limited nature of these training programs makes it difficult to see a clear cause and effect relationship between the training offered and the actual performance of troops trained under them in the field.[63] Moreover, the disproportionate focus on the training of U.S. allies at the expense of all AU member states affects the rapid impact on African peacekeeping. The nature of the relationship between the AU and the United States has also not been clearly defined. The relationship between the two has largely been ad hoc and crisis-driven, partly due to the U.S. failure to construct a coherent or sustained policy toward Africa. This is actually reflected in the shifting and changing nature of its security strategies toward the continent. Instead of giving more substantial support to the AU, the United States has rather focused on supporting individual countries that benefit its interests.[64] This for example, has reinforced the perception that AFRICOM is meant to serve U.S. interests rather than Africa, and makes some Africans even question the real motivations behind the creation of AFRICOM. Moreover, despite the objectives of AFRICOM that suggest that it will go beyond traditional security concerns by addressing nontraditional security issues, it remains essentially a military organization.

Like its predecessor programs, AFRICOM is also threatened by inadequate funding and political commitment, insufficient interagency coordination, as well as a failure to harmonize activities with international partners to achieve maximum impact and eliminate duplication.[65] In particular, the financial support of AFRICOM has been vulnerable to raids from other budget lines, and remains uneven from year-to-year.[66] But this is not surprising, given the parlous state of the economy inherited by President Obama and the fact that his administration has to focus on the recovery of the U.S. economy. The inconsistencies in U.S. military engagement in Africa have also raised serious

359

concerns about its commitment to the attainment of peace and stability on the continent. While the United States was quick to intervene in the crisis in Libya, it was largely absent when it came to the post-electoral violence in La Cote d'Ivoire; again reflecting the dominance of security interests in U.S. engagement with Africa, including the removal of "out of favor" regimes, in this case Muammar Gaddafi, and replacing them with loyal governments with the aim of controlling resources.[67] Thus, though in Libya, the United States adopted a military posture to oust President Gaddafi, this was not the case in Cote d'Ivoire where the main approach used was a combination of quiet diplomacy and economic sanctions even when people were dying from clashes between Alassane Ouattara's supporters and that of Gbagbo.

CONCLUSION

To a great extent, AFRICOM has significantly enhanced and improved the tactical and operational dimensions of AU peacekeeping missions. Nevertheless, it is necessary for the Command to consider how it can effectively complement rather than undermine the efforts of the AU's nascent peace and security architecture. Evidently, U.S. policy toward Africa has remained largely intact without any dramatic change under the Obama administration. It is quite clear that President Obama is following the militarized and unilateral security policy that had been pursued by the Clinton and Bush administrations toward Africa.[68] But it is significant for the United States to note that its security needs in Africa would be best assured by looking to meaningfully address and reconcile its interest with the continent's human security needs such as poverty, high levels of unemployment, access to clean water, and the HIV/AIDs pandemic.[69] These are the issues that confront and threaten the survival and the existence of most African states and make them vulnerable to terrorist groups such as al-Qaeda.

It is also important for the United States not to see Africa at the periphery of its foreign policy engagements. Now opportunities for progress in Africa abound due to rising regional institutions, expanding economies, increasing democratization, and emerging security institutions. For example, the International Monetary Fund (IMF) notes that in 2011, against a threatening global backdrop, most economies in sub-Saharan Africa turned in a solid performance with a growth rate averaging more than 5 percent.[70] Most importantly, the AU and the RECs, especially ECOWAS, have developed very robust peace and security architectures to deal with African security challenges. It is therefore imperative that Africa is not seen or engaged by the United States as a conflict-ridden continent but as a continent that is advancing democratically, economically, and developmentally.

ENDNOTES - CHAPTER 13

1. See "National Security Review 30: American policy towards Africa in the 1990s," Washington, DC: The White House, June 15, 1992.

2. Kwesi Aning, "African Crises Response Initiatives and the New African Security (DIS) Order," *Africa Journal of Political Science*, Vol. 6, No. 1, 2001, p. 45; Benedikt Franke, *Enabling a Continent to help itself: US Military Capacity Building and African Emerging Security Architecture*, Monterey, CA: Center for Contemporary Conflict, 2007, p. 2.

3. Alhaji Sarjoh Bah and Kwesi Aning, "US Peace Operation Policy in Africa: From ACRI to AFRICOM," *International Peacekeeping,* Vol. 15, No. 1, 2008, p. 119.

4. *Ibid.;* for more information, see Adekeye Adebajo, *UN Peacekeeping in Africa: From Suez Crisis to the Sudan Conflicts,* Boulder, CO: Lynne Rienner Publishers, Inc, 2011.

5. *Ibid*; see also Ivor H. Daalder, "Knowing When to Say No: The Development of US Policy for Peacekeeping," William Durch, ed., *UN Peacekeeping, American Politics, and the Uncivil Wars of the 1990s,* New York: St. Martin's Press, 1996, pp. 35–67.

6. Mark Malan, "US Response to African Crises: An Overview and Preliminary Analysis of ACRI," *ISS Occasional Paper,* No. 24, 1997.

7. Bah and Aning, 2008; Kwesi Aning, Thomas Jaye, and Samuel Atuobi, "The Role of Private Military Companies in US-Africa Policy," *Review of African Political Economy,* Vol. 35, No. 118, 2008, pp. 613-628.

8. *Ibid.*

9. *Ibid.*

10. Franke, "Enabling a Continent to help itself."

11. "African Contingency Operations Training and Assistance (ACOTA)," Washington, DC: U.S Department of State, available from *www.state.gov/p/af/rt/acota/.*

12. Aning, Jaye, and Atuobi.

13. *Ibid*; see also Eric G. Berman and Katie E. Sams, "Peacekeeping in Africa: Capabilities and Culpabilities," Geneva, Switzerland/Pretoria, South Africa: United Nations Institute for Disarmament Research, 2000, pp. 267–290.

14. U.S. AFRICOM Public Affairs, "FACT SHEET: Africa Contingency Operations Training and Assistance (ACOTA)," Stuttgart, Germany, June 15, 2008.

15. For more information, see Sarjoh Bah and Aning, p. 122.

16. Aning, Jaye, and Atuobi.

17. Nina M. Serafino, "The Global Peace Operations Initiative: Background and Issues for Congress," CRS Report for Congress, Washington, DC: Congressional Research Service, 2009.

18. *Ibid.*, p. 1-2; Bah and Aning, p. 123. More information is available from *www.state.gov/t/pm/ppa/gpoi/*.

19. *Ibid*; Aning, Jaye, and Atuobi.

20. Niall Ferguson, "Wanted: A Grand Strategy for America," *Newsweek*, February 13, 2011.

21. Colin Dueck, "New Perspectives on American Grand Strategy: A Review Essay," *International Security*, Vol. 28, No. 4, 2006. See also Charles Kupchan, "Grand Strategy: The Four Pillars of the Future," *Democracy: A Journal of Ideas*, Issue No. 23, Winter 2012.

22. Peter Feaver, "What is Grand Strategy and Why Do We Need It?" *Foreign Policy*, January 6, 2012.

23. Anna Field and Geoff Dyer, "The 'Obama Doctrine' Begins to Take Shape," *Financial Times*, October 24, 2011, p. 6.

24. Field and Dyer, p. 6.

25. Available from *www.africom.mil/AboutAFRICOM.asp*.

26. "President Bush Creates a Department of Defense Unified Combatant Command for Africa," Washington, DC: The White House, available from *www.africom.mil/getArticle. asp?art=3152&lang=0*.

27. *Ibid.*

28. Christopher Isike, Ufo Okeke-Uzodike, and Lysias Gilbert, "The United States Africa Command: Enhancing American

Security or Fostering African Development?" *African Security Review*, Vol. 17, No. 1, 2008, p. 31.

29. EUCOM had responsibility for most of the continent, thus 42 states out of the 54 in Africa; PACOM administered military ties with Madagascar, Comoros, Mauritius, and other Islands in the Indian Ocean; and CENTCOM oversaw Egypt and the Horn of Africa region, together with the Middle East and Central Asia.

30. See "U.S. Creating New Africa Command to Coordinate Military Efforts," Washington, DC: U.S. Department of State, available from *usinfo.state.gov/xarchives/display.html?¼washfile-english&y¼2007&m¼Febaruary*; Secretary of Defense Robert Gates, Testimony before the Senate Armed Services Committee, Washington, DC: U.S. Senate, February 6, 2007.

31. See "AFRICOM Mission Statement," USAFRICOM, Stuttgart, Germany, 2008, available from *www.africom.mil/AboutAFRICOM.asp*; Lauren Ploch, "Africa Command: U.S. Strategic Interests and the Role of the U.S. Military in Africa," CRS Report for Congress, Washington, DC: Congressional Research Service, 2011, pp. 1-4.

32. *Ibid.*

33. They include the U.S. Army Africa (USARAF), Vicenza, Italy; U.S. Naval Forces, Africa (NAVAF), Naples, Italy; U.S. Air Forces, Africa (AFAFRICA), Ramstein Air Base, Germany; U.S. Marine Corps Forces, Africa (MARFORAF), Stuttgart, Germany; Special Operations Command-Africa (SOCAFRICA), Stuttgart, Germany; and the Combined Joint Task Force-Horn of Africa (CJTF-HOA), Camp Lemonnier, Djibouti.

34. See "About U.S. Africa Command," available from *www.africom.mil/AboutAFRICOM.asp*.

35. See "OEF-TS Fact Sheet and the TSCTP Fact Sheet," available from *www.africom.mil/AboutAFRICOM.asp*.

36. "About U.S. Africa Command."

37. See "IMET Fact Sheet and PMHAP Fact sheet," available from *www.africom.mil/AboutAFRICOM.asp.*

38. *Ibid.* For critical articles on the efficacy of these programs, see Alhaji Sarjoh Bah and Kwesi Aning, "US Peace Operations Policy in Africa: From ACRI to AFRICOM," Ian Johnstone, ed., *US Peace Operations Policy: A Double-Edged Sword?* London, UK, and New York: Routledge, 2009; Kwesi Aning, Thomas Jaye, and Samuel Atuobi, "The Role of Private Military Companies in US-Africa Policy," *Review of African Political Economy*, 2008.

39. See "FACT SHEET: United States Africa Command," available from *www.africom.mil/getArticle.asp?art=1644.*

40. Ploch.

41. On May 25. 2004 (Africa Day), the PSC was officially inaugurated with fanfare to replace the "Mechanism on Conflict Prevention, Management and Resolution," which had been established in June 1993 in Cairo, Egypt, under the umbrella of the OAU.

42. AU doc. PSC/AHG/ST(X, para. 1, May 25 2005.

43. Kwesi Aning, "The African Union's Peace and Security Architecture: Defining an Emerging Response Mechanism," *Lecture Series on African Security*, No. 3, Uppsala, Sweden: The Nordic African Institute, and Stockholm, Sweden: The Swedish Defense Research Agency, FOI, 2008.

44. *Ibid.*, p. 3.

45. See the Solemn declaration on a Common African Defense and Security Policy (CADSP), 2004, available from *www.iss. co.za/AF/RegOrg/unity_to_union/pdfs/au/cadspjan04frm.pdf;* see also Aning, p. 5.

46. See the AU's CADSP, p. 3.

47. *Ibid.*

48. Paul D, Williams, "The African Union's Conflict Management Capabilities," Working Paper, New York: Council on Foreign Relations, October 2011.

49. *Ibid.*, p. 6.

50. See Protocol Relating to the Establishment of the Peace and Security Council (PSC); See also Kwesi Aning, "The UN and African Union's Peace and Security Architecture: Defining and Emerging Relationship?" *Critical Currents*, No. 5, October 2008.

51. See PSC, Articles 3, 4, 7.

52. Paul D. Williams, "Thinking about Security in Africa," *International Affairs*, Vol. 83, No. 6, 2007, pp. 1021-1038.

53. See PSC, Article 7; see also Kwesi Aning and Samuel Atuobi, "R2P in Africa: An Analysis of the African Union´s Peace and Security Architecture," *Global Responsibility to Protect*, Vol. 1, 2009.

54. Anthoni Van Nieuwkerk, "The Regional Roots of the African Peace and Security Architecture: Exploring Centre-Periphery Relations," *South African Journal of International Affairs*, Vol. 18, No 2, August 2011, pp. 169-189; Tim Murithi, "The African Union's Foray into Peacekeeping: Lessons from the Hybrid Mission in Darfur," *Journal of Peace, Conflict and Development*, Issue 14, 2009.

55. Article 4 (h) of the Constitutive Acts states that the AU has the right to intervene in member state conflicts with respect of grave circumstances, namely war crimes, genocide, and crimes against humanity; while Article 4 (j) gives the right to member states to request the intervention from AU in order to restore peace and security.

56. Williams, "Thinking about Security in Africa," p. 10.

57. See International Peace Institute, "Operationalizing the African Standby Force," Meeting Note of the High Level African Civilian and Military Leaders Retreat in Kigali, Rwanda, January 2010.

58. Since its establishment in 2004, the MSC has been engaged in providing advice on the PSC's authorized peace operations in Burundi, Sudan, Darfur, Comoros, and currently Somalia.

59. See "U.S. Mission to African Union Shows Commitment to Africa," available from *www.usau.usmission.gov/commitment-to-africa.html*.

60. Combined Joint Task Force: Horn of Africa (CJTF-HOA) personnel, for instance, provided military training and assistance to Burundian and Ugandan forces who were deployed to Somalia. Since 2007, the United States has contributed over $250 million to AMISOM. See Paul D. Williams, "The African Union's Conflict Management Capabilities," Working Paper, New York: Council on Foreign Relations, 2011.

61. See "TRANSCRIPT: Ambassador Anderson on African Union Peacekeeping Operations," available from *www.africom.mil/getArticle.asp?art=5475&lang=0*.

62. Ploch.

63. Aning, Jaye, and Atuobi.

64. Stephanie Hanson, "The African Union," available from *www.cfr.org/africa/african-union/p11616*.

65. Ploch.

66. For more information, see Alexis Arieff *et al.*, "U.S. Foreign Assistance to Sub-Saharan Africa: The FY2012 Request," CRS Report for Congress, Washington, DC: Congressional Research Service, May 20, 2011.

67. For more information, see "The Crisis in Libya: the Imperative of rushing the ASF," available from *www.currentanalyst.com/index.php/opeds/158-the-crisis-in-libya-the-imperative-of-rushing-the-asf*.

68. See Daniel Volman, "Obama Expands Military Involvement in Africa," available from *ipsnews.net/news.asp?idnews=50898*.

69. Bah and Aning; Isike, Okeke-Uzodike, and Gilbert.

70. Available from *www.imf.org/external/pubs/ft/survey/so/2012/car011012a.htm*.

CHAPTER 14

U.S. GRAND STRATEGY AND THE SEARCH FOR PARTNERS: SOUTH AFRICA AS A KEY PARTNER IN AFRICA

Abel Esterhuyse

In an age of austerity, the United States needs partners. More specifically, for a grand strategy to be effective, a country like the United States should be able to shape its security and foreign policy environment in cooperation with key partners. South Africa and the United States are both important role players in Africa in general, and in African security in particular: South Africa as regional and to some extent also continental hegemon, and the United States as the sole hyper power in the world. Neither South Africa, nor the United States necessarily has a long positive history of constructive engagement in Africa. Yet, their involvement in Africa, and African security, raises questions about a possible competition or confluence of security and other interests and questions about similarities and differences in their approaches in the pursuance of these interests. More importantly, are they cooperating in the case of a confluence of interests, or are the United States and South Africa, even in cases of a confluence of interests, each walking its own path in pursuing these interests?

This chapter aims at providing a descriptive analysis of the divergence and/or cooperation between South Africa and the United States in their contributions to African security. The first section considers the role of Africa in South African security and foreign policy outlook in general and in the worldview of the reigning African National Congress (ANC) government in particular. In the second section, a brief analysis is provided of U.S. involvement in African security. The discussion concludes with a consideration of possible cooperation and/or discord between South Africa and the United States in Africa.

INTO AFRICA: SOUTH AFRICA'S STRATEGIC OUTLOOK

The focus on Africa in South Africa's foreign policy is undeniable. The strategic plan of the South African Department of International Relations and Cooperation is explicit in noting that South Africa's foreign relations are anchored in a prioritization of the African continent and in strengthening the political and economic integration of the South African Development Community (SADC).[1] However, South African interests in Africa are not that clear. South Africa does have economic interests in Africa.[2] However, those interests are limited and more or less restricted to the SADC region.[3] There is also, for example, a considerable imbalance in South Africa's trade relationship with Africa. This ranges from 9:1 in trade with SADC countries, and 5:1 in trade with Africa as a whole.[4] Compared to its economic relations with other parts of the world, its economic relations with Africa are growing, although they are still relatively limited.[5] At the same time, South Africa's security is not being challenged by any African country or specific threats. In short, there is reason to doubt whether the South African focus on Africa is interests-driven.

It is possible, though, to explain the South African foreign policy focus on Africa in terms of a number of considerations. The first is domestic politics. The worldview of the South African (ANC) government is shaped by the need for a so-called "National Democratic Revolution." Linking the three words, *national*, *democratic*, and *revolution*, is in itself of great significance and provides at least some insight into the ANC mindset. Like most South African political concepts, the National Democratic Revolution is rooted in the legacy of apartheid and, in this case, a revolutionary-oriented East-bloc approach to politics that was formed during the Cold War anti-apartheid struggle.[6]

Today, the South African domestic political landscape is still colored by the legacies and realities of apartheid. Apartheid defines the ANC's view of the country and the world. Apartheid is still the tool for mobilization of the masses, on which the ANC as a political party relies. The ANC, as the government, thus manages a unique paradox. On the one hand, they need to cleanse the South African society of apartheid and eradicate the legacy and influence thereof. On the other, though, keeping the "fight against apartheid" alive is an integral part of the ANC's philosophy and, more specifically, keeping the tripartite-alliance[7] together. The fight against apartheid has always been the central organizing concept for the ANC and the reason for its existence. The ANC has to use the structural legacy of apartheid to explain the disparity between what is, or what was, and what could have been.

At present, the process to address the legacies of apartheid is playing itself out predominantly in an economic policy of black economic empowerment (BEE) and the application of affirmative action (AA) to ensure representivity[8] and deal with the economic inequalities in society. The National Democratic Revolution, thus, needs to provide many who have been excluded from the productive economy with a pathway to, what in the West at least, would be considered as development and life improvement. Representivity and AA action have become important pathways in making this happen for the masses. Of course, a small number of so-called "black diamonds"[9] have benefitted from BEE. Certain elements within the ANC are, however, increasingly calling for more drastic measures and, as a consequence, the debate on nationalization is heating up in South Africa.[10]

As a matter of irony, the need for representivity and AA have driven many experienced and capable workers out of the public sector, leading to serious service delivery problems for the ANC government — especially in the rural areas.[11] A growing bureaucratic inefficiency increasingly underpins a view of government as ineffective and incompetent. Many South Africans thus tend to view the National Democratic Revolution with skepticism and as a metaphor for government inaptitude.[12] The need for representivity and AA, at the same time, developed into an attitude of entitlement in the constituency of the ANC-led tripartite government. Of course, an attitude of entitlement absolves people from action, while the service delivery problems reinforce an attitude of powerlessness and victimhood.[13]

Why is this important? The need for a national democratic revolution, AA policies, and the acceptance of inadequacies in many areas of government is informed by the importance of Africa. It underpins a government approach that highlights the need to emphasize the African dimension and identity in South African society to the detriment of many considerations that others may consider more important. The ANC domestic political discourse and the domestic political agenda of the ANC government are informed by "Africa" and the need to emphasize the importance of Africa. This orientation toward Africa in domestic politics, by design, also informs the foreign policy stance of the South African government. In a multicultural and multiethnic society, this is an important message from government to both its domestic and foreign audiences.

A second consideration is geography. A previous South African president, Thabo Mbeki, found it necessary to deliver a speech on "I am an African" in the South African parliament.[14] He had to make the point explicitly in the South African parliament that South Africa is part of Africa! Why? From a geographical perspective, South Africa is not only part of Africa, but its position at the southern tip of the continent is also a blessing and a curse. With some of the world's most important minerals, the country has very long open borders to the north and has to police a coastline of more than 3,000 kilometers (km) on one of the naval choke points of the world. The recent instabilities in the oceans around East and West Africa, together with subsequent increase in sea traffic around Africa, highlight this reality.

Geopolitics dictate that the South African government should commit itself to a prioritization of the African continent in general and in strengthening of the political and economic integration of the SADC in particular. It is no surprise, then, that South Africa's foreign policy has a very explicit focus on Africa in general, and the SADC in particular, in "consolidation of the African Agenda."[15] The geographical emphasis on Africa, like the domestic political agenda, also encases South Africa's African identity. This explicit alignment with Africa is in stark contrast to the focus of the apartheid government that projected itself as part of the European civilization. The apartheid government projected the South African sea lines and minerals as important to the West. For the ANC government, it is part of Africa's rich reserve. Thus, identity politics drive the South African geostrategic orientation toward Africa.[16]

History is a third consideration in South African foreign policy orientation toward Africa. The apartheid government never steered away from political, economic, and military coercion in Southern Africa. The ANC is inspired by the need to mend these injustices. Its history of resistance against apartheid (the so-called struggle history) left the ANC with a responsibility to repay many African countries for their services as sanctuaries to ANC cadres during the anti-apartheid struggle.

History, of course, also shapes South African strategic engagement with the rest of the world: from support to controversial "underdogs" such as the Palestinians and, more recently, Muammar Gaddafi, to a very strong anti-American and anti-West stance in general, and an emphasis on South-South relations in particular.[17] The South African orientation to the West in general, and the United States in particular, is driven by Africa's colonial heritage and U.S. support to the apartheid government during the Cold War. The very strong anti-American sentiments of the South African government were clearly demonstrated through the latter's reactions to the creation of the U.S. Africa Command[18] (AFRICOM) and the positioning of the Libyan crisis as American neo-colonialism.[19] In both cases, the South African government furiously denounced the decisions and actions by the U.S. Government.[20]

South African foreign policy therefore contains a very explicit grounding in an Africanist and anti-imperialist agenda. Greg Mills notes, for example, "there is a visceral genuflection to interpret, label and dismiss Western actions on the African continent as imperialistically intended."[21] Thus, an Africanist and anti-imperialist stance is, in essence, about being anti-West. This foreign policy agenda contains an implicit expression of both anti-Americanism and solidarity with allies around the world from the period of national liberation. Liberation movement politics of sentiment and solidarity are also an important drivers of the South African strategic orientation toward Africa and its role on/toward the African continent.[22]

The nature of global governance is a fourth factor underpinning the emphasis on Africa in South African foreign policy. Liberation politics and the Africanist and anti-imperialist agenda support the strong emphasis of the ANC government on a just global order and an effort to change the international structure. South Africa's aggregate capabilities in terms of economic, diplomatic, and military capacities in relation to other African countries led to a view of South Africa's role in Africa as that of pivotal state, regional power, and hegemonic state. Of course, each description contains some truth about South Africa's role in Africa. At the same time, though, this also masks a constraint of South African involvement in Africa: the possible perception of South Africa as a big brother using bullying tactics. The perception explains, at least partly, South Africa's cautious handling of the Zimbabwean crisis in general and Robert Mugabe in particular.[23] It is a reality that the South African government deliberately portrays a selective image of multilateral engagement through political partnerships and (sometimes) regional leadership. This self-imposed perceptual constraint is a reality of South Africa's engagement and role in Southern Africa.

South Africa, supported by others, mainly Nigeria, has become the key driver and competitor in the reconstruction of Africa's institutional architecture. This specifically pertains to the creation of the African Union (AU) and the hosting of the African Parliament in South Africa. In July 2001, the Assembly of African Heads of State and Government in Lusaka, Zambia, also reached a decision on the New Partnership for Africa's Development (NEPAD) as an overarching vision and policy framework for accelerating economic cooperation and integration among African countries. This corresponded with the vision of the then South African president Mbeki of an African Renaissance to confront the challenges of the African continent. South Africa was also the key actor in transforming the South African Development Coordinating Conference into the South African Development Community, which, in August 2008, launched the Southern African free trade area. These continental and regional institutions became an important part of South Africa's approach of multilateral engagement in shaping its immediate geostrategic environment. The country's support for and role in the establishment of regional and continental institutions, together with the substantial financial support to the AU, the NEPAD Secretariat, and the Pan-African Parliament, not only demonstrate South Africa's leading role in Africa, but also the country's commitment to the African agenda (identity politics) and in helping Africa (enlightened self-interest).[24]

South Africa uses its geopolitical position in (Southern) Africa as a means to popularize Africa's potential and challenges on global forums and institutions. As a result of South Africa's efforts, Africa features increasingly on the agenda of the United Nations (UN), the G8 (France, Germany, Italy, Japan, the United Kingdom [UK], and the United States), the World Trade Organizations (WTOs), the International Monetary Fund (IMF), and the World Bank. The extent to which South Africa, for example, was willing to give up or sacrifice reputation and respect outside of Africa during its tenure at the UN Security Council in its search for a mediated solution in Zimbabwe, once again demonstrated South Africa's commitment to the African continent.[25]

Compassion and humanitarian considerations may provide a fifth explanation for South Africa's focus on Africa. There is no doubt that South Africa under ANC leadership is committed in its search for an end to conflict and violence and a move toward sustainable peace on the African continent. Over the last number of years, South Africa has provided considerable funding, military resources, and political energy in places such as Burundi, the Democratic Republic of the Congo, and Sudan to create what can only be considered fragile peace settlements. Conflict resolution and the utilization of its military in peace missions in Africa have come to symbolize South Africa's search for African solutions for African problems. The military has become, specifically under the Mbeki regime, the most prominent (and preferred) South African foreign policy tool in Africa. With the decision by the South African government to make the military once again responsible for the safeguarding of South Africa's borders, the South African military presence in Africa is set to decline. The South African military is overstretched, underfunded, and, the Army in particular, in dire need of new equipment. The South

African government will continue its role as a peace broker on the continent and to use the country's considerable political leverage as a means to stabilization. In this regard, the South African military places a high emphasis on so-called defense diplomacy.[26]

South Africa is without doubt a key state, not only in the SADC region, but also on the Africa continent as a whole. South Africa's position in Africa is to a certain extent comparable to that of the United States in the global arena — if you act, you are in the wrong, and if you do not act, you are also in the wrong. A key strategic question pertains to the extent to which South Africa has to prove its commitment to Africa — a continent that is already suffering under the burden of a continent-wide inferiority complex and bad leadership in its interaction with the rest of the world. On a continent that is in dire need of constructive leadership, South Africa seems to offer itself as a willing leader; often to the detriment of its own position and image.

In the absence of clear identifiable interests and a wide variety of factors underpinning South Africa's explicit commitment to the African continent, a lack of focus is to be expected. It is thus no surprise that a mixture of geopolitical and historic realities, domestic and liberation politics, and Africanism and anti-imperialism seems to drive the unpredictable and inconsistent nature of the ANC government's foreign policy agenda in general, and on the African continent in particular. Such an array of factors is responsible for the description of South African foreign policy as a "bit of this, bit of that." Making sense of such a foreign policy approach will always be difficult.

INTO AFRICA: THE U.S. (RE)DISCOVERY OF AFRICA

Until fairly recently, Africa did not feature very prominently on the political radar screens in Washington.[27] This has always been a logical outcome of U.S. global strategic, political, and economic interests, which are profoundly Eurocentric by nature. Salih Booker, for example, argues that there has always been a denial of most U.S. interests in Africa.[28] Booker is of the opinion that America reluctantly identifies with Africa in spite of the dramatic changes that have taken place in Africa over the last decades and also in the status of Africa's descendants in the United States itself.[29]

Except for the slave trade, the United States does not really have historical ties with Africa. For a variety of reasons, the United States has not been involved in the "scramble for Africa." America did not challenge European influence in Africa; in exchange, it is argued, for dominance in the Western hemisphere.[30] In the aftermath of World War II, Africa became more important for the United States, not only because of the creation of the UN and the independence of so many (UN-voting) African states, but in particular because of the geopolitics of the Cold War. The creation of the Bureau of African Affairs in 1958 serves as an example of the growing concern in Washington at the time about what was happening in Africa, the increasing Soviet influence in Africa in particular.[31]

The end of the Cold War led to renewed disengagement of the United States from Africa, reinforced by the 1993 "Black Hawk Down" incident in Somalia. The 1994 Rwanda genocide did not attract much political attention (or action) in and from the United States.

Until the creation of AFRICOM in 2007, the U.S. approach to Africa was characterized by the promotion of democracy and the development of trade relations by means of initiatives such as the African Growth and Opportunity Act.[32] During most of these times, two particular considerations shaped U.S. foreign policy toward Africa. First, the color line has always been an important factor. Before and during the Cold War, America predominantly identified with Europeans in Africa.[33] Second, economic factors reign supreme. The question of how America will gain economically from Africa has always directed its foreign policy toward the continent.

The United States always experienced some difficulty in developing a coherent policy toward Africa. This difficulty is rooted in a number of realities. First, before the eruption of the War on Terror, the United States had few concrete, material interests in the continent.[34] Africa is perhaps the only sizable inhabited geographical region that has never really been vital to U.S. security interests. While clear identifiable interests provide policy with a solid foundation and coherence, a lack thereof normally leads to ambiguity, debate, and vulnerability to changing political moods. In the case of Africa, this particular reality linked U.S. policy closely to global geopolitical developments. In addition, U.S. African policies very often reflect an indifference to indigenous African political realities and an inability to predict the probable impact of specific policies on interstate relations among African states.[35]

Second, it is difficult for the average American citizen to relate to the diverse, sometimes chaotic or anarchic, and often depressing realities of the African continent.[36] The public idea of Africa, so successfully sustained by Western media, is rooted in an image of conflict, disaster, challenges, and hopelessness. In the United States, no news is better than good news from Africa. Thus, many Americans have a "National Geographic" image of "Africa" — as if Africa does not consist of different countries with a huge diversity of nations and peoples, rich and poor, developed and underdeveloped, who have a variety of interests, opinions, and prejudices. U.S. involvement in Africa is underpinned by media coverage of humanitarian catastrophe and public pressure on the U.S. Government to react to the human need. U.S. engagements in Africa are mostly episodic, short-lived, and inconsistent. Egregious suffering without media coverage will most probably be ignored.[37] Washington deals with "Africa" as if it is a single country and search for "a single African voice" to guide them in dealing with this diverse continent. The search, of course, is both futile and dangerous.[38] Though hegemonic states such as South Africa have tried to do this in the past, there is nobody who speaks for or who can speak on behalf of "Africans."[39]

Third, there is an absence of a powerful and cohesive domestic constituency in the United States to maintain pressure on Washington for an effective policy toward different countries in Africa.[40] This reality has its roots in the lack of common personal and professional commitments, interests, and linkages between the civil societies of most African countries and the United States. Many Americans refer to themselves as "Afro-Americans" as if Euro-Africans or Arab-Africans do not exist and as if Afro-Americans have closer ties with the African continent than their fellow Americans.

Last, until the creation of AFRICOM, U.S. policy toward the majority of African countries was, to a large extent, the responsibility of the bureaucratic middle echelons in Washington that practiced the art of bureaucratic conservatism. These bureaucrats operate within a framework of do not spend too much money, do not take a stand that might create domestic controversy, and do not let African issues complicate policy toward other, more important, parts of the world.[41] This bureaucratic approach to U.S. policy formulation led to a situation where the United States had to "rediscover" Africa at several junctions during the post- World War II era.[42] U.S. engagement with Africa has often reflected rather different approaches and intensities between the Department of State, the U.S. Agency for International Development (USAID), and the Department of Defense (DoD). This very often results in some confusion about U.S. interests, objectives, and motives.[43]

Obviously, the September 11, 2001 (9/11) terrorist attacks, the consequent U.S. War on Terror, and more specifically, U.S. military involvement in Iraq and Afghanistan dramatically impacted the U.S. geostrategic outlook. It is possible to argue that U.S. foreign policy is shifting attention away from the Middle East to, *inter alia*, Africa. There is a clear growth of U.S. interests in Africa, and Africa is on the rise on the U.S. security agenda. Different factors are driving current U.S. interests in Africa: oil and global trade, maritime security, armed conflicts, violent extremism, and HIV/AIDS.[44] This growth in interests is rooted in two very specific global geostrategic considerations: the continuing global economic meltdown that, specifically in Europe and the United States, reached new heights during 2011, and the power shift away from the north Atlantic to the Indian Ocean rim with India and China as the two main players. These two considerations are closely interwoven in the competition for African resources and markets.

There is no clearer indication of " a more focused strategic approach toward the continent"[45] than the creation of AFRICOM and, more specifically, the nature of that command. The unique blending of the U.S. military and diplomatic apparatus in AFRICOM is itself a reflection of the elevation of U.S. security and other interests in Africa, a more aggressive U.S. foreign policy toward Africa, and, most importantly, a new militarized approach in dealing with Africa.[46]

SOUTH AFRICA AND THE UNITED STATES IN AFRICA: PARTNERS OR COMPETITORS

The most outstanding feature about both U.S. and South African involvement in African security is the prominent role of the military. Of course, neither of the two would like to be seen as being overtly militarily involved in African security. There is also no doubt that there is a confluence of U.S./South Africa interests in African security. U.S. interests in Africa have a visible focus on security. This specifically concerns the need to address maritime security, armed conflicts, and violent extremism in Africa.

The Strategic Plan of the South African Department of International Relations and Cooperation explicitly identified the "continued prioritisation of Africa" as the first of its "overarching priorities."[47] The Plan continues to explain that the focus of South Africa's engagements on the African continent is to promote development, contribute to the resolution of conflicts, and build an environment in which socio-economic development can take place. Whereas in the case of the United States, the emphasis in their engagement with Africa is centered on security, in the case of South Africa, it is on development.

Of course, it is quite easy for both the United States and South Africa to identify Africa as a strategic priority. However, explaining why Africa is or should be of vital strategic interest is not that easy. From an African perspective, U.S. interests in Africa, irrespective of what is said in the halls of politics, are rooted in access to African oil and mineral riches, the need to pursue the War on Terror in the African battlespace, and the continued inroads into African markets by peer competitors such as China and India. Identifying the interests of a fellow African country is a more sensitive and complex issue. Not only is African politics sometimes difficult to disaggregate, but South Africa is in many ways Africa's economic super power with a history of destabilization on the continent. South African interests in Africa center on the history of the governing party, identity politics, and geostrategic realities. The South African government, very much like that of the United States, is very cautious not to be seen as "exploiting" Africa for its own selfish economic interests. Thus, South African economic interests in Africa (and these are real vital interests!) are coated in the jargon of socio-economic development since "socio-economic development is critical for addressing the root causes of conflict and instability" in Africa.[48] This difference (security vis-à-vis socio-economic development) may provide an important first clue in understanding the reluctance of the South African government in working with the United States in Africa.

The U.S. 2010 *National Security Strategy* stresses the need to "embrace effective partnerships" and for a consultative approach on the African continent to facilitate access to open markets, conflict prevention, global peacekeeping, counterterrorism, and the protection of vital carbon sinks.[49] Similarly, the February 2010 U.S. *Quadrennial Defense Review* highlighted the fact that American efforts in Africa "hinge on partnering with African states . . . to conduct capacity-building and peacekeeping operations, prevent extremism, and address humanitarian crises."[50] The need for partnerships is also highlighted in the most recent U.S. *National Military Strategy* to preserve stability, facilitate resolutions to political tensions that underlie conflicts, and to foster broader development. The *National Military Strategy* stresses the need to:

> identify and encourage states and regional organizations that have demonstrated a leadership role to continue to contribute to Africa's security.[51]

The 2010 *National Security Strategy* placed specific emphasis on South Africa as "a critical partner" in "charting a course toward improved governance and meaningful development" in Africa. According to the *National Security Strategy*, South Africa often serves as a springboard to the entire African continent. Thus, the U.S. need is to work with South Africa to "pursue shared interests in Africa's security, growth, and the development of Africa's human capital."[52]

The United States, however, does not feature in South African foreign policy documents as a key partner in Africa. The first priority for the South African government is to pursue the so-called African Agenda through the political and economic integration of Africa and to defend Africa's geostrategic interests to be "among equals in the global architecture."[53] The European Union Strategy for Africa, the New Africa-Asia

Strategic Partnership (NAASP), the Tokyo International Conference for African Development (TICAD), and the Africa-India Forum and the Forum for China Africa Cooperation (FOCAC) are mentioned as key pathways for development and cooperation in Africa. This raises questions about South Africa's perception of the U.S. role in Africa. An outstanding feature of South Africa's involvement in Africa is the emphasis that is placed on the role of SADC, the AU, and the UN "to bring peace, security, and stability to the African continent."[54] In the description of its relations with the United States, the need is emphasized to maintain the key U.S. role in the fight against communicable and infectious diseases and to nurture and utilize the U.S. commitment to Africa to promote peacekeeping, post-conflict reconstruction and development, skills development, capacity building, and trilateral cooperation.[55] Nowhere is the need expressed to work with the United States in Africa. From a geopolitical perspective, the South African disregard or indifference toward the U.S. role in Africa is quite obvious. Clearly, although the United States recognizes the importance of South Africa on the African continent and the need to work with South Africa in addressing African challenges, the same cannot be said of the South African government. Partnering with the United States is not only bad domestic politics for the ANC government; it also does not resonate and correspond very well with South Africa's image in the rest of Africa.

There is no doubt that the current South African ANC government has what the United States would see as "a terrorist background." The ANC, to be specific, not very long ago, was listed by the United States as a terrorist organization.[56] South Africa has not been the most energetic partner in the U.S. War on Terror.

Concerns have obviously been raised—at least by the U.S. intelligence community—about South Africa as a possible recruiting and training area for international terrorists. South African passports are relatively easily available on the black market and have been found in the possession of al-Qaeda suspects.[57] Moreover, while South Africa is not directly threatened with international terrorist activity, it may well be a safe haven for international terrorists. The most important issue concerning the U.S./South Africa terrorism nexus, though, is the reality that South Africa does not share the U.S. outlook on terrorism. In the ANC worldview, at least, a sharp distinction is made between international terrorism and the use of terror as a weapon in the armed struggles of the anti-colonial and national liberation movements. The use of terror in these struggles for liberation is morally and legally just in the ANC worldview. The ANC, thus, distinguishes between international and revolutionary terrorism. Terrorist violence is described as "indiscriminate, violent attacks on the civilian population."[58] According to the ANC, these kinds of attacks are not being used by armed liberation movements and run counter to their ethos.

Thus, the ANC viewed the 9/11 attacks against the United States as wrong but, at the same time, the terrorist tactics of the Taliban and the revolutionary forces against the United States in Afghanistan and Iraq as justified. This also holds true for the support by the ANC for terror tactics by the Palestinians against Israel. There is no doubt that the ANC government in South Africa, albeit tacitly, views the U.S. security objectives in Africa in the War on Terror as imperialist by nature.[59] According to this view, the United States used the events of 9/11 very cleverly to its own advantage. Instead of focusing on those immediately responsible for the attack, the United States used military expansionism to strengthen its economy through the acquisition of markets and oil-rich areas. The War on Terror, according to ANC logic, has become a U.S. excuse to gain control of strategic oil supplies and markets in Africa.

The perceptions of the ANC are grounded in its revolutionary background and experiences. Whether those perceptions are rooted in reality is absolutely irrelevant. The ANC understands the notion that there is always, at least, some truth in any perception. The perceptions about the creation of AFRICOM are a good example in this regard. To be more specific, the interwoven nature of the military and diplomatic instrument within AFRICOM positioned the U.S. military as the primary instrument of U.S. foreign policy on the African continent. The U.S. military is thus seen as the lead instrument of U.S. foreign policy in Africa—or it is portrayed by the South Africans as the leading foreign policy instrument. The reaction from the South Africa government to the creation of AFRICOM was one of outrage. At its 2007 Polokwane Conference, for example, the ANC accepted a resolution that "urges Africa to remain united and resolute in the rejection of the African Command Centre (sic) (AFRICOM)."

At the same time and as a matter of irony, though, the South African National Defence Force became, for all practical purposes, the leading South African foreign policy instrument in Africa during the Mbeki administration.[60] The human security paradigm is supposed to inform South African military involvement on the continent, and the South African armed forces:

have to be transformed from an instrument of aggression to an instrument of protection [in] the development of the individual and the community.[61]

As a consequence, both the U.S. and the SA militaries are actively involved in African security. Yet,
the South Africans view their military involvement as
human security-related and that of the United States
as military security-orientated. For the ANC government, South African military deployments into Africa
are meant as a force of good, while the U.S. military
instrument in Africa is seen as a force of destruction.
More specifically, the U.S. force utility, according to
ANC logic, is shaped by conventional warfighting applications, while South African military involvement
is driven by the human security and peacetime applications of military force. The differences between
perceptions and reality in the South African and U.S.
military involvement in Africa may thus raise questions of South African hypocrisy in the United States.

CONCLUSION

This discussion was intended to provide an overview of possible areas of cooperation or disagreement
between the United States and South Africa in Africa
in general and African security in particular. South
Africa's economic and security interests are to a large
extent restricted to Southern Africa. Yet, Africa features very prominently as a foreign policy focus area
in South African foreign policy. The explicit focus on
Africa has very little to do with South African interests
in Africa and is only explainable within the context of
domestic politics, geostrategic realities and identity
politics, historical considerations of struggle politics

and alignment with the underdogs of the world, the current imbalances in global governance, and a commitment to end conflict and violence in a search for peace and stability on the African continent. This conglomerate of factors makes the development of consistency in the South African foreign policy toward Africa extremely difficult and the policy itself very complex and complicated. It is difficult to understand and to predict future actions and reactions.

Until fairly recently, Africa did not feature very strongly on the U.S. political agenda. That, though, seems to be changing, and Africa is increasingly becoming a priority region for the U.S. Government. The increasing prioritization of Africa seems to be rooted in geopolitical changes and the rising interest of China and India in African resources and markets in particular; the U.S. need to achieve its objectives in the Global War on Terror in Africa; and to secure access to Africa's oil resources. Thus, both the United States and South Africa seem to have limited but growing interests in Africa. As a non-African country, the U.S. approach to Africa is rooted in caution and a search for key partners, South Africa being one. The military-political nature of AFRICOM demonstrates the U.S. caution toward and recognition of the uniqueness of Africa.

South Africa, as an identified key partner in Africa, has not always been very positive about U.S. military involvement in Africa. South Africa is using its own military as a key component of its own foreign policy engagement on the African continent. Though South Africa seems to be more open and accommodative of U.S. economic involvement in and support to Africa, U.S. security involvement in Africa is not very positively considered. More specifically, South Africa appears to look toward its own military use in Africa as something positive that is contributing toward peace and security in Africa. That is not necessarily its view of U.S. military involvement in Africa—something that is perceived as neo-colonial in nature.

ENDNOTES - CHAPTER 14

1. South African Government, Department of International Relations and Cooperation, *Strategic Plan, 2010–2013*, 2010, Pretoria, South Africa, p. 7, available from *www.dfa.gov.za/department/strategic%20plan%202010-2013/index.htm*.

2. For statistics in this regard, please see the South African Department of Trade and Industry, available from *apps.thedti.gov.za/econdb/raportt/rapregi.html*.

3. The Southern African Development Community (SADC) is an intergovernmental organization in Southern Africa and is headquartered in Gaborone, Botswana. The purpose of SADC is to further socio-economic cooperation and integration as well as political and security cooperation among its 15 member states. The member states are Anglo, Botswana, Democratic Republic of the Congo, Lesotho, Malawi, Mauritius, Mozambique, Namibia, Tanzania, Swaziland, Zambia, Zimbabwe, South Africa, Seychelles, and Madagascar.

4. S. Naidu and J. Lutchman, "Understanding South Africa's engagement in the region: Has the leopard changed its spots?" *Stability, Poverty Reduction, and South African Trade and Investment in Southern Africa*, Proceedings of a conference presented by the Southern African Regional Poverty Network and the EU's CWCI Fund, Human Sciences Research Council, Pretoria, South Africa, March 29–30, 2004, p. 12.

5. See C. Alden and M. Soko, "South Africa's economic relations with Africa: hegemony and its discontents," *Journal of Modern African Studies*, Vol. 43, No. 3, 2005, pp. 367–392.

6. This is clearly demonstrated through the ANC's political lingua franca, addressing each other, for example, as comrades.

7. The South African government consists of the ANC, the Congress of South African Trade Unions (COSATU), and the South African Communist Party (SACP) in a tripartite alliance.

8. The word representivity (*verteenwoordiging* in Afrikaans) is deeply imbedded in the South African lingua franca as a way to explain the need for representativeness in society at large. It is widely used throughout society and is seen as the driving need underpinning affirmative action and equal opportunities for all in society.

9. The term "Black Diamonds" is a collective term used in South Africa to refer to members of the new black middle and ruling class who, in many instances, benefited from the affirmative action policies of the post-1994 ANC government and who became very rich and influential in a relatively short period of time. Depending on the circumstances, it is used in a derogatory, complimentary, or lighthearted manner.

10. The voice of the ANC Youth League and its leader, Juluis Malema, has been very strong in this regard.

11. See the service delivery plans of the Department of Public Service and Administration, available from *www.pmg. org.za/minutes/20070528-service-delivery-improvement-plans-sdip-dpsa-closeout-report*.

12. See, for example, the opinion piece of Moeletsi Mbeki on South Africa's "Tunisia Day," available from *www.businessday. co.za/articles/Content.aspx?id=133902*. Also see the view expressed by the Rector of the University of the Freestate, available from *www.iol.co.za/news/politics/government-has-f-you-attitude-1.1182705*.

13. A. Van Zyl, "Hope can help overcome 'conditional helplessness' in SA," *The Sunday Independent*, Opinion and Analysis, November 6, 2011, p. 17.

14. Speech by the Deputy President TM Mbeki, on behalf of the ANC, on the occasion of the adoption by the Constitutional

Assembly of The Republic of South Africa Constitution Bill 1996, May 8, 1996, available from *www.info.gov.za/aboutgovt/orders/ new2002_mbeki.htm.*

15. Department of International Relations and Cooperation, *Strategic Plan, 2010–2013*, Pretoria, South Africa: South African Government, 2010, p. 7, available from *www.dfa.gov.za/department/ strategic%20plan%202010-2013/index.htm.*

16. E. Sidiropoulos, "South African foreign policy in the post-Mbeki period," *South African Journal of International Affairs*, Vol. 15, No. 2, p. 114.

17. See, for example, the negative reference to the United States in terms of the "unique dominance of one 'hyper power'" in the world. African National Congress (ANC), *Resolutions*, 52nd National Conference, Polokwane, South Africa, 2007, p. 37, available from *www.anc.org.za/ancdocs/history/conf/conference52/.*

18. *Ibid*, p. 43. It is noted that "[t]he conference urges Africa to remain united and resolute in the rejection of the African Command Centre (sic) (AFRICOM)."

19. T. Mbeki, "Africans must guard as new colonialism walks roughshod over international law and human decency," *The Sunday Independent*, Analysis, November 6, 2011, pp. 8–9.

20. For a detailed exposition of the South African reaction to the creation of AFRICOM, see A. J. Esterhuyse, "The Iraqization of Africa? Looking at AFRICOM from a South African Perspective," *Strategic Studies Quarterly*, Vol. 2, No. 1, Spring 2008, pp. 111-130.

21. G. Mills, "SA's 'bit of this and bit of that foreign policy," *Sunday Times*, Times Live, November 27, 2011, available from *www.timeslive.co.za/opinion/columnists/2011/11/27/sa-s-bit-of-this-bit-of-that-foreign-policy.*

22. Sidiropoulos, p. 116. Also see African National Congress (ANC), *Resolutions*, p. 37.

23. South Africa is often criticized for its preference to remain silent on the controversial land distribution and other contentious policies of Robert Mugabe's ZANU-PF government in Zimbabwe. The Mbeki Administration was known for its so-called "Silent Diplomacy" toward the Zimbabwe crisis.

24. Sidiropoulos, p. 116.

25. This is a typical example where the importance of development and democracy had to bend the knee and make provision for African solidarity, Africanism, and a general anti-colonial and anti-western sentiment.

26. Department of Defence, *Strategic Plan (MTEF FY 2010/11 to FY 2012/13)*, Pretoria, South Africa: South Africa Government, p. 23, available from *www.pmg.org.za/files/docs/100303dodplan.doc*.

27. See, for example, the *United States Security Strategy for Sub-Sahara Africa*, Washington, DC: Department of Defense, Office of International Security Affairs, August 1995. For a chronology of U.S. involvement in Africa, see U.S. Africa Command, "Fact sheet: U.S.-Africa relations chronology," available from *www.africom.mil/getArticle.asp?art=1645*.

28. Booker is the executive director of the Washington-based Africa Policy Information Center and the New York-based Africa Fund (ACOA).

29. S. Booker, "The colour line: US foreign policy and national interests in Africa," *South African Journal of International Affairs*, Vol. 8, No. 1, Summer 2001, p. 2.

30. A. J. Esterhuyse, *Die militêre betrokkenheid van die Verenigde State van Amerika in sub-Sahara Afrika: 1993-2001* (The Military Involvement of the United States of America in Sub-Saharan Africa: 1993-2001), Unpublished MSS thesis, University of Pretoria, Pretoria, South Africa, September 2003, pp. 52–53.

31. See the Bureau of African Affairs, May 14, 2007, available from *www.state.gov/p/af/*.

32. J. E. Frazer, "African affairs," *US foreign policy in the 21st century: Regional issues*, Washington, DC: U.S. Department of State, September 2006, pp. 4–5, available from *usinfo.state.gov/journals/itps/0906/ijpe/ijpe0906.pdf.*

33. Booker, p. 3; D. A. Dickson, *United States Foreign Policy Towards Sub-Sahara Africa*, Lanham, MD: University Press of America, 1985, p. 172.

34. M. Clough, *Free At Last? US Policy Towards Africa and the End of the Cold War*, Lawrenceville, NJ: Africa World Press, 1992, p. 3.

35. Dickson, p. 173.

36. Clough, p. 3.

37. E-mail correspondence with Dr. Dan Henk, U.S. Air War College, July 30, 2007.

38. Clough, pp. 20–25.

39. Dickson, p. 170;

40. Clough, p. 3.

41. *Ibid*, p. 2.

42. P. J. Schraeder, *United States Foreign Policy Towards Africa: Incrementalism, Crisis, and Change*, London, UK: Cambridge University Press, 1994, p. 2.

43. See the discussion of this phenomenon in D. Henk, "The environment, the US military, and Southern Africa," *Parameters*, Summer 2006, pp. 101–102.

44. L. Ploch, "Africa command: U.S. strategic interests and the role of the U.S. military in Africa," *CRS Report for Congress*, Washington, DC: Congressional Research Service, July 22, 2011, pp. 13–19, available from *www.fas.org/sgp/crs/natsec/RL34003.pdf.*

45. *Ibid.*, p. 14.

46. M. Malan, *AFRICOM: A Wolf in Sheep's Clothing?* Washington, DC: Refugees International, Testimony before the Subcommittee on African Affairs, Committee on Foreign Relations, U.S. Senate, August 1, 2007, available from *foreign.senate.gov/imo/ media/doc/MalanTestimony070801.pdf.*

47. *Strategic Plan, 2010–2013,* p. 7.

48. *Ibid.,* p. 8.

49. *National Security Strategy,* Washington, DC: The White House, May 2010, p. 45.

50. Secretary of Defense, *Quadrennial Defense Review Report,* Washington DC: Department of Defense, February 2010, p. 61.

51. Chairman of the Joint Chiefs of Staff, *The National Military Strategy of the United States: Redefining America's Military Power,* Washington DC: Joint Chiefs of Staff, February 8, 2011, p. 12.

52. *National Security Strategy,* p. 45.

53. *Strategic Plan, 2010–2013,* p. 8.

54. *Ibid.,* p. 9.

55. *Ibid.,* p. 17.

56. BBC News, *Mandela taken off US terror list,* available from *news.bbc.co.uk/2/hi/americas/7484517.stm.*

57. F. Osman, "Is South Africa joining the American-led war on terrorism?" *Media Review Network,* March 19, 2008, available from *www.mediareviewnet.com/index.php?option=com_content&task =view&id=20&Itemid=38.*

58. J. Duncan, "With us or against us? South Africa's position in the 'War against Terror'," *Review of South African Political Economy,* Vol. 34, No. 113, September 2007, p. 514.

59. Many ANC leaders were explicit in labelling the NATO action against the regime of Muammar Gaddafi as imperialist.

In South Africa, a clear line is not necessarily drawn between what NATO is doing and what the United States is doing as part of NATO. See, for example, the article in the influential *Business Day*, available from *www.businessday.co.za/articles/Content.aspx?id=156734.*

60. See the consecutive strategic plans of the South African Department of International Relations and Cooperation, formerly known as the Department of Foreign Affairs. For the most recent strategic plan, see South African Department of Relations and Cooperation, *Strategic Plan 2009–2012* (n.d.), available from *www.dfa.gov.za/department/stratpla2009-2012/strategicplan2009%20-%20 2012.pdf.*

61. "Chapter 6: Defence — A defence perspective on the 2007 State of the Nation address," *Strategic Plan of Parliament*, Pretoria, South Africa: Parliament of the Republic of South Africa, 2007, available from *www.parliament.gov.za/content/07_Chapter% 206~2.pdf8.*

CONTRIBUTORS

FOUZIE MELANIE ALAMIR has worked as an academic researcher and lecturer at the University of the Armed Forces and the German Federal Staff and Command College from 1997 to 2002. After an assignment with the Federal Ministry of Defense from 2002 to 2004, she joined the German Agency for Technical Cooperation as a Program Manager for Security Sector Reform. From 2006 to 2011, she worked for the private enterprise, IABG, as Head of Comprehensive Security. Following a period of work as a private consultant from 2011 to 2012, she assumed the position of Head of Competence Centre "Security Sector" at the German Agency for International Cooperation in January 2013. Dr. Alamir has field experience in Afghanistan, Azerbaijan, Ghana, and Indonesia, among others. In 2006, she worked as a Political Advisor to the Senior Civilian Representative of the North Atlantic Treaty Organization (NATO) in International Security Assistance Force (ISAF) HQ, Kabul. Her fields of expertise cover a broad range of security policy issues, including the security-development nexus, civil-military interfaces, aspects of comprehensive security and interagency cooperation in the context of international crisis management and peacebuilding. She is familiar both with military and civilian approaches to crisis management and peacebuilding at the strategic, operational, and tactical levels. Dr. Alamir has published numerous articles in books and scientific journals.

EMMANUEL KWESI ANING is a Clinical Professor of Peacekeeping at Kennesaw State University and the Provost and Academic Vice President for all academic programs at the Kofi Annan International Peacekeeping Training Centre (KAIPTC), Accra, Ghana. His rich experience in security issues has been tapped by a number of organizations including the United Nations (UN), where he wrote a Secretary-General's report in 2008 for the UN Security Council on the relationship between the UN and regional organizations on peace and security, especially the African Union, leading to the establishment of the Prodi Commission; the African Union, where he served as its first Expert on Counter-terrorism, peace, and security; and the Economic Community of West Africa States (ECOWAS). Dr. Aning is currently a member of the World Economic Forum's Council on Conflict Resolution. He has written numerous book chapters, monographs, and articles in several international peer reviewed journals. Dr. Aning holds a B.A. from the University of Ghana, a Master of Philosophy (Cand. Phil) and a Ph.D. from the University of Copenhagen, Denmark.

MICHAEL ASHKENAZI is the Program Leader for SALW Control at the Bonn International Center for Conversion, a German applied research center focusing on security and development. He has conducted research in Afghanistan, China, Guinea Bissau, Japan, Korea, Liberia, Nepal, South Sudan, Timor Leste, and Uganda. Dr. Ashkenazi's current research interests range from traditional security providers through arms and ammunition storage, disarmament, demobilization, and reintegration (DD&R), security sector reform (SSR), to the effects of small arms and light weapons (SALW) on societies and development. He has previously worked on Japanese religion, food culture, and business culture, and on migration. Dr. Ashkenazi's research has been disseminated through numerous publications, including the Training and

Education on Small Arms (TRESA) publications and numerous courses across the world, including in Colombia, Germany, Ghana, Mozambique, South Sudan, and UN Headquarters. Audiences range from police and military officers through nongovernmental organization (NGO) members to parliamentarians. Previous to working for BICC, Dr. Ashkenazi was professor of anthropology, teaching graduate and undergraduate students at universities in Canada, Israel, and the UK. He has also served as infantryman, platoon and company commander, and in staff positions. Dr. Ashkenazi was educated in Israel, Japan, and the United States.

FESTUS KOFI AUBYN is a Research Fellow at the Faculty of Academic Affairs and Research (FAAR) of the Kofi Annan International Peacekeeping Training Centre (KAIPTC), Ghana, and a Doctorial Candidate in Peace and Conflict Studies at the University of Ibadan, Nigeria. His research interests are in the areas of conflict, peace and security in Africa with a particular focus on transnational organized crimes, peace operations and election security. Among Mr. Aubyn's recent publications are "Ghana" in Alex J. Bellamy and Paul D. Williams (eds.), *Providing Peacekeepers: The Politics, Challenges and Future of UN Peacekeeping Contributions* (Oxford University Press, 2013); "Unconstitutional Changes of Government: Confronting Africa's Democratic Paradox" (*AU Herald,* Vol. 3); and "Africa's Resistance to Peacekeeping's Normative Change" (CSS ETH Zurich and Geneva Centre for Security Policy, Policy Paper, 2013).

ROBERT H. "ROBIN" DORFF is Dean of the College of Humanities and Social Sciences (CHSS) and Professor in the Department of Political Science and International Affairs. He joined KSU as Dean of CHSS in July 2012 from the Strategic Studies Institute (SSI) at the U.S. Army War College (USAWC), where he was Research Professor of National Security Affairs (2007-12) and also held the General Douglas MacArthur Chair of Research since 2009. Dr. Dorff held faculty positions at Michigan State University and North Carolina State University. He has served on the US-AWC faculty as a Visiting Professor (1994-96) and as Professor of National Security Policy and Strategy in the Department of National Security and Strategy (1997-2004), where he also held the General Maxwell D. Taylor Chair (1999-2002) and served as Department Chair (2001-04). Dr. Dorff has been a Senior Advisor with Creative Associates International, Inc., in Washington, DC, and served as Executive Director of the Institute of Political Leadership in Raleigh, NC (2004-06). Dr. Dorff remains extensively involved in strategic leadership development, focusing on national security strategy and policy, and strategy formulation. His research interests include these topics as well as failing and fragile states, interagency processes and policy formulation, stabilization and reconstruction operations, and U.S. grand strategy. He has published and lectured frequently on these topics and has spoken all over the United States and in Canada, Europe, Africa, and Asia. Dr. Dorff holds an M.A. and Ph.D. from the University of North Carolina-Chapel Hill.

CHARLES J. DUNLAP, JR., is a Visiting Professor of the Practice at Duke Law School and the Executive Director of its Center on Law, Ethics, and National Security. Prior to retiring as an Air Force major general in June 2010, he assisted in the supervision of more than 2,500 military and civilian attorneys worldwide. His 34-year career included tours in both the United Kingdom and Korea, and he deployed for military operations in Africa and the Middle East. Totaling more than 120 publications, General Dunlap's writings address a wide range of topics, including various aspects of national security law, airpower, counterinsurgency, cyber power, civil-military relations, and leadership. General Dunlap speaks frequently at professional conferences and at numerous institutions of higher learning, to include Harvard, Yale, MIT, UVA, and Stanford, as well as the National Defense University and the Air, Army, and Navy War Colleges. He serves on the Board of Advisors for the Center for a New American Security. General Dunlap is a distinguished graduate of the National War College and holds an undergraduate degree from St. Joseph's University and a law degree from Villanova University.

ABEL ESTERHUYSE is an associate professor of strategy in the Faculty of Military Science of Stellenbosch University at the South African Military Academy. Before joining the Faculty of Military Science, Professor Esterhuyse served as a lieutenant colonel in the South African Army. He teaches a wide variety of courses in the School for Security and Africa Studies of Stellenbosch University, regularly publishes on contemporary military issues, and has a keen interest in (South African) military history. He is the editor of *Scientia Militaria: The South African Journal of Military Studies*. Professor Esterhuyse is a graduate of the summer program in military history at the U.S. Military Academy, West Point, and the program on the analysis of military operations and strategy (SWAMOS) of Columbia University's Saltzman Institute of War and Peace Studies. He holds an M.S.S. from Pretoria University and a Ph.D. from Stellenbosch University.

WILLIAM FLAVIN is the Division Chief of the Doctrine, Concept, Education, and Training Division at the U.S. Army Peacekeeping and Stability Operations Institute (PKSOI), located at the U.S. Army War College in Carlisle, PA, since July 2007. Previous assignments include a senior foreign affairs analyst with Booz Allen and Hamilton on contract to assist PKSOI for doctrine development. From 1995 to 1999, he was a colonel in the U.S. Army serving as the Deputy Director of Special Operations for the Supreme Allied Commander of Europe at the Supreme Headquarters, Allied Powers Europe. He was a senior fellow at CSIS for his Army War College year and then taught at the Army War College. Colonel Flavin holds a B.A. in History from VMI and an M.A. in History from Emory University.

VOLKER C. FRANKE is Special Assistant to the Vice President for Research and Graduate Dean for Strategic Partnerships and Associate Professor of Conflict Management at Kennesaw State University. He is the Founding Director of the Ph.D. program in International Conflict Management at Kennesaw State University (2010-12) and served as Director of Research at the Bonn International Center for Conversion (BICC), one of Germany's premier peace and conflict research and capacity building institutes (2006-08). From 1998 to 2007, he was Director and Managing Editor of the National Security Studies Case Studies Program at Syracuse University's Maxwell School of Citizenship and Public Affairs. Dr. Franke is the author of *Preparing for Peace: Military Identity, Value-Orientations, and Professional Military Education* (Praeger 1999) and more than 30 journal articles, book chapters, case studies, and research reports on issues related to peace and security studies, conflict management, civil-military relations, development policy, and social identity. He is also the editor of *Terrorism and Peacekeeping: New Security Challenges* (Praeger 2005), *Security in a Changing World: Case Studies in U.S. National Security Management* (Praeger 2002), and co-editor (both with Robert H. "Robin" Dorff) of *Conflict Management and "Whole of Government:" Useful Tools for U.S. National Security Strategy?* (SSI, 2012). Dr. Franke holds an MA in political science and sociology from Johannes Gutenberg University in Mainz, Germany; an M.P.A. from North Carolina State University; and a Ph.D. in political science from Syracuse University's Maxwell School.

KARL-THEODOR zu GUTTENBERG served as German Federal Minister of Defense from 2009 to 2011 and as Federal Minister of Economics and Technology from February 2009 to October 2009. As Minister of Defense, zu Guttenberg led the most significant structural reform to the German Bundeswehr since 1955, particularly leading the effort of transforming the Bundeswehr from a conscription-based army to an all-professional military. He also served as a member of the German parliament or Bundestag from 2002 to 2011 and as a leading member of the Bundestag's Foreign Affairs Committee from 2005 to 2008. Minister zu Guttenberg is leading a new transatlantic dialogue initiative at the Center for Strategic and International Studies (CSIS) which will bring European and American thought-leaders, practitioners, and officials together on a variety of security and economic related issues to develop a bold, new strategic vision to reinvigorate the transatlantic relationship and prevent strategic drift. By exploring the global shift of power, the increased global economic and market instability and the challenge to multilateral institutions, the focus of the project will examine how the transatlantic relationship can lead in this increasingly complex geopolitical setting.

CHRISTOPHER HOLSHEK is an international peace and security consultant focusing on civil-military relations in policy and practice as well as peace operations related civil-military training and education. A Senior Fellow with the Alliance for Peacebuilding and a civil-military strategic analyst with Wikistrat, he was recently a Senior Associate with the Project on National Security Reform as well as Country Project Manager in Liberia for the U.S. Department of Defense's Defense Institutional Reform Initiative working in Africa on defense ministerial capacity development in order to promote civilian oversight of the military. A retired U.S. Army (Reserve) Civil Affairs (CA) officer, Mr. Holshek has 3 decades of civil-military experience at the strategic, operational, and tactical levels in joint, interagency, and multinational settings across the full range of operations, among them command of the first CA battalion to deploy to Iraq in support of Army, Marine and British forces, as the Kosovo Forces (KFOR) Civil-Military Liaison Officer to the UN Mission in Kosovo, and in the Balkans in the mid-1990s, and as Senior U.S. Military Observer and Chief of Civil-Military Coordination (CIMIC) for nearly 2 years in the UN Mission in Liberia, where he broke new ground in applying CIMIC concepts central to the development of UN civil-military policy and training. In his final tour as Military Representative at the U.S. Agency for International Development for USEUCOM/SHAPE, Mr. Holshek helped link security and development at the national strategic level in an interagency setting as well as stand up the National Response Center for the Haiti earthquake.

ROBERT KENNEDY, a former senior government official, returned to his position as Professor in the Sam Nunn School of International Affairs, Georgia Institute of Technology, Atlanta, GA, in January 2003 after serving as director of the joint German-American George C. Marshall European Center for Security Studies in Germany. In nearly 35 years of government service, Dr. Kennedy has also served as Civilian Deputy Commandant, NATO Defense College, Rome, Italy; Dwight D. Eisenhower Professor of National Security Studies at the USAWC, researcher at the U.S. Army SSI, Foreign Affairs Officer, U.S. Arms Control and Disarmament Agency; an enlisted man in the Army; and a command pilot on active duty with the U.S. Air Force and later with the Reserve forces. Dr. Kennedy's most recent works are *Of Knowledge and Power: the Complexities of National Intelligence* (2008), "The Elements of Strategic Thinking" in Gabriel Marcella, ed., *Teaching Strategy: Challenge and Response* (2010), *The Road to War: Congress' Historic Abdication of Responsibility* (2010), and "National Security Reform: 12 Central Questions for Responding to the Security Challenges of the 21st Century," in Volker Franke and Robin Dorff, eds., *Conflict Management and "Whole of Government:" Useful Tools for U.S. National Security Strategy* (2012).

MICHAEL LEKSON is director of gaming for the Academy for International Conflict Management and Peacebuilding, United States Institute of Peace. United States Institute of Peace. He joined the Institute's Professional Training program in 2003 as a program officer. He came to the Institute following a 26-year career in the Department of State, where he was deputy assistant secretary of state for arms control, overseeing all multilateral arms control negotiations and treaty implementation. Prior to that, Mr. Lekson was deputy to the special representative of the president and the secretary of state for implementation of the Dayton Peace Accords. He was also director of the Office of European Security and Political Affairs, where he helped develop and implement policies to adapt NATO to the post-Cold War world, and of the Office of United Kingdom, Benelux, and Ireland Affairs, where he worked intensively on the Northern Ireland peace process. During his Foreign Service career, Mr. Lekson served as a consular officer in Bilbao, Spain, and as a political officer in U.S. embassies in Costa Rica, Peru, and the United Kingdom. He was deputy U.S. representative to the Organization for Security and Cooperation in Europe (OSCE) during that organization's augmentation of its democracy building, conflict prevention, and conflict management efforts in formerly communist countries, especially in the Balkans and Central Asia. Prior to joining the Department of State, he served 2 years in the U.S. Army as a field artillery officer. Mr. Lekson has a B.A. in English from Princeton University and a master's in linguistics from Stanford University.

LISELOTTE ODGAARD is an Associate Professor at the Royal Danish Defence College. Her most recent international position was in 2008-09, when she was a residential fellow at the Woodrow Wilson International Center for Scholars, Washington, DC. Her areas of expertise include International Relations, Asia-Pacific Security, and China Studies. Ms. Odgaard's most recent monograph is *China and Coexistence: Beijing's National Security Strategy for the 21st Century* (Woodrow Wilson Center Press/Johns Hopkins University Press, May 2012). Ms. Odgaard has been selected to be a contributor to the 2014 Nobel Symposium.

DWIGHT RAYMOND joined PKSOI at the USAWC in July 2009 after retiring from the Army as an infantry colonel. His military assignments included infantry leadership, command, and staff positions; faculty positions at the United States Military Academy and the USAWC; theater-level plans positions in Korea; and training and advisory assignments at the National Training Center and in Iraq as an advisor to an Iraqi Army brigade. He has developed military doctrine related to the Protection of Civilians, and is one of the primary authors of the Mass Atrocity Response Operations (MARO) Military Planning Handbook. Mr. Raymond has a Bachelor's Degree from the United States Military Academy and master's degrees from the University of Maryland's School of Public Affairs, the U.S. Army School of Advanced Military Studies, and the USAWC.

F. WILLIAM SMULLEN III is Director of the Maxwell School's National Security Studies Program and a member of the faculty of Syracuse University's S.I. Newhouse School of Public Communications as a Professor of Public Relations. Prior to his appointment at Syracuse University, he was the Chief of Staff to Secretary of State Colin L. Powell beginning in January 2001. A veteran of 30 years in the U.S. Army, his last active duty assignment was Special Assistant to the 11th and 12th Chairmen of the Joint Chiefs of Staff.

NATHANIEL L. WILSON is a Program Assistant in the Academy for International Conflict Management and Peacebuilding, U.S. Institute of Peace. He currently works on development of a Countering Violent Extremism course curriculum to be delivered internationally. Previously, he was a Research Assistant at the Partnership for Global Security in Washington, DC, and at a different position, he spent a summer working on civil rights issues in Israel. Mr. Wilson also undertook translation work and research for the National Consortium for the Study of Terrorism and the Reponses to Terrorism (START) at the University of Maryland-College Park. He has an abiding interest in the Middle East and is learning Arabic. Mr. Wilson holds a B.A. in political science from the University of Missouri-St. Louis and an M.A. in international relations, U.S. foreign policy specialization, from American University's School of International Service.